WOODY ALLEN
Profane and Sacred

by
Richard A. Blake

The Scarecrow Press, Inc.
Lanham, Md., & London

SCARECROW PRESS, INC.

Published in the United States of America
by Scarecrow Press, Inc.
4720 Boston Way, Lanham, Maryland 20706

4 Pleydell Gardens, Folkestone
Kent CT20 2DN, England

British Cataloging in Publication Information Available

Library of Congress Cataloging-in-Publication Data

Blake, Richard Aloysius.
Woody Allen : profane and sacred / by Richard A. Blake.
p. cm.
Filmography: p.
Includes bibliographical references and index.
1. Allen, Woody—Criticism and interpretation. I. Title.
PN1998.3.A45B63 1995 791.43'092—dc20 95-3312

ISBN 0-8108-2993-2 (cloth : alk. paper)

Printed in the United States of America

The paper used in this publication meets the minimum requirements of American National Standard for Information Sciences—Permanence of Paper for Printed Library Materials, ANSI Z39.48-1984.

CONTENTS

PREFACE: THE PRESS RELEASE PUBLICITY

Cliff Stern, the Woody Allen hero in CRIMES AND MISDEMEANORS suddenly discovers that the philosopher Louis Levy, the subject of his projected documentary film, has committed suicide. Cliff is shattered. Levy's message of hope would have made a wonderful film, but now the thousands of feet of film Cliff has shot about this articulate, optimistic survivor of the death camps have been rendered useless.

Cliff Stern and I are kindred spirits. Less than two weeks after I had signed a contract to produce a book on the religious dimensions of Woody Allen's thought, the allegations began to appear in the tabloids. Was the project doomed? Why would anyone want to produce a book-length treatment of the religious ideas of an accused child molester? In such circumstances, the very notion of linking Woody Allen with religion bristles with incongruity, if not irony.

The decision to go ahead was not difficult. From the beginning, this book was conceived as a study of the films, not the man. Regardless of the sensational charges, denials and counter-charges the newspapers carried, the record of the films offers a legitimate and intriguing body of material for study. The public's feelings about the man as a person seemed to change for better or worse with every new rumor leaked to the press, but the films remain an immutable record of his artistic achievement stretching back a quarter of a century. Although the films carry the freight of autobiographical references, still they stand on their own merits apart from the life of the artist. Even though the task was difficult at times, it was nonetheless possible to prescind from the headlines and go ahead with the study of the films.

Even so, the project still held an element of risk. In a nightmare scenario, the courts would have substantiated the worst of the allegations, and at the end of this bitter suit for custody and visiting rights for his family, Woody Allen might even have been required to face criminal charges. This distasteful business would have dragged on for months. If that had happened, and fortunately it did not, a critic would be forced to ask whether Allen's personal life casts a shadow of cynicism over the religious questions he poses in the films. To pose the critics' question another way: How seriously could Allen inquire about moral structures in the universe through his films, if in his own life he blatantly disregards the very moral structures he is trying to discover and validate? Is he self-deluded, a hypocrite or charlatan?

If these terrible allegations had been proved true, it is sobering and a bit disheartening to realize that Allen would not have been a unique phenomenon. Poets may write quite movingly about love while cruelly abusing those who love them. Should readers abandon Shakespeare's lovely romantic sonnets if scholars one day prove definitively that he was homosexual, or celibate, or profligate, or abusive? Or should they continue to cherish the poetry for its unique beauty regardless of the type of person who composed it? In other words, I believe that even if the worst rumors about Woody Allen's personal life had been verified, his films would still constitute a priceless part of the world's artistic heritage.

Fortunately, the nightmare never materialized, and the most uncomfortable questions never had to be asked. As might have been predicted from the outset, the findings of the long judicial process were ambiguous. Allen never denied a romantic involvement with 20-year-old Soon-Yi Previn Farrow. But since she is daughter of Mia Farrow by adoption and since he never married Ms. Farrow, the 57-year-old Allen vigorously denied the accusation of incest. While a team of child psychologists from Yale could not substantiate Ms. Farrow's charges that Allen had sexually abused other children in her extensive family, Judge Elliott Wilk of the New York State Supreme Court awarded custody of the children to Ms. Farrow and noted some reservations about the exonerating report of the psychologists. In addition, the court's decision of June 7, 1993 included a decidedly negative assessment of Mr. Allen's character to explain its denial of custody to Allen.

The personal life of Woody Allen, then, remains a mystery, and rightly so. Mr. Allen, like everyone else in the world, has a right to his privacy, and a fair-minded critic also has the right to respect that privacy and confine his efforts to the public record contained in the films. Even though the subject matter of this study was deliberately limited to the Allen films, the temptation to engage in after-the-fact psychologizing was powerful, largely because of Allen's own frequent references to psychotherapy, neuroses, and even sexual deviation in the scripts. The clinical references, however, pertain to fictional characters, however tempting it might be to draw parallels to their creator.

Since Woody Allen is one of the foremost artists of this generation, these films deserve careful scrutiny. They tell us a great deal about the artistic development of a significant film maker, a topic of far more interest to a serious critic, than his psychosexual development, which is a matter for Woody Allen and his analysts.

Several fine studies of Allen's films have appeared over the years. In my own preparation of this book, I found the comments of Douglas Brode and Maurice Yacowar extremely helpful. Nancy Pogel and Graham McCann have also provided insightful critical studies relating Allen's films to other arts and artists, while Stephen J. Spignesi's book is an invaluable resource for factual information about the films. Eric Lax's recent biography combines material about the Woody Allen, the man, and his works, and thus offers rare glimpses into Allen's artistic processes. Without burdening the reader with extensive critical apparatus, I have tried to acknowledge the contributions of these authors where appropriate. Their work underlies many of my observations throughout this book.

The pages that follow build on earlier criticism, but there is a difference. This study narrows its focus to Allen's religious and philosophic ideas as they develop through the years in the films. A great deal of other interesting material had to be treated like distractions and dropped. For example, had this been a more generalized treatment, it would have contained many references to the wonderful songs Allen uses on his sound tracks. Often the words of the song comment shrewdly or ironically on the scene. This is a wonderful topic, but not for present purposes. Similarly, the brilliant contributions of the cameras of Carlo Di Palma, Sven Nyquist, and Gordon Willis manifestly deserve extensive study, but not here, unfortunately. And the same could be said for the designs of Santo Loquasto, the casting of Juliet Taylor and the performances of dozens of actors who agree to be overworked and underpaid just for the privilege of appearing in an Allen film, where they know they will probably give the best performances of their careers.

Most regrettable of all is the omission of Woody Allen's comedy. With few exceptions, his movies delight audiences with their remarkable one-line jokes and outrageous comic situations. Even the most serious of scholars can occasionally lighten their ponderous academic prose with a deft quotation from the script. The decision to concentrate exclusively on the ideas affords no such luxury in this present study. Woody Allen is a genius of comedy. His movies are very, very funny, a fact that may be lost in this specialized discussion of his religious ideas.

Since this study is limited to the ideas of Woody Allen, it includes only those films that Allen both wrote and directed. These are the films over which Allen exercised an extraordinary degree of artistic control. With this guideline in operation, several films, which Allen either wrote or appeared in as an actor and thus are often thought of as Allen films, receive very little notice. Readers may regret the sparse comments on WHAT'S NEW, PUSSYCAT? (Clive Donner, 1965), CASINO ROYALE (John Huston and others, 1967), DON'T DRINK THE WATER (Howard Morris, 1969), PLAY IT AGAIN, SAM (Herbert Ross, 1972), THE FRONT (Martin Ritt, 1976) and SCENES FROM A MALL (Paul Mazursky, 1991). In these films, others not sharing Woody Allen's concerns obviously had their own ideas to bring to the work. Disentangling the respective contributions of the various artists would lead to an extensive exercise in production analysis, which again would offer a distraction from the specialized discussion at hand.

When one views over a relatively short period of time all the 23 films that can be called truly Allen films, several remarkably consistent religious preoccupations become apparent. These few sketchy generalizations can provide a useful preamble for more detailed analyses of his individual works.

Unquestionably, Allen sees his universe as a hostile environment. Even in his most delightful comic moments, this conviction remains unshaken. His heroes or heroines tend to be frail, vulnerable people who are victims of the world and its more self-confident inhabitants. He wonders why life is so unfair, and the question leads to an unresolvable dilemma for him: If there is a God who has created and rules the universe, how could he allow evil like the Nazis or human suffering to exist? If there is no God, then how is one to find meaning in life and a moral structure to direct one's actions? Since these questions cannot be resolved with absolute certitude, how are people to live?

Allen consistently explores the human responses to this situation. One solution is to cease living. Attempted and threatened suicide appears as a constant motif in the films, often in an incongruous comic setting. Yet despite the frequent presentation of suicide as an option, only two people succeed: Eve, the deranged mother in INTERIORS, and Louis Levy, the death-camp survivor and philosopher in CRIMES AND MISDEMEANORS. In fact, death in any form occurs very rarely in Allen's films—LOVE AND DEATH is the obvious exception—even though many of the characters seem morbidly preoccupied with their own mortality and aging. Despite his belief in the difficulty of living in this hostile world, his characters generally have the courage to decide to go on with the task of living.

Allen almost invariably tries to justify this option for life in one of three ways. First, falling in love gives one a reason for living, even though invariably his characters fail to form a lasting relationship with their ideal loved one. In this case, they learn to settle for a far-from-perfect love, or end one relationship and move on to another, hoping for more success the next time, or simply cherish a few happy memories from past loves. While it would clearly be an overstatement to regard the search for human love as a metaphor for the human yearning for the divine, Allen's gallery of failed lovers documents his belief that this is a universe where love does not appear easily. How could such a world be created and governed by a God who is supposed to be loving?

Art in its many forms provides a second excuse to opt for life. If the real world is intolerable and unknowable and love is ever-elusive, then it may be necessary to withdraw into the world of the artistic imagination. By the act of human creation artists know the answers and give purpose to the creatures in their own artificially constructed universe. Many of Allen's later figures are writers, scholars and film makers who retreat into their work when their real world overwhelms them and love constantly escapes them. Others, at times the less gifted, are consumers of art who find in the movies an escape from the cruelties of the world that makes life endurable.

Finally, on occasion, Allen has even explored religion itself and the option of faith in its many guises. In several films, he treats his

Jewish heritage as an added burden in life. It casts him as an outsider in a closed and vaguely hostile gentile world. Gradually his feelings mellowed, however, and he begins to find a supportive identity in his Jewishness. He moves from a cruel stereotypical presentation of cultural Judaism to a form of affection for it. On a few rare occasions, he even began to look at Judaism as a religious tradition that might hold the answers to his questions about death, meaning and morality. Even more rarely, Allen asks whether Christianity may provide some assistance, but this option is closed to him by virtue of both his rationalist philosophy and his Jewishness.

The questions that have remained with Woody Allen over the past quarter century are ultimately religious questions. The language he uses to address these problems, however, is with rare exception a secular language, and thus the answers he proposes and tests are secular as well. Through his many characters he professes a rejection of religion and an inability to make the faith commitment demanded of a religious person. Invariably he wants philosophic or even scientific answers, but as he repeatedly admits, reason is an inadequate tool for dealing with the mysteries that bedevil him. Like most modern, secular people who reach the limits of reason, Allen suspects that the answers he craves lie beyond the capabilities of reason, but again like most contemporary intellectuals, he cannot accept any solution that is not the result of modern scientific analysis. In A MIDSUMMER NIGHT'S SEX COMEDY, a world of unseen realities is reduced to a child's fantasy realm of sprites and fairies.

Religion, for thinkers like Woody Allen, remains a collection of myths and fantasies, comforting perhaps for those who can believe them, but essentially unknowable or unacceptable to any thinking person today. Fascinating in his own right, Woody Allen thus becomes especially important as a representative of modern, post-religious inquiry into the meaning of life and morality. As a spokesperson for the contemporary urban agnostic, Allen in his work embodies Alexander Pope's famous definition of wit: "What oft was thought but ne'er so well expressed."

As a final prenote, let me express my gratitude to Professor Ingrid Shafer, professor of philosophy and religion at the University of Science and Arts of Oklahoma, who as guest editor invited me to contribute an article for a theme issue of the *Journal of Popular Film & Television* (Summer 1991) on the religious imagination. I chose Woody Allen as an example of the contemporary religious imagination, and most of that article is reproduced in the first chapter of this book. Without Professor Shafer's gentle but insistent encouragement, neither the article nor this project would have come to completion.

My thanks, too, to Professor Joan D. Lynch, professor of communication arts at Villanova University, who asked me to introduce and moderate a discussion on CRIMES AND MISDEMEANORS as part of the sesquicentennial lecture series "Film, Faith and Philosophy" at the University. The resulting evening provided both the new ideas and the resolve to move ahead with the manuscript. Finally, Professor Herbert J. Ryan, S.J., professor of theology at Loyola Marymount University in Los Angeles, was kind enough to read through an early version of the typescript of the first chapter to help me avoid formal heresy. If the Inquisition confiscates and burns all copies of this book, it is because I failed to follow his astute suggestions.

The first version of this study was completed and sent to the publisher in July 1993. Then the nightmare began. Requests for permissions to use frame enlargements, quotations from the eight published screenplays and from the films were met with delay and ultimately emphatic rejection in the form of a gratuitously offensive fax from Mr. Allen's office expressing contempt for research and scholarship, even if it presents an enthusiastic critical appreciation of the works. Since the academic world lacks the resources to contest commercial giants, it was clear that all direct quotations would have to be replaced by my own paraphrases, although as a service to other scholars, the page references to the eight published screenplays remain. It is a highly unusual and unsatisfactory form of documentation for what had been intended as a close analysis of the texts.

Among the acknowledgments then must be included the legal department of Orion Pictures in Los Angeles, several executives and their staffs at Random House/Vintage, Mr. Allen's staff in New York and finally Woody Allen himself, with whose reasonable cooperation this might have been a better book.

WOODY ALLEN
PROFANE AND SACRED

Sacred and profane are two modes of being in the world, two existential situations assumed by man in the course of his history. These modes of being in the world are not of concern only to the history of religions or to sociology; they are not the object only of historical, sociological, or ethnological study. In the last analysis, the sacred and profane modes of being depend upon the different positions that man has conquered in the cosmos; hence they are of concern both to the philosopher and to anyone seeking to discover the possible dimensions of human existence.—Mircea Eliade[1]

I. INTRODUCTION

Theological film criticism is a dangerous business, for theologian and film critic alike. If pursued with vigor, it can tempt the eager critic to work violence upon the text of the film by imposing religious meanings on perfectly secular films and unearthing religious symbols which are neither intended by the film makers nor congruent with the narrative and thematic intent of the film. In its most extreme forms, it reduces film to a catechetical or homiletic exemplum, which is fine for discussion groups but questionable for criticism.

It is, for example, possible for a religiously inclined critic to argue plausibly that SUPERMAN (Richard Donner, 1978) retells the story of the Messiah. The hero is, after all, sent from another world by his benevolent father, succumbs for a while to the powers of darkness, then through his heroic agon rises from apparent death and restores love to earth, as imaged in his union with the life symbol, Lois Lane. The comparison is interesting, but it reveals little about the film. Similar messianic interpretations could be imposed on any number of genre films, especially Westerns. A critic could more profitably deal with SUPERMAN by reflecting on the science-fiction genres, comic-book fiction, the other works of Richard Donner, the lush John Williams score and the imagination of the screen writer Mario Puzo.

Theologians also run risks when they turn their attention to screen images. For a Christian theologian, the Incarnation of Jesus as Man marks the beginning of a unique messianic event, one whose uniqueness can be lost or trivialized by overly facile comparisons to the icons of pop culture. The notion of a loving God rests at the core of the Judaeo-Christian tradition, but it is a love of such power that only at the risk of cheapening it can it be readily mirrored in every love story that involves some element of self-sacrifice. Many romantic stories in film can be called examples of "redemptive" love, but that is quite different from saying the story is a parable of the Redemption, which for a Christian is a privileged instance of love on a scale that defies the imagination.

There precisely lies the dilemma for the film critic who is a believer and the theologian who "uses" films. Since human intelligence is finite, and thus incapable of grasping the infinity of God, the imagination must serve where reason falters. From the beginning of recorded history artists in every conceivable medium have tried to present their gods in human terms, and many believers have undoubtedly come closer to the divine through the senses—through color and form, through song and story and dance—than through the precise verbal formulations of their theologians, through Bach's Mass in B Minor, for example, rather than through the *Summa Theologica* of St. Thomas Aquinas. Must the makers and audiences of popular films alone be denied a role in this ancient human enterprise of making God manifest in artistic creation?

The dilemma becomes particularly cruel, however, since the validity of the imagination's presentation must be tested by reason's cold, analytic scrutiny. Put another way, how can believing critics be sure they are not bringing their own subjective set of beliefs into their reading of the film, and how can theologians not take out of a film the predetermined meanings that they want to find? Can some methodology be devised to permit a faith dimension to be found in film, as it is in the other arts, while preserving the integrity of the text? Because of their subjective character, these questions may never be resolved with complete clarity, but devising some canons of critical methodology must precede any discussion of individual films or their religious content.

Before beginning a film-by-film comment on each of the Allen films, it will be important to establish a few ground rules for this style of "theological" criticism. In the pages that follow I would like to propose a way to apply some fairly current but traditional theology as a basis for approaching the films, then for purposes of illustration apply the method in a general way to the very different religious preoccupations of Ingmar Bergman and Woody Allen.

I. THE CATHOLIC PROBLEM

For the purposes of this exploration, awareness of one's own defined religious tradition is extremely important for both the critic and the theologian. Finding theology in a film implies having a theology to begin with, at least a strong awareness of God and creation as understood through a coherent, articulated body of beliefs. For a serious religious critic, experiencing "God" in a film should be somewhat different if the critic is a Jew, a Christian, Muslim, or a Buddhist because the religious sensibilities of each are correspondingly different. Neither critic nor theologian can be satisfied with an awareness of God that is little more than a vague motivating force for good in the activities of movie characters. They must rather be attuned to their own religious heritage and experience as well as that of the film makers. Without that awareness, there can be no clear dialogue between the theologian/critic and the film.

The Catholic tradition provides a suitable place to begin devising a methodology for this kind of dialogue. Catholics have an extraordinarily well articulated sense of their own identity, and although this clarity has led to problems in dealing with the extra-Catholic world throughout the centuries, it has also put Catholic theologians in a strong position to evaluate the strengths and weaknesses in their own heritage as they enter into dialogue with other traditions today. In the last quarter century especially, they have confronted issues like historic intolerance, and their work has provided the basis for a new style of exchange with non-Catholic traditions. By adaptation, this kind of theological development can be useful for the encounter of critic and film maker.

Since Catholics believe that the revelation of God in Jesus Christ is the privileged moment in human history and one that has been preserved infallibly through the centuries, they found themselves historically assuming a superior stance in dealing with others. The logic of their position is unassailable. Since all salvation comes from Jesus Christ and the Catholic Church alone is the body of Christ in time, then outside His Church there is no salvation. This was never a comfortable position, and Catholic writers have long struggled to reconcile the apparent exclusivity of this tradition with the presumed intent of an all-loving God to save the entire race.[2] From the voyages of discovery in the fifteenth century through the communications revolutions in our own day, the discomfort has grown acute as theologians have tried to reconcile the logic of their belief with the obvious fact that the vast majority of the world's citizens have no association with Christ or His church. In fact, as the world has shrunk they have become aware of the obvious fact that many other traditions have produced equally coherent views of the world and call their adherents to equally rich spiritual lives.

For present purposes, the theological question is not as important as the methods proposed for resolving it. According to Richard McBrien, a prominent theologian at the University of Notre Dame, since the time of the Second Vatican Council (1962–65), Catholic theologians have in general taken one of three approaches to the problem.[3] These three methods have application for the believing film critic searching for a religious meaning in films.

The first affirms the primacy of the Christian faith but accepts the possibility that other religious bodies communicate authentic values to their members. Since Jesus Christ is the mediator of all grace and the Church is necessary for salvation, persons "outside" the visible Church enjoy "lesser and looser ways of belonging to Christ and to the Mystical Body of Our Lord which reaches concrete form in the [Catholic] Church."[4] People in such a condition could be referred to as "anonymous Christians," a phrase that gained great currency during the time of Vatican II. It was a convenient theological concept for Christians, but still held overtones of religious imperialism that non-Christians found simply offensive. A devout Jew would quite properly be outraged at the notion that he is somehow anonymously a Christian.

The second approach accepts the indisputable value of other religious traditions in and of themselves and does not try to force them under the umbrella of anonymous, virtual or implicit Christianity. At the same time, it affirms the Church as the primary source of grace and salvation, while other traditions are relative and lesser, although extraordinary sources of grace. McBrien comments: "This is the teaching, for the most part, of the Second Vatican Council and perhaps the majority of Catholic theologians today."[5]

The third approach goes one step further. It not only accepts the intrinsic value of non-Christian traditions, but finds them suitable partners in dialogue. It sees the revelation of God as taking many forms, and it holds to the principle that the various traditions have a great deal to offer one another. One adhering to this approach remains steadfastly Catholic, yet appreciates the riches of other traditions as enriching Catholicism, as it hopes that Catholicism can enrich other traditions without either forcing conversion or leading to relativism. Such a person will not view other traditions as anonymously Christian or flawed, incomplete versions of Christianity, but as authentic religious traditions valid in their own right.

For film critics these theological considerations can be helpful. Critics, too, stand on a middle ground between their own religious beliefs and those presented in the film. It helps to understand the rules of engagement.

Those who view films in a manner analogous to the first approach would invariably face the temptation to baptize what they view. It holds the presumption that the good Jewish, atheistic or agnostic director is really an anonymous Christian, who presents a profoundly Christian message, but sadly does not recognize the fact. For such critics, love between man and woman is redemptive, heroes are messianic and shared lunches are eucharistic. Making films and film makers anonymously Christian is a kind of religious imperialism, and many Jewish film makers would be amused or infuriated to discover the Christian content some claim to discover in their work.

The second understanding of the relationship between religious traditions often leads to a kind of homiletic film viewing in which the human action on the screen is but a lesser version of the divine. The love or heroism in the film is but a pale reflection of God's activity in the world. Critics of this type see human conduct as of a value inferior and relative to the ultimate values the film maker portrays on the screen in quasi-parable form. Human love and human accomplishments can become cheapened by comparison with ultimate Christian values. Japanese, Indian or African films have a certain edifying religious content, but it is still to be measured against the Christian norm, which can be seen in an inchoate form in the nonchristian films in question. Such critics distrust the beauty of the human and the artistic. They are too eager to go upstairs to divine realms, when the film is content dealing with earthbound questions of fidelity, love and malice.

Finally, in keeping with the third approach, critics with religious interests can enter into respectful and fruitful dialogue with non-religious films. They can see the secularist films as often having something to say to Christian tradition. They need not look for Christ-symbols because the human images on the screen already have value in themselves. For them the need to translate action into Christian terms not only robs the film of its own identity but lapses into a form of religious imperialism. When religious elements are present in the text of the film, they can be savored and explained; when they are not, critics can find the film's values in its own internal text, not in a predetermined religious agenda they bring to the film from without.

While the first two methods have their place in some circumstances, such as an undergraduate philosophy or theology class, it is this third approach that holds the most value for the film critic. Uncovering religious content can help illuminate a film, but critics who undertake the task must be sensitive to their methods and purposes.

2. INGMAR BERGMAN AND WOODY ALLEN

Joining this unlikely pair of film makers clarifies the method to some degree. The operative presumption is that religious criticism is a form of dialogue between the viewer and the film, and dialogue serves its purpose best when each side understands, respects and appreciates what the other holds. Most films are resolutely secularist enterprises, created by people who invariably want to earn money, frequently make an artistic statement and occasionally succeed. Religious content must be considered suspect, until it can be identified as such from either the text of the film or from the intent of the film maker as demonstrated in other projects or in recorded statements of intent.

A critic, in this instance a Catholic, will try to approach the films of both Lutheran and Jewish film maker not only with a sensitivity to their respective Protestantism and Judaism but also with due appreciation of the nonsectarian and secularist values each individual film embodies. If the dialogue between believing critic and artifact is authentic, then the Catholic viewers can find their own appreciation of the human condition enriched without having to translate the content of the films into Catholic categories. In fact, these attempts at translation into alien conceptual frameworks risk compromising meanings that are intrinsically valuable in their own terms. It is crucial to ask what the film maker attempts to say and what language he uses to say it before one can offer a response in one's own theological language and one's own conceptual framework.

Few would doubt, for example, that Ingmar Bergman created a number of extraordinary religious statements. His childhood experiences with his father, a Lutheran pastor, have been exhaustively documented.[6] At the height of his career, he created a series of explicitly religious films, beginning with THE SEVENTH SEAL (1956) and including THE VIRGIN SPRING (1959), THROUGH A GLASS DARKLY (1961), WINTER LIGHT (1962) and THE SILENCE (1963). This series surely substantiates the director's own oft-quoted statement: "To me religious problems are continuously alive. I never cease to concern myself with them; it goes on every hour of every day."[7]

With this body of evidence in mind, a critic would not be unreasonable to read WILD STRAWBERRIES (1957) or THE MAGICIAN (1958), both non-religious films from this highly religious period, as having some overtones of the sacred. In WILD STRAWBERRIES perhaps Prof. Isak Borg travels not only through the countryside to receive his academic honors but also is really reviewing his life on the way to receive his eternal reward. The dour old man must learn how to love in order to find his salvation, and perhaps, too, his daughter-in-law Marianne in her selfless devotion to him actually "redeems" him. In the context of Bergman's other works from the period, the critical assumption of religious content is justifiable, and in fact a fruitful way to read the film, as long as the text of the film supports the interpretation.

Further, if due care is exercised, it is possible to move beyond the explicitly religious period and uncover an implicitly religious content in some of the earlier or later films. One could argue that the films of the angry young rebel, like THIRST (1949), SUMMER INTERLUDE (1950) or SAWDUST AND TINSEL (1953) reflect an emptiness of life without God, or at least without the love that God brings and the certainty that comes from faith. Similar lines of inquiry can be put to the later films, like CRIES AND WHISPERS (1972), THE SERPENT'S EGG (1977) or AUTUMN SONATA (1978). A viewer then indeed could view love between humans as "redemptive" in the theological sense and its absence as a form of damnation. The speculation is valid because of the explicit interest of the film maker in questions of God and the Spirit. One can document in the text of the films Bergman's rising and declining interest in God questions. One may accept or reject the hypothesis of the presence of virtual theological content in the non-religious films, but it cannot be dismissed out-of-hand as imposing spurious meanings on the films.

Bergman's notion of God emerges from a Swedish and Lutheran milieu. His characters are solitary figures searching for God in a private quest whose main arena is the intellect. For Lutherans redemption comes from faith alone, and so it is terribly important for a Bergman protagonist to know whether there is a God or whether the leap of faith is reasonable. In the absence of such evidence, one goes mad, as in THROUGH A GLASS DARKLY, perseveres in rituals that have lost their meaning, as in WINTER LIGHT, or simply continues life's journey alone in the face of God's silence, as in THE SILENCE. For the Italian Catholic Fellini, by contrast, God appears in clowns and crowds and Nino Rota's bouncy circus music, as in LA STRADA (1954) or NIGHTS OF CABIRIA (1957). God's absence brings not bleak despair but boredom touched with a hope for meaning in some future time, as in LA DOLCE VITA (1959) or JULIET OF THE SPIRITS (1965). Both directors address their questions from a Christian perspective, but Catholic and Lutheran frame the question in different contexts and with different imagery. Similarly, too, both seem to have gradually lost interest in religious issues in the later years of their careers.

For the Lutheran, without the saving power of Christ, the human person is thoroughly corrupt. Bergman's later work, once he has exorcised his God from his thought through the God Trilogy, reflects this bleak outlook: THE HOUR OF THE WOLF (1967), SHAME (1969), CRIES AND WHISPERS (1972) and THE SERPENT'S EGG (1977) and FROM THE LIFE OF THE MARIONETTES (1979). By the time he reached his last films, like the gentle FANNY AND ALEXANDER (1982), he could find peace only by reverting to childhood and family. In even these most secular films, his negative, almost despairing view of life is conditioned by his theological presumptions.[8] Paradoxically, once he has satisfied himself in his films that God is at best unknowable and therefore meaningless, his theology remains to shape his grim, but thoroughly secular picture of life.

Given the record of Bergman's concerns, the critic is perfectly justified in asking theological questions of his secular films, and the reflections that emerge from this exercise offer a sensitive, nuanced understanding of his work.

In stark contrast, Woody Allen presents an entirely different critical and religious context for his films. Since his primary medium has been comedy, it is understandable that few critics have tried to approach the serious or, more precisely, the theological side of his work. While Bergman acknowledged that "to me religious questions are continuously alive," when asked about his Jewishness, Allen, who attended Hebrew school for eight years, maintains, "It's not on my mind; it's no part of my artistic consciousness."[9]

Jewishness, as it generally appears in Allen's films, is a cultural phenomenon, a relic of childhood that he has dragged into adult life. Bergman in the mid-1950's directly confronted his early Lutheran background and gradually grew away from it. Allen for his part has used humor to distance himself from his past. Here a distinction is very important. Allen's humor springs from the external and visible surfaces of Judaism as an organized religion. In a fantasy in ANNIE HALL (1977), for example, Alvy Singer joins Annie's family for a traditional Easter dinner of baked ham. As he listens to their politely anti-Semitic comments, he suddenly imagines himself sitting in their midst dressed in Hasidic garb, complete with fur hat and side locks. The target of the humor is more the anti-Semitic stereotyping of the Halls than his own ethnic roots. In RADIO DAYS (1987) Joe, the Woody Allen character as a child, has been into mischief, and the rabbi and Joe's parents argue about who has the right to discipline him. They punctuate each phase of the argument by slapping him on the head, as though both family and rabbi are responsible for pounding good Jewish guilt into his youthful psyche.

The internal spirit of Judaism, however, is scarcely the material of comedy. While Allen makes cultural Jewishness, the externals, a rich source of his humor, he treats the philosophic and even theological concerns of Judaism with extreme seriousness, even in his comedies. He tries to understand the cost exacted from a people "chosen" to be different from the majority culture. For him, the ultimate cost of being the outsider is the Holocaust, which Allen refers to in such odd places in the films that it seems ever in the background of his consciousness. Alvy Singer in ANNIE HALL takes Annie to THE SORROW AND THE PITY, a four-hour documentary on Nazis, and when Mickey Sachs, in HANNAH AND HER SISTERS, tries to explain his contemplated conversion to Catholicism to his parents, he tells his hysterical mother that he needs answers to the questions of God and moral evil. He is driven to discover how a loving God could allow Nazis in the world."[10] This is a contemporary expression of the dilemma explored in Hebrew Scripture in the Book of Job: How can a just and loving God permit horrible suffering to fall upon a devout man like Job? For Woody Allen God's simultaneous love for humanity and tolerance for unspeakable evil present a supreme theological mystery, even when he reflects upon it in comic terms.

Even in his earlier comedies, like BANANAS (1971) and SLEEPER (1973), the comic character finds himself an alien amid a hostile majority culture, which he can neither escape or assimilate to. In the later comedies, like ZELIG (1983), the Allen character adjusts so perfectly to his milieu that he disappears into the culture and becomes whatever people want him to be, but Leonard Zelig knows he cannot be happy until he discovers his own personality. In BROADWAY DANNY ROSE (1984), the character blends into a tiny subculture of Jewish comedians that gathers at the Carnegie Delicatessen in Manhattan, but runs into trouble when he crosses the Hudson River into the alien and gentile land of New Jersey and tangles with the Mafia.

Ingmar Bergman writes from a homogeneous Swedish culture, and as the son of a Lutheran pastor who once served as chaplain to the Swedish royal family, he, if anyone, grew up knowing that he was respectable, an insider, in the upper levels of Swedish society.[11] Thus, if Bergman's characters are outsiders, the alienation is the result of choice or internal compulsion. As a result, the Bergman quest is private. These tormented characters find themselves unable to accept the superficial social norms of their less perceptive colleagues, and thus a gulf of loneliness grows as they search for unambiguous knowledge of God or meaning in a world that holds little interest in such questions.

Living as outsiders in a larger society, Allen's Jewish characters, in contrast, embark on a quest that is social. Bergman's heroes yearn for knowledge; Allen's for acceptance and love. Both artists focus their attention on self-absorbed characters, but while Bergman's withdraw from the commerce of daily living, Allen's face their anguish while holding a job, preparing meals and dealing with families and friends who have their own problems. Bergman concentrates on the individuals and pares away everything that could distract from the central person. Allen's dramatic narratives interweave several stories at once, underlining the complex, social nature of the quest. Bergman generally reserves complex plots and ensemble acting for comedy, like SMILES OF A SUMMER NIGHT (1955), NOW ABOUT ALL THESE WOMEN (1964) or FANNY AND ALEXANDER (1982). For Bergman the quest is intellectual: "How do I know if there is a God?" For Allen, it is ethical: "How do I live, whether there is a God or not?"

When trying to evaluate the religious concerns of Ingmar Bergman and Woody Allen, a critic sees them like the proverbial ships passing in opposite directions. Bergman began with a clearly articulated religious heritage which he treated in his films through several years and then abandoned. His concerns can be traced in a parabola. Before THE SEVENTH SEAL (1956) one looks for preludes, after THE SILENCE (1963) for vestiges. Woody Allen's concerns are far more tentative, but they seem to rise in a straight line from his early madcap comedies to his later use of comedy to explore several serious questions in life. His thinking has been shaped by a Jewish tradition, to be sure, but since he refers explicitly to religion so rarely, a religious critic must deal with the films very delicately and very, very respectfully.

3. COMING ATTRACTIONS

In entering into a religious dialogue with Woody Allen's films critics must be aware of their own preconceptions of what constitutes religion or God or Judaism. In keeping with the third style of interaction, as described above, one should regard these films, at least initially, as purely profane, or secularist, statements. Secularity covers a wide variety of philosophic patterns, but here the term connotes nothing more than a world view that is perfectly intelligible on its own terms without any reference to a personal God, as understood by the ordinary religious traditions. The dialogue between critics with theological concerns, in this instance stemming from a Roman Catholic tradition, and the films, secularist statements growing from a Jewish tradition, can lead to a greater appreciation of the films without compromising the integrity of either the critic or the film.

Thus, it is not necessary and in fact it would be dishonest to impose religious meanings on the films. At the same time, however, if such elements do appear in the text of the film and emerge in the dialogue of the Jewish Allen and his secular films on one side and his Catholic critic on the other, then there is no reason to refrain from acknowledging their presence for fear of imposing an alien meaning on the works. If the films do have a demonstrable religious content, one need not be embarrassed by identifying it.

Several other presumptions ought to be made explicit. The survey of the Allen films to follow grows out of the auteur method of film criticism. The auteur method, called "politique des auteurs," was born in France and imported into the English-speaking world by Andrew Sarris and others in the 1960's.[12] It forces attention almost exclusively on directors. These critics view individual films merely as examples of a director's artistic autobiography. The body of work of an individual director must be studied in the context of his or her entire artistic output on the assumption that the genuine auteur exercises a certain degree of control over the product from early story conferences to release print, at least to the degree that one's individual preoccupations and style appear even in the most routine genre films. An auteur critic would argue, for example, that a Howard Hawks Western, like RIO BRAVO (1958), has more in common with a Howard Hawks romantic comedy, like BRINGING UP BABY (1938) than with a John Ford Western. The explicit objective of such criticism is an increased understanding and appreciation of Howard Hawks through analysis of the entire body of his works rather than an elucidation of any particular film.

This critical method in its pure form is now largely discredited. American scholars like Thomas Schatz have understandably reacted passionately against this French-born style of criticism, because it fails to account for the complexity of the Hollywood production system and the demands of the market place. Even the most independent of film makers collaborates with producers, writers, actors, camera operators, musicians and scores of other creative people. If such a director does exercise "control," it is control through creative compromise with the other artists on the set. In addition, if a director's personal vision and special project hold little chance of attracting a ticket-buying audience, business interests, not artistic ones, will be the determining factors. The film will not be made. In rejecting the auteur method Schatz writes: "Auteurism itself would not be worth bothering with if it hadn't been so influential, effectively stalling film history and criticism in a prolonged stage of adolescent romanticism."[13]

Even with this cautionary note from contemporary film critics, however, a modified auteur method can be a fruitful approach to the films of Woody Allen. As writer, director and leading actor in many of his films, he has exerted enormous control over his own works, perhaps more than any other American director. He claims to keep himself relatively isolated from critics and audience alike, and he probably does.[14] Despite the frequent absence of critical and popular support, he claims that he continues to try to please only himself. Few of his films have been enormously profitable, and many have received decidedly mixed reviews. Yet he continues to experiment and stretch with different film genres and styles, and some of his films he dismisses as failures, but worth the effort because they allowed him to grow as an artist.[15]

This study owes a methodological debt to auteur criticism in that it presumes and will develop the notion that all the Allen films, from the early comedies to the ponderous "Bergmanesque" dramas, bear the mark of their creator to a certain degree. Moreover, a careful reading of the films can uncover a consistency in style and theme that matures consistently through the years.

The survey of the Allen films to follow will provide a discussion of these themes under the umbrella term "theology." In particular, Allen's "theology" provides a useful tool for undertanding and appreciating his preoccupations: love, death, intelligibility, a meaning and purpose in the universe and finally, the existence of God. His films reveal an imagination that turns continually to the mysteries of life that lie beyond the power of the intellect alone to penetrate. This most profane artist continually reveals a continuing fascination with the sacred.

Woody Allen's films provide a textbook illustration of the human approach to the sacred described by Rudolf Otto in his seminal essay *The Idea of the Holy,* originally published in German in 1917 and translated into English five years later. Otto explains that in the face of mystery, one experiences a sense of dependence: "It is the emotion of a creature, submerged and overwhelmed by its own nothingness in contrast to that which is supreme above all creatures.[16] The mystery of the sacred is both "fascinans" and "tremendum"; it leaves the beholder both fascinated and trembling in awe at the same time. This reaction is understandable. The ordinary arena for humankind in this industrialized postreligious age is profane in Eliade's sense of the term, outside ("pro," literally "in front of") the sacred space occupied by the "fanum," or "altar."[17] In their encounter with mystery, the unknowable, ordinary, workaday "profane" people are out of their proper element.

At the same time, the holy place, as a forbidden territory is ever attractive, while it is ever horrifying. Children rush to explore dark attics with curiosity and fear held in precarious balance. If worrisome parents forbid them to enter, the forbidden place becomes all the more attractive. Otto cites the example of adults, "even persons of high all-round education," who delight in ghost stories.[18] Like curious children or ghostly readers, Allen repeatedly explores the topics that most intrigue him, not quite certain what he will find at the top of the creaking staircase.

How does the ordinary person react to the terror and fascination of mystery? In many ways a committed believer has the easiest time of it. Through assent to a formulated body of religious or philosophical traditions—Judaeo-Christian, Muslim or Marxist—it is possible to take refuge in dogma. In this way many of the mysteries are solved, and the believer learns to cope with those that remain: In most Bible religions, God rewards the good and punishes the evil, if not in this world then in the next. In large part, then the mystery of evil becomes a more manageable problem for many believers.

Likewise, those living with some level of non-belief can also find an easy way out. They can simply shrug their shoulders, proclaim themselves agnostics, materialists or rationalists—without necessarily using those terms—and get on with the business of living without giving mystery another thought. Families, bills and health provide enough challenge for most people to try to cope with in one lifetime, and such preoccupations usually leave little time or energy for being awed or fascinated in the face of mystery. Understandably, then, these two alternatives are the ones most frequently chosen by the bulk of the world's citizens.

An artist like Woody Allen does not have this luxury granted to the majority. He cannot retreat from the fear and allure of mystery. His reaction is brilliantly diverse. At times he must laugh at the absurdity of the human condition and thus at himself. His comic characters, especially in the early films, struggle under the burden of anxiety in the face of loneliness, death or human cruelty. These frantic little people are funny precisely as they stumble through life balancing their neuroses with their will to live. The comic genius—Charlie Chaplin, Buster Keaton or Harold Lloyd, for example—reveals the heroic struggle of the puny human protagonist against the ruthless, impersonal forces of the universe as essentially very funny. When their audiences realize how much life is stacked against them, the result is comic, and their plucky, even manic attempts to overcome the odds are heroic and gratifying. Woody Allen fits into this tradition.

Comic genius, however, is a rare commodity. Most artists, like Poe or Melville, O'Neill or Bergman, view the universe as anything but funny. Their vision is the stuff of horror and tragedy. Only giants can rise above the forces of destiny, but even their momentary triumph must be tempered by recollections of human mortality. In several films, Woody Allen presents this brooding vision as well. His "serious" films, often prematurely dismissed by critics as ponderous or derivative (of Bergman), deal with the same topics as the comedies, but the tormented protagonists are more likely to weep than laugh at the smallness and emptiness of their lives.

In many ways the tragedian's work is easier. Tragic heroes are literalists; they say what they feel and think about the limits of the human condition. Their pain lies closer to the surface where it can be translated into words and images. They weep and howl in their torment. The artist transcribes what is there. Comic artists deal on the same level of seriousness as tragedians when they contemplate humanity, but their characters counterattack life through laughter. They, too, find the human condition painful, even terrifying, but it is laughable at the same time. Armed with a sense of humor, the human species survives and triumphs.

The challenge for the critic is to discover the serious content of the comedies and appreciate the consistency of Woody Allen's "theological" vision. A look at two nonfilmic works will illustrate the convergence of theological content and the comic style. It will thus provide a methodological model for scrutinizing the films. In these works, Allen relies on his usual irreverent comedy style, but all the while he is asking serious theological questions, a technique he will follow consistently in the films.

MR. BIG was added to the collection of pieces largely from *The New Yorker* published under the title *Getting Even* in 1971.[19] At this stage in his career, Allen was known for his acting, stand-up comedy and successful comic film scripts, like WHAT'S NEW, PUSSYCAT? (1965) and TAKE THE MONEY AND RUN (1969). The humor is often brilliant, and often, too, embarrassingly crude and sophomoric. The short pieces of the collection spoof serious subjects, like "Death," the character from Bergman's THE SEVENTH SEAL (1957), philosophy and psychoanalysis. Some familiarity with the object of the satire adds to the enjoyment of the work, but for the most part the humor is fairly obvious.

MR. BIG parodies THE MALTESE FALCON (John Huston, 1941), but it too has its own serious agenda. Huston's Sam Spade, played by Humphrey Bogart, becomes Allen's Kaiser Lupowitz, who mimics the Spade/Bogart dialogue but bumbles through the case as a Woody Allen alter ego.[20] The beautiful but deadly femme noire, played by Mary Astor in the film, goes through a series of name changes as Spade becomes more entangled in her web. Initially, she is Miss Wonderly, described by Spade's secretary as a "knockout." This description is fair, and her beauty is wonderful enough to lure Spade and his partner into her trap. For the next contact Miss Wonderly becomes Miss LeBlanc, a mysterious blank sheet, a woman with no identity. Finally, she appears as Brigid O'Shaughnessy, whose down-to-earth Irish name stereotypically unites her with violent crime, deceit and murder.

Allen's femme noire goes through a similar series of name changes, but with an entirely different purpose. When she enters Lupowitz's office to start him on his search for Mr. Big, who is God, "The Creator, the Underlying Principle, the First Cause of Things," she has the crude name Heather Butkiss, who claims to be a "nudie model." Almost immediately, she admits that this is a lie and she is really Claire Rosensweig, a philosophy major at Vassar. Later, Lupowitz discovers that Claire is not really a student, but a teacher at Radcliffe, who got involved with a philosopher. Finally, he learns that she is in fact Ellen Shepherd, professor of physics at Bryn Mawr.

Allen uses the changes of identity to mark a progression in his comic search for God. Heather offers the perfect erotic fantasy of the idealized female, providing beauty and the promise of sexual

fulfillment, but in a quest of such seriousness, amoral, instant sexual gratification offers little of lasting importance. Claire, the undergraduate, is merely doing a paper for "History of Western Thought." Her interests are sincere, but superficial. She needs an "A" in the course so that her father will buy her a Mercedes. Claire the philosopher and Ellen the physicist are committed to the search for God, but Claire is said to have been misled by a philosopher who used to be a drummer in a jazz trio, while Ellen's need for mathematical certainty renders all philosophic speculation worthless. Claire, posing as a philosopher, actually hints at her true identity as a scientist. As she and Lupowitz are engaged in love-making, she dismisses as "absurd" Kierkegaard's thesis that one cannot know God, but must have faith. Thus she reveals herself as a hardcore rationalist. Allen uses both of the intellectual personae of his femme noire to criticize his own search for certainty on the question of God. Once he enters the quest on the terms of the academic, he has no alternative but to conclude that God is unknowable, or simply dead.

In his search, Allen ventures outside the philosophic realms and examines the conclusions of familiar religious traditions as well. After his first interview with Claire, he immediately visits Rabbi Itzhak Wiseman. Wiseman's name is ironic. He explains that God has been running a celestial protection racket with his chosen people for centuries. God takes care of His people for a price that is so terrible the Rabbi will not even mention it. One might speculate that the Rabbi is hinting that part of the price is Jewish guilt, which has always been a staple of Allen comedy. His reluctance to name the price also has darker suggestions of centuries of persecution leading up to the Holocaust. The interview between Lupowitz and Wiseman ends abruptly.

The trail leads next to Chicago Phil, a committed atheist, who assures Lupowitz that God is a Sicilian syndicate run by the Pope. After his liaison with Claire, Lupowitz visits the Pope as he dines at Giordino's Italian restaurant. The Pope, surrounded by gunmen, assures Lupowitz that God does indeed exist, but he, the Pope, alone can communicate with God because he owns the red suit. (Allen may be confused on his Catholic lore: The Pope wears white, while the cardinals wear red.) When Lupowitz asks if the existence of God is really "hype," the Pope shrugs off the question by admitting that the God business can be highly profitable.

In these exchanges with the rabbi and the pope, Allen reveals skepticism with both the traditions of Judaism and the organized side of Catholicism. In his quest, neither religious body offers much help: One is a joke and the other is cynical.

The search does have an ending of sorts. Lupowitz has received word from the police that God is dead, murdered by an existentialist. The detectives deduce this from the haphazard technique of the murderer. Lupowitz himself may be a suspect. At Claire's apartment, Lupowitz confronts her with her real identity as Ellen, the physicist, and accuses her of murdering God. She denies the charge, but Lupowitz reasons that since she is a scientist only posing as a philosopher, she coldly killed off all the philosophic systems even as they tried to explain God. Finally, he concludes, she, the scientist, killed God herself. Confronted with her guilt, she tries first to seduce Lupowitz, and failing that, she draws a forty-five so that she can end the argument with a bullet. Lupowitz shoots first, and as Claire/Ellen dies, he offers an explanation of being and nothingness that parodies the convoluted language of Jean-Paul Sartre.

At the end of this brief short story, the mystery of God remains, and the usual solutions—philosophy, religion and science—are dismissed as meaningless or, worse, destructive. The philosophers contradict one another, religion is a fraud and science, attractive as it is to the modern searcher, tries to seduce him with its wiles while sneakily planning to kill him just as it had killed God with its demand for quantifiable certitude. These are serious religious questions explored by the comic muse. Woody Allen has thus entered the realm of the sacred on a tourist visa; he remains a citizen of the profane world where such questions fascinate and terrify to such an extent that they provoke laughter, the nervous giggle of one not quite sure what he will find at the end of his search.

Some years later, in 1975 after the successful comedies PLAY IT AGAIN, SAM (1972), EVERYTHING YOU ALWAYS WANTED TO KNOW ABOUT SEX* (*BUT WERE AFRAID TO ASK) (1972) and SLEEPER (1973), Allen returns to the themes of MR. BIG in his one-act play "God."[21] In many ways even the structure of the play is similar to the earlier story.

Not only does "God" feature the device of the Greek comedies by presenting a play-within-a-play, but the actors also interact with modern, New York characters planted in the audience as theater-goers. In this spoof of the Greek New Comedy, an actor and the playwright frantically try to discover a plot and meaning in their play, but as the opening approaches, they still have no clue. The actor is Diabetes and the writer Hepatitis. Later, another actor Trichinosis will join them. The Greek-sounding names are familiar English words, and as names of diseases surely provide a comic touch. At the same time, precisely as names of diseases, they introduce a suggestion of human mortality.

The hapless characters even try to contact the author, Woody Allen himself as an off-stage voice. Allen plays the part of the heartless creator of this dramatic universe and provides no help whatever as the cast tries to discover what to do. From the outset of the play, then, Allen is linking his search for God to an ethical dimension. If God, the author (presuming that he does exist), cannot or will not tell us what to do, how are we humans supposed to know how to live?

Doris Levine, a philosophy student from Brooklyn College, provides the occasion for the earthy humor, but she is a more marginal character than Heather/Claire/Ellen. She is a member of the audience from Great Neck, a name that suggests either anatomy, erotic activity or both. Like the Heather character, Doris is a sexual object, and her confused preoccupations and contradictory statements about orgasm seem as inane as her philosophic truisms. In exasperation, Hepatitis comments that she must have formulated her ideas in the Brooklyn College cafeteria.

When he enters the scene, Trichinosis, an actor and inventor, offers to save the play by providing an ending. As a man of science, he has devised a machine holding Zeus with his thunderbolts. At the end of the play, he explains, the machine will be wheeled onto stage, and the god will descend from a pulley to rescue the actors, who are grateful for his intervention but distressed at the recognition of their own powerlessness. He is prepared to rent his invention at a reasonable hourly rate. They agree to try the device. It works nicely in rehearsal, but during the actual performance the machine jams, leaving Zeus suspended high above the arena of mortal concerns. Once again, Allen voices his skepticism of claims that science or God can provide answers for the human condition. Neither can provide the *deus ex machina* ending to rescue people from an impossible situation.

Another character known as Blanche DuBois, having left a deliberately unnamed Tennessee Williams play because she needs a

God in her artistic universe, agrees to join the cast of the new play. Bursitis will play Zeus, and the new play is entitled "The Slave," a comment on the subservient position of mortals in a universe ruled by a remote God, who may or may not exist.

The Slave, played by Diabetes, rejects the idea presented by the chorus that, like all slaves, he longs for freedom. He prefers slavery because without freedom he can simply do what he is told without having to make any ethical decisions. When Doris, now playing a fellow slave, challenges him, he repeats his belief that freedom is dangerous; one can make mistakes and get into trouble. His master, however, gives him the power to change his condition. If he undertakes a dangerous journey and delivers a message to the king, he will receive his freedom. Doris urges him to accept the arrangement, but with little success. Finally, the off-stage voice of Woody Allen, once more in his role of creator of this dramatic universe, persuades him to accept the challenge. Once he leaves the confines of his servitude and begins to experience the wider horizons of life, he confides to his audience that he is beginning to feel nauseous. Diabetes is clearly cast into a role that he does not enjoy. Paradoxically, freedom for him is slavery. He longs to be free from inquiry, responsibility and knowledge, the burdens of a free man. Slavery frees him from such concerns. He is afraid of his humanity.

The message itself poses a cruel dilemma for the slave. Learning that kings routinely murder the bearers of bad news, Diabetes has good reason to worry. The message is the single word "yes." Since he does not know the question, Diabetes cannot imagine what his answer means, and if the king will take his message as good news or bad news. A true slave would be ignorant of such complications and simply say what the master wants; with freedom, one must decide what to say, even though put in the unfair position of not knowing the questions. In theological terms, the thinking person in Allen's view, must act without knowing what God wants from him—presuming of course that there is a God to begin with.

The question, Diabetes eventually discovers, is the central theological question: Does God exist. He blurts out his affirmative answer, and the King is shaken. He is terrified, since if there is a God who passes judgment, his deeds will condemn him for all eternity. God can also possibly rescue his servants, but the machine bearing Zeus jams, spilling the actor on the stage, who dies of a broken neck. God, then, has ceased to exist; he is dead. Without a God, the two original actors, Diabetes and Hepatitis conclude that the play has no meaning. The entire episode has been ridiculous.

Allen's moral dilemma arises directly from his metaphysics: If God exists, then human actions are trivial and judged by a Being that offers very few clues about his own existence and his expectations for his creatures. In such a world, freedom is a terrible burden. On the other hand, if God does not exist, then the human person, as an individual, becomes the sole measure of the good, but the universe as a whole is meaningless and human actions, however heroic and altruistic, are likewise meaningless.

In one guise or another, this dilemma is restated in several of Allen's recent films. For example, Cliff Stern (Woody Allen) and Judah Rosenthal (Martin Landau) in CRIMES AND MISDEMEANORS (1989) are a modern-day Hepatitis and Diabetes. Near the end of the film, they sit in a quiet side room at a wedding reception and discuss an imaginary script for a film about moral responsibility. They cannot resolve the question posed by their would-be script. Does the presence of God make people more or less moral, more or less tragic. Similarly, Kleinman, literally "the little man" (Woody Allen), the anti-hero of SHADOWS AND FOG (1991) is forced to wander though a murky, urban landscape searching for an unseen murderer, but has no hint from any higher authority as to what he must do to protect himself and the city from the random evil of the killer. Because he understands so little and offers confused answers to the authorities, he becomes a suspect himself. Some believe that even if he did not commit the murders himself, Kleinman is surely a collaborator, and the little man begins to understand that he is inextricably involved in an evil that he cannot stop or even comprehend. He longs for someone, like God, to enlighten him and show him what he must do, but of course his hopes are never fulfilled.

Nor are his hopes for moral certainty fulfilled in any of his films. His characters laugh or whine, face crises or run away from them, turn neurotically inward or run about in impulsive activity that serves as a distraction from themselves, but at the end, the doubt remains. Woody Allen and the people he creates can never pass from their profane realm into the sacred despite all their efforts. In their attempts they are funny, or tragic or both.

NOTES

1. Mircea Eliade, *The Sacred and the Profane: The Nature of Religion,* tr. Willard S. Trask, (New York: Harcourt Brace Jovanovich, 1959), p. 15. The classic study suggests not only the title of this present study but it has provided a great deal of the context for these reflections. A contemporary author and translator would certainly be more sensitive to the use of gender inclusive language.
2. Karl Rahner, "Membership in the Church," *Theological Investigations II,* tr. Karl-H. Kruger (Baltimore: Helicon, 1963) 38–45 supplies a summary of the history of the dilemma.
3. Richard P. McBrien, *Catholicism* I (New York: Winston, 1980), 269–70, provides the summary of the three approaches at the conclusion of lengthy discussion of religious pluralism.
4. "Membership," p. 55.
5. McBrien, p. 270.
6. For examples, Ingmar Bergman, *The Magic Lantern, An Autobiography,* tr. Joan Tate (New York: Viking, 1987), pp. 1–24; Vernon Young, *Cinema Borealis* (New York: Equinox, 1971), pp. 7–15; and Peter Cowie, *Ingmar Bergman: A Critical Biography* (New York: Scribner's, 1982) 3–19. Virtually every other study of Bergman alludes to his childhood experiences in the vicarage.
7. Ingmar Bergman, "Introduction: Bergman Discusses Film Making" in *Four Screenplays of Ingmar Bergman,* tr. Lars Malmstrom and David Kushner (New York: Simon and Schuster, 1960) p. xxi.
8. Richard A. Blake, *The Lutheran Milieu of Ingmar Bergman's Films* (New York: Arno, 1978), pp. 41–53. This section relates the dark vision of Ingmar Bergman in his early films to his experience of popular Lutheran piety. The analysis is equally applicable to the pessimism found in the films of the later, post-God period.
9. Nancy Pogel, *Woody Allen* (Boston: Twayne, 1987), p. 25.
10. Woody Allen, *Hannah and Her Sisters* (New York: Vintage, 1987), p. 133
11. Frank Gado, *The Passion of Ingmar Bergman* (Durham: Duke Univ., 1986), p. 7
12. Andrew Sarris, "The American Cinema" and "Directorial Chronology," *Film Comment,* No. 26 (Spring 1963), pp. 1–68, is generally credited with turning the attention of the American critical establishment to the auteur method. These twin essays were subsequently greatly expanded and published in book form: *The American Cinema: Directors and Directions 1929–1968,* (New York: Dutton, 1968.
13. Thomas Schatz, *The Genius of the System: Hollywood Filmmaking in the Studio Era,* (New York: Pantheon, 1988), p. 5.

14. Eric Lax, *Woody Allen: A Biography* (New York: Knopf, 1991), pp. 369–372.
15. Lax, p. 279.
16. Rudolf Otto, *The Idea of the Holy: An Inquiry into the non-rational factor in the idea of the divine and its relation to the rational,* tr. John W. Harvey, (New York: Oxford, 1958), p. 10.
17. Eliade, pp. 22–24.
18. Otto, p. 16.
19. Woody Allen, *The Complete Prose of Woody Allen* (New York: Wings, 1991), pp. 283–292, contains a reprint of "Mr. Big."
20. Maurice Yacowar, *Loser Take All: The Comic Art of Woody Allen* (New York: Continuum, 1991), pp.92–93, presents an insightful commentary of this story as a step in Allen's search for meaning, one aspect of which is his search for God.
21. Woody Allen, *God* (New York: Samuel French, 1975).

CHAPTER II. THE CARTOONS

Woody Allen did not burst into the pantheon of great directors with a sudden flash of genius, as did, for example, Orson Welles in 1941 with CITIZEN KANE. His stature grew slowly and unexpectedly, and this is probably a major reason that some critics and the mass audience alike are still reluctant to recognize the serious side of his work. Once pigeon-holed as a vulgar, borscht-belt comic, he had to struggle to establish his reputation as a major talent, dealing with topics that could fit reasonably under the heading of "philosophic" or "religious."

A survey of the early comedies, colored by an awareness of the themes that gradually surfaced in Allen's later work, adds to the appreciation of his films as a whole. This is the critical method the auteur critics have proposed for years. WHAT'S NEW, PUSSYCAT? (1965) is not technically an Allen film, since he merely provided the screenplay for a film that Clive Donner directed. Even so, it offers hints of themes that will emerge later when Allen assumes more control over his own films. WHAT'S UP, TIGER LILY? (1966) and TAKE THE MONEY AND RUN (1969) are spoofs of popular film genres, and thus their originality lies hidden beneath the surface of their generic conventions. These can, of course, be criticized as derivative, but derivation is the whole point of parody.

EVERYTHING YOU ALWAYS WANTED TO KNOW ABOUT SEX* (*BUT WERE AFRAID TO ASK) (1972) spoofs not only several familiar film genres, but American culture itself for its making the book of the same title a national best seller. Sex in America, according to Allen, was being reduced to a business. Finally, in BANANAS (1971) and SLEEPER (1973), Allen begins to emerge as an important creative artist, whose ideas are beginning to evolve into serious personal statements. The medium remains comedy, but the questions he explores are quite significant by any standard.

During this period, Woody Allen was involved in other projects as well. He acted in CASINO ROYALE (1967), a limp parody of the then popular James Bond movies. Its lack of focus may be attributed to the fact that it suffered through many writers and many directors, including John Huston, before it stumbled onto the screen. His stage play, "Don't Drink the Water" became a film directed by Howard Morris in 1969. He also adapted his stage play for the screen and starred in PLAY IT AGAIN, SAM, a spoof of Humphrey Bogart films directed by Herbert Ross. Although he made varying contributions to these generally lackluster films, Woody Allen was gaining exposure to both movie-going audiences and to Hollywood professionals. In film he had found his medium of preference.

WHAT'S NEW, PUSSYCAT? (1965) marks Allen's first involvement with the world of big-budget film making. Although he did not direct it, he provided the script for director Clive Donner, but claims that the final version was far different from his original.[1] Regardless of the confused comic styles, resulting from Donner's direction of Allen's script and the improvised comic dialogue provided by co-stars Peter O'Toole and Peter Sellers, the film both introduced Allen to a new medium, and it hardened his resolve to gain complete control over future films by directing his own screenplays. In addition, WHAT'S NEW, PUSSYCAT? became one of the most profitable films of the year, and thus it made Woody Allen a bankable commodity in the industry.[2]

Even with its mixture of styles—silent-movie slapstick, Marx Brothers mayhem and burlesque crudeness—several of the later, familiar Allen themes lurk quietly beneath the surface. The female characters represent a goal to be sought, and the quest becomes an attempt to live out an erotic fantasy. The actresses (Romy Schneider, Capucine, Paula Prentiss, Catherine Schaake and Ursula Andress) are extraordinarily beautiful women, voluptuous and more or less available. The characters they play seem eager to be disencumbered of their clothing on the flimsiest of pretexts, a process that Donner the director and Allen the writer encourage with amazing regularity.

In the make-believe world of bedroom farce, where the moral considerations of the real world hold little sway, the male characters might be expected to delight in their edenic surroundings. In Woody Allen's farces, however, they are too neurotic to take full advantage of their fantasy situations. Beautiful women are both objects of desire and sources of frustration or terror. For example,

Michael James (Peter O'Toole), the editor of a fashion magazine, inhabits a world populated by gorgeous, ambitious and accommodating models, but since he is afraid to pursue Carol (Romy Schneider), the one idealized woman in his life, he finds them a bother. Victor (Woody Allen) helps dress the strippers at The Crazy Horse Saloon, but the disdain by the minimally attired ladies of the chorus brings him only a sense of rejection and self-pity. Paradoxically, he is successful with several women outside the theater, but his frustration is deepened by his failure with Carol, who is the woman of *his* dreams as well. Finally, Dr. Fritz Fassbinder (Peter Sellers) is married to a huge, dominating woman (Edra Gale), who wears the horned helmet of a Valkyrie, but Fritz loves Renee, one of his patients (Capucine).

All of these characters lead lives of lost opportunity, missing the occasions of love near at hand, while pursuing an unattainable ideal. The sequence of failed love affairs is a striking portrait of the limitations and futility of the human condition, but it is also potentially very funny. Allen will not permit his audiences to brood about human foolishness and isolation. He invites them to enjoy the joke.

The religious critic must be very careful in dealing with this theme of unrequited love. In the films of Ingmar Bergman, by contrast, one might easily and productively slip into a metaphorical understanding of thwarted sexual attraction. For Bergman, at least in his religious period, woman, the source of life, mirrors in some way the elusive presence of God, Creator and Redeemer. The longing of a hero for one particular beloved person offers some suggestion of the human yearning for fulfillment in the presence of God. Finding love with a redeeming woman is tantamount to finding salvation. On the other hand, failure to reach the object of one's quest hints at the absence of God in a universe that becomes harsh and unloving without Him. Such themes reflect the dictum from the *Confessions* of St. Augustine: "My soul is restless, 'till it rests in Thee." In his theological films, Bergman continually explored the possibility of faith and the emptiness of a world without God.

The Woody Allen of WHAT'S NEW, PUSSYCAT? is neither Ingmar Bergman nor Augustine of Hippo. He is a comic writer borrowing, perhaps unconsciously, from a series of earthy traditions that stretches from the bawdy Roman theater of Terence, Plautus and Juvenal through American burlesque, vaudeville, movies and television, seasoned by the indefatigable summer-resort comedians of the Catskills. If he is derivative, it is from these, not from any definable theological sources.

Rejecting overt religious content in an early farce, like WHAT'S NEW, PUSSYCAT?, however, does not preclude a few tentative but important theological reflections on the work. One need not impose a reading upon the film to note that the male characters are self-centered and seek sexual fulfillment only for their own gratification. They are bumbling and incompetent in reaching their goals in life. The women tend to be cartoon characters, beautiful objects to pursue and possess. Even when these females become aggressive in chasing the men, they are at best little more than male fantasies come to life and at worst threatening nightmares. Mutuality, sharing and giving hold little place in Allen's world of madcap comedy. At this stage in his thought, Allen creates male characters, certainly born of his own personal reflection rather than formal study, who are isolated and seem capable of relieving that isolation only by possession of an unattainable object. Frustration is therefore inevitable. His early portrayal of human sexuality has an adolescent, self-centered and self-defeating quality about it.

The comic character, called the nebbish, the schlemiel or simply "the little man," provides access to Allen's view of the human condition in a potentially hostile but very funny universe.[3] The hero is powerless in his search for fulfillment. Alone and burdened by neurosis, he is programmed for failure. The only reasonable response to this pitiable condition is laughter, laced with cynicism. The only other obvious but less reasonable response is death. This is, of course, a thoroughly secular conception that is perfectly intelligible without any reference to religious thinking whatever. At the same time, one searching for the means to understand Allen's religious imagination, especially as it surfaces in the later films, may be excused for finding scattered religious implications in this comic characterization of the human condition. It gives a preview of things to come.

WHAT'S UP, TIGER LILY? (1966) is generally considered Allen's directorial debut, even though he really supervised very little of the photography and acting. As Allen explains on screen, the film about to be shown had already been released in Japan as an adventure movie, but he as director and author added a completely different story to the English-language sound track. Unsuspecting audiences invariably wait to be let in on the gag, but there is no punch line to the spoken prologue. Allen tells them exactly how the film made its way to English-speaking audiences.

American International Pictures held the American rights to a third-rate Japanese spy movie KAGI NO KAGI (KEY OF KEYS), directed by Senkichi Taniguchi in 1964. Rather than dub in an English-language translation that approximates the Japanese script by Hideo Ando, A.I.P. called in Woody Allen, then known mainly as a television writer and nightclub monologist, to create his own story by adding a thoroughly inappropriate comic dialogue to the images on the screen.[4] As a result, the dubbed dialogue has no relationship to the original story line. The characters belong to a predictable James Bond spin-off with Japanese flavor, but the English words that come out of their mouths are Jewish low comedy. The conceit wears thin very quickly, however, and despite some brilliant comic touches, the film as a whole rapidly becomes more tedious than inventive.

The film opens without dialogue during a classic movie chase of the James Bond variety: luxury cars screaming through the night, gun fire and even a flame thrower. For reasons unexplained, a beautiful female victim dressed in yellow is tied to a conveyor belt and is being fed into a bench saw. At the last possible second, the police arrive and rescue her after a rousing Kung-Fu battle with the unidentified miscreants.

The hero of the battle is a Japanese detective, who introduces himself as "Phil Moskowitz, lovable rogue" (Tatsuya Mihashi). The Japanese version of 007 shares the near invincibility of the English prototype. He is handsome, competent, suave and ever successful with the ladies, but with his Jewish name, he is cast as something of an outsider to Japanese society. The audience may be struck by the incongruity of the name, but the actors scarcely notice. Allen's use of obviously Jewish characters will become a signature in his comedies, and in many of them the name itself marks the character as somehow apart from the majority culture. In the Japanese setting, of course, the alienation of the characters is even more complete and more comedic than it is in Allen's later New York settings. During several of the athletic fist fights during the film, the Japanese combatants insult each other by hissing ethnic insults: "Saracen pig! Spartan dog!"[5] Casting the adversary as the alien is a part of the strategy of hostility and aggression.

As Moskowitz demonstrates, the littleness of "the little man" then need not be physical, and he need not be a bumbler either. The Moskowitz character even carries a certain heroic quality over from the Japanese version. In many Allen films, even when the hero is successful in the ways of the world, he somehow remains an outsider by the very fact of his Jewishness. References to the Holocaust, Hitler and Nazis throughout Allen's work, often in comedic settings, underline his notion that life is precarious for such outsiders.[6] And in a hostile, unforgiving universe, Tokyo as well as New York, everyone is an outsider, a "little man," and thus everyone is in danger.

The incongruity of the Jewish name and Japanese actor provides a laugh—at least the first time the name is used—but it also presents an image of the human person cast adrift and alienated from his surroundings. Later on, Allen will ask if there is a God to sustain and protect such creatures, but even in this mishmash of a comedy, he reveals some of his fears about his own human status. First in a long series of Allen misfits, Moskowitz, an Allen surrogate, is obviously successful, yet not fully at home in his world. What must a character possess, or do or be to feel secure in his surroundings?

As Woody Allen the director finishes his on-screen explanation of his seemingly lunatic idea of dubbing his unrelated comic dialogue onto a pre-existing spy film, the titles begin and Allen becomes a cartoon caricature, complete with red hair and glasses. The animated figure races around the screen, pulling titles out of the bodies of beautiful, living female dancers and snidely covering the bare breasts of an exotic dancer with cartoon X's. The first two juxtaposed sequences point out an odd paradox: Allen as writer and director in charge of the film and Woody reduced to the status of a cartoon in his own film. In other words, Allen suggests, a man may be in charge, but he's still a joke.

After the titles, the action returns to Phil Moskowitz and the usual, now cliché package of Bond adventures. While this Oriental Bond seems to be an indefatigable lover, he is never completely successful. In one adventure Phil's female companion retires to the bathroom to prepare for their encounter, but before she rejoins him, bullets rip through the window, and Phil must depart on another harrowing chase. Later, apparently the same evening, Phil is locked in a passionate embrace in a car parked in the shadow of a prison wall. An escaping female prisoner, however, jumps from the wall and crashes through their roof, thus interrupting his amorous activity once more. Phil takes up with the escaped convict, but before they can fulfill their desires, high technology ruins their tryst. The home office calls on a space-age transmitter to warn Phil about the gang who is after his romantic companion. Almost immediately, two gang members break into the bedroom and kidnap both would-be lovers.

Wing Fat, a villainous gambler, is similarly thwarted. After a successful evening at the tables in a shipboard casino, he is encouraged to spend some of his winnings on one of the ladies-in-waiting upstairs. Walking slowly along a row of staterooms, each one decorated with a beautiful potential partner, he surveys the offerings coolly, but when he comes to the last door, he appears to recognize the woman. While we wait to discover their past relationship, he calls her "Mother!" and punches her in the face. Kvetching like a comic Jewish mother, this beautiful young Japanese actress explains that she turned to prostitution because he didn't write.

Even Allen the on-screen director joins in this dance of failed love. At one moment, after the film apparently breaks, the action returns to the director's screening room, where the audience discovers him in the projection booth, passionately preoccupied with an otherwise anonymous woman (Louise Lasser, his second wife). The broken film, of course, interrupts their activity, and they are duly embarrassed by the intrusion of the movie audience. They are first seen as projected silhouettes on the screen, and again unsuspecting audiences would need time to realize that the film break and shadows are part of the movie. By adding this bit of business to the Japanese film, Allen identifies himself with his movie characters in the ludicrous spy story and at the same time he suggests that in film making, the would-be auteur is actually placing himself on the screen. This scene gives a hint of Allen's future use of film as a medium of personal expression: If his films consistently contain autobiographical elements, as is widely believed, he intended from the start to add his own life to the fiction on the screen.

Frustrated love is common enough in bedroom farce, but in addition to its comedic possibilities it also provides an image of a world where one's desires for love are constantly thwarted. At this stage of Allen's development, love and sex are used interchangeably. The self-centered male characters want sex, preferably without any other involvement. As Allen's ideas mature, his notion of love and human desires will become more nuanced, and thus more human. The sex, as a goal in itself, will become less important.

The simplicity of Allen's understanding of love is underlined by his controlling metaphor used in several forms throughout this film and many others. He equates sex and food.[7] The ridiculous premise of the caper, as Allen rewrites the story, is the recovery of a stolen recipe for perfect egg salad. The madcap chase, in its metaphorical sense, is the quest of perfect love/sex. When Shepherd Wong, the fabulously wealthy operator of a gambling boat and suspected owner of the stolen recipe, prepares to take a woman of his choice into his quarters, he promises her "a perfect egg-salad sandwich." Again, Phil's two partners in his quest are attractive sisters: Terry Yaki (Mie Hanna) and Suki Yaki (Akiko Wakayabayashi), two Japanese dishes popular at least with Americans who occasionally are brave enough to try Japanese food.

Finally, the themes are united in the last scene, when the Woody character, the on-screen director of the film, lounges on a sofa, eating an apple and commenting on the action of the film as the final credits roll and China Lee, a professional striptease artist, does her act on the right side of the screen in front of him. At first he is more interested in the apple, but as the routine continues, he reaches out and tries to bite her. In this final shot, he unites visually the two human appetites that dominate the motivations of his characters. Satisfaction of these two primal drives, virtually indistinguishable in the film, provides a purpose to life, perhaps the only purpose.

Allen reprises the theme of futility in love in the final scene of the original adventure movie. After Moskowitz has located the recipe and cracked the code, he should in the manner of all James Bond characters win "the girl" as well. The Japanese movie ends with a jet airliner taking off, presumably in the original version carrying the lovers to some romantic vacation land to enjoy the fruits of their success. In Allen's version, rather than offer the expected explanation that the hero is flying off into the sunset with his mission accomplished and heroine in tow, the script announces that Moskowitz now thinks he is a Boeing 707, the ultimate identity crisis for a hero alienated from his culture and the ultimate frustration for one seeking human companionship.

TAKE THE MONEY AND RUN (1969) brought Woody Allen the control he believed necessary for his film making. It is more properly the real directorial debut of the auteur in the making. Thanks to the box-office success of WHAT'S UP, TIGER LILY?, Palomar Pictures gave Allen the go-ahead to direct and star in a film produced from the script he had written. Still groping for his own authentic voice, Allen created a parody of the gangster films of the 1930's. He retold the story of the failed criminal, Virgil Starkwell (Allen), according to the style of television news documentaries.

The original gangster films generated controversy and eventually brought about their own demise very quickly because they made romantic heroes out of criminals.[8] While films like PUBLIC ENEMY (William Wellman, 1931) and SCARFACE (Howard Hawks, 1932) claimed to preach the message that crime does not pay, the central characters, dashing criminals played by James Cagney and Paul Muni respectively, tended to overwhelm the stated moral. These heroic figures were skilled, colorful and courageous, and against all the odds they were winners. Audiences loved seeing them rise to the top of the mob, outsmart the police and their rivals, take over the city and enjoy the good life, until the last few minutes when they received their long overdue punishment for their crimes. Virgil Starkwell's life offers rich possibilities for a classic gangster biography, but Virgil was a loser who muffed every opportunity for criminal greatness. Much of the comedy stems directly from the audience's familiarity with what gangsters do on their way to the top and its amazement when Virgil invariably fails to do it.

While the content of the film comes from the 1930's, the cinematic style is a parody of the television biography. Before the titles, the stentorian voice-over of Jackson Beck, the familiar disembodied narrator of Paramount newsreels, summarizes Virgil's early life, a chronicle of bungled petty crimes that eventually leads to his arrest for trying to rob an armored car. The grainy, black-and-white footage suggests the newsreel, and periodically Virgil's parents appear on screen to offer the audience childhood reminiscences through an interview with an off-camera reporter. This is the treatment accorded important people, but Virgil is, according to Kay Lewis (Louise Lasser), an old girlfriend, a life-long failure. He is noteworthy only because television is making a film about him, a fact that impresses Kay and offers a glimpse into what Allen, one of the entertainment industry's legendary mediaphobes, thinks of media-generated celebrity.[9]

Virgil's gentile name is unusual for an Allen hero, but the character remains resolutely Jewish.[10] As the television reporter interviews Virgil's parents, the stereotypical comic Jewish accents and mannerisms are quite clear.[11] They wear Groucho Marx noses and mustaches because they are ashamed of their son, the failed criminal. They recount the story of a medical experiment in prison that temporarily transformed Virgil into an Orthodox rabbi. The father recalls that Virgil is an atheist, despite the family's violent efforts to make a believer out of him. These gags will reappear in later films. In BANANAS (1971) Fielding Mellish will try to talk to his parents, noted surgeons, while they operate on an anonymous patient. Like the Starkwells, they are hidden behind surgical masks, a metaphorical cover for their shame at their son's failed career as a products tester. In ANNIE HALL (1977), Alvy Singer again assumes the appearance of a rabbi as an imagined response to the genteel Wasp anti-Semitism of the Halls. Virgil Starkwell's cultural and religious roots are Jewish, despite the gentile name.

Virgil's Jewishness, however, is only a minor source of his alienation. No matter what he attempts, Virgil relentlessly misjudges himself and his surroundings, and as a result becomes a universal failure. Not knowing what any sensible criminal would do, he invariably does something outrageously wrong, and must pay the price. Despite his thick glasses, he simply does not see reality as other people do, and as a result he does not know what he ought to do. Thus, this semi-blindness has ethical implications for Virgil Starkwell.

People continually smash his signature dark-rimmed eye glasses, as a suggestion that hostile forces conspire to rob him of vision and condemn him to his sadly distorted images of himself and his world. First, the boys in the neighborhood (his peers) break them during a fight, then the action is repeated by an ice-delivery man (representing his elders) and by the judge who sentences him to prison (the law). In effect, as a young man he experiences a moral myopia, and others frustrate his search for clarity. Since Virgil cannot "see" moral values, the criminal life is as attractive as any other. As an added pessimistic comment, after a scene of passionate love-making, the glasses suddenly appear on his partner Louise (Janet Margolin). Has love blinded him, however gently, or through their association has Louise's moral vision become as impaired as Virgil's? The defective vision is, of course, Virgil's to begin with, but society, with its cruelty and avarice, does not help the situation. Two decades later, the hero's moral vision will be distorted by SHADOWS AND FOG (1991) to such an extent that Kleinman, an older version of Virgil, cannot discover whether he is implicated in a crime or not.

Not seeing clearly, physically or spiritually, Virgil cannot negotiate terms with his world. As a young man, Virgil fails as a cellist, first because he tries to blow into the instrument, and when he finally learns to use the bow, he joins a marching band with it. When he sits down to play a few notes, the parade passes by. As a prisoner, he is outwitted by a shirt-folding machine in the prison laundry. Testing a career as a shoe shine boy, he attempts a spit shine, misses and hits his customer's pants leg.

It is as a criminal, however, that his failure is most apparent. Since Virgil has no identity of his own, he borrows his criminal roles from the movies. He tries to be a pool hustler, like Paul Newman in THE HUSTLER (Robert Rossen, 1961), but he clearly has no talent. He draws a switchblade, like the gang members in WEST SIDE STORY (Robert Wise, 1961) but the blade falls out of his knife. He escapes from prison still in chains, like Paul Muni in I AM A FUGITIVE FROM A CHAIN GANG (Mervyn LeRoy, 1932), but while the other convicts ride bicycles to freedom, Virgil, still in leg irons, runs frantically beside them.

Despite his disastrous career as a thief, Virgil does have a certain degree of success in love. He meets Louise, a professional laundress, while he is planning to steal her purse. They fall in love instantly, marry and have a son. The child has a potential for introducing a theme of life-giving for Virgil, but its presence is all but ignored in the narrative. In addition, the characteristic food/sex metaphor shows that his marriage scarcely offers the kind of gratification that Virgil needs to bolster his self-esteem. Louise pours coffee over teabags, cremates the roast, incinerates the toast and tries to fry a steak in its styrofoam package. The failed meals indicate a failed marriage. When Louise visits Virgil in prison, she pulverizes a hard boiled egg by pushing it through the screen toward him. The steel between them illustrates their separation, and by being smashed the egg, a common image of potential life, provides a visual comment on their ruined marriage.

Louise also takes an active role in Virgil's demise. On the day of his planned bank robbery, her leisurely morning shower, which keeps Virgil out of the bathroom, and her nagging him about his selection of clothes, delay his arrival for the hold-up. Because he falls behind schedule, another gang appears and stages its own more successful robbery. Virgil's futile attempts to find love with Louise bring not only emptiness in his search for a rewarding relationship, but they cause him to fail in everything else as well.

Virgil has a history of bungled bank robberies. In one of the most effective scenes, he hands a note to a teller demanding money, but the teller, and later other bank officials, cannot read his writing: "I've got a gun" becomes "I've got a gub." This very funny scene underlies Virgil's problem with even the most rudimentary form of human communication. He is closed in upon himself to such a degree that he cannot make known even his worst and most obvious intentions.

After establishing Virgil's record of unadulterated failure, Allen wanted to end the film with a bloody shoot-out, with his hero's being killed in the manner of BONNIE AND CLYDE (Arthur Penn, 1967). The veteran editor, Ralph Rosenblum, brought in as an editorial consultant for the inexperienced Allen, persuaded him to opt for a gentler ending.[12] In the final version, Virgil attempts to mug a man, who turns out to be both an old friend from Virgil's cello and marching-band days and an undercover police officer. Even to the end, crime pays no dividends for Virgil.

Woody, the comic persona that is beginning to develop, embodies a frightening view of the human situation. The character is small and powerless, without love, vision or self-understanding. His world is hostile and self-contradictory; he finds it impossible to discover and develop a sense of personal morality. Without a personality of his own, this "hollow man" tries to borrow one from others, even from movie figures, while acknowledging that these pretenses are nothing more than comic fantasies. Passing from a ruined past to a hopeless future, Virgil, loser and nothing, has no way out but violent death. As Allen develops the Woody character and probes the questions of death and love in later films, it is important to recall his utterly bleak vision of the world in the earliest films.

BANANAS (1971) can be considered a political satire of the trendy revolutionary movements of the 1960's, a period when the entire world seemed to "go bananas." In the context of Allen's development as an artist, however, the film contains much more than political satire. In its rejection of political remedies to the world's problems, the comedy seems on first viewing to echo the nihilism and despair of TAKE THE MONEY AND RUN. In his search for happiness, however, Fielding Mellish, the Woody character in BANANAS, represents a considerable advance over Virgil Starkwell in MONEY. Allen does not offer escape from failure only in death, as in the original treatment of MONEY, nor does his life continue on a treadmill of despair, as in the release print. In BANANAS, by contrast, Allen seems to be reaching toward a truce with reality.

Fielding, like most of the world's denizens, is trapped in a workaday world. In his opening scene, after the prologue and credits, he demonstrates an Execuciser, a work station rigged with exercise equipment to enable the busy executive to have a vigorous workout without leaving the desk. During the sales pitch, the machine goes berserk, nearly killing him. The concept itself is a comment on the dehumanizing effect of work, and it echoes both thematically and visually Charlie Chaplin's eating machine in MODERN TIMES (1936).

Fielding longs to escape from the tedium of his life through sex, but he is doomed to frustration. Even the receptionist, reputed to be the most accommodating woman in the office, rejects his advances. She tells him that she prefers to watch porn films at home with her friends. Later, despite his obvious embarrassment, Fielding tries unobtrusively to buy a pornographic magazine for himself, but the cashier shouts out the title, *Orgasm,* and his nasty little secret is out. A woman looks at him with pity and contempt. On the way home on the subway, Fielding hides behind a copy of his other magazine *Commentary,* when a gang of thugs, including a very young Sylvester Stallone, tries to mug an elderly woman on crutches. After initially ignoring the violence, Fielding rescues her, but the gang reboards the train and turns on him. As he escapes, Fielding runs past the erstwhile victim, who smiles broadly as she reads his abandoned copy of *Orgasm.*

At the start of his story, Fielding Mellish wants nothing more than an "orgasm." This level of gratification, which he sees as an escape from his humdrum life, seems easily available to everyone else including crippled old ladies on the subway, but the world conspires to lock Fielding into his loneliness and frustration. At this point in the film, communion with another person and much less love are far beyond his capabilities. He wants sex, pure and simple, in whatever form he can find it. The partner and the means are irrelevant to him.

Fielding's luck begins to change when Nancy (Louise Lasser), an earnest philosophy student at City College, appears at the door to enlist his support for a Marxist revolution in Latin America. They trade intellectual inanities, but a spark of romance enters when Allen falls back on his food/sex metaphor. Fielding offers Nancy food and dinner invitations, which she politely refuses, for the present. He admits that he is not a student, but he claims to have eaten once in the cafeteria at City College, where he caught trichinosis. In Allen vocabulary of love/sex, Fielding's comment reveals his failure with both studies and female students.

Nancy finally does respond to his initiatives. They eat together, participate in demonstrations and eventually engage in love-making in Fielding's apartment. Even as they prepare for their first romantic engagement, something is wrong. Fielding powders and sprays himself, as though trying to mask his own body. Nancy complains about the heat and the light in the room. He wants to be perfect, while she nitpicks about everything. It is not long before Nancy ends their relationship, telling him simply that the romance isn't working for her. Through Nancy's words, Allen recognizes that Fielding's problems cannot be blamed entirely on the hostile world. Fielding is a selfish little man. His lack of concern, and hence his lack of love, for the outside world, is the personal problem that keeps him from having more satisfying and permanent relationships with individual women.

Eager to fill the emptiness in his life and thus to have something to offer Nancy, Fielding travels to San Marcos to become part of the revolution. He is, however, co-opted by the rightist dictator who plans to set him up to be murdered by his own henchmen so that his death can be blamed on the Marxists. When the news of the kidnapped American reaches Washington, General Vargas (Carlos Montalban) believes American arms and money will flow into his government to help him repress the insurgents. Things do not go according to plan, however. The General's planned ambush fails, and Fielding is rescued by the revolutionaries and by default joins their cause. Fielding's love scene with Yolanda (Navidad Abascal), a beautiful rebel soldier, follows a meal whose sensuality rivals the dinner scene in TOM JONES (Tony Richardson, 1963). Despite the passionate gustatory prelude, Yolanda, it seems, has been bored by her experience with Fielding. The camera pulls back from her empty expression as she smokes the traditional postcoital cigarette, and the audience learns that she has not even bothered to take off her thick-soled army boots.

At least this relationship, as unsatisfying as it was, is a start for Fielding. He devotes himself to his military training, and proves as inept in war as in love. He learns that Esposito (Jacobo Morales), the rebel general is just as corrupt and crazy as the old dictators. Even so he has found a cause to dedicate himself to, and he goes along with the revolution and its lunatic leader. Fielding even helps organize mass executions for him, and he becomes an official of the new government. In an obviously phony red Castro beard, Fielding travels to New York to foster support for the revolutionary regime of San Marcos. He meets his old girlfriend Nancy, and despite the obvious transparency of his disguise, she fails to recognize him. She is captivated by the revolutionary fervor of her unknown hero. They arrange a meeting and spend a passionate, mutually satisfying night together. The Fielding who has come back to her is a different man in some ways, it is true, but the man Nancy loved was not Fielding. The revolutionary persona is only a cheap, unconvincing disguise. Nancy, for her part, falls in love with an idea, an illusion, more than the real man.

Is Allen offering the cynical view that love is nothing more than pretense and deception, and that happiness is the result of successful disguises and stupidly accepted illusions? If the romance were to end at this point, this bleak conclusion would be unavoidable. The love story continues, however, with Howard Cosell covering their wedding night as though it were a boxing match. According to Nancy in a post-bout interview, the sex was not great, but it was all right, and that seems to be enough to bring the story to a happy conclusion. Fielding is free from his obsessive self-centered search for the spectacular "orgasm" as his goal in life. Nancy has stepped back from her naive political commitment to idealized revolutionary heroes. They are a married couple, who have learned to accept one another as real persons. And they have discovered a way to find joy in life's small, but real dividends.

The Woody character in BANANAS still fumbles his way through life, and the universe still bears a grudge against him, but he now knows enough to shed unrealistic expectations of finding a heaven on earth, even a revolutionary paradise in San Marcos. Gone are the disguises. Gone too are the self-inflating illusions of Virgil Stark, disguised with his gentile name, the would-be marching cellist and notorious criminal who never made the F.B.I.'s Ten-Most-Wanted list. Fielding Mellish accepts Fielding Mellish and realizes that he needs love, not just sex. These discoveries will not make him a happy man, but they do offer a certain level of peace.

Other Allen themes show a mellowing. He still remains alienated from his world, but this does not lead him to destructive behavior, as it did Virgil Stark. Mellish remains the Jewish outsider. Even when he becomes a Christ-figure being carried on a cross, according to a dream he recounts to his psychiatrist, he does not quite fit in. The band of monks, carrying Fielding and his cross through the streets of New York, cannot even find a parking place because another Christ-figure with *his* monks has nosed in ahead of them. A monastic fist fight breaks out. Even as Christ on the cross, Fielding is not Christian enough, and thus does not gain acceptance in the majority culture.

In San Marcos, however, Fielding escapes from the police by stealing a cross-shaped lug wrench from a man fixing a tire. He holds it over his head like a processional cross and joins a group of clerical pilgrims. It would be overstating the case to impose a Christian meaning on the scene by suggesting that Fielding had been "saved" by the cross, but at the same time, Allen does bring the key Christian symbol into his comic escape.

Christian imagery appears once more, near the end of the film when a newscaster (Roger Grimsby) reporting Fielding's trial for being a New York, Jewish, intellectual communist, breaks for a commercial message. A priest distributes communion and looks up urging his communicants to smoke New Testament cigarettes. The juxtaposition of image and message suggests that religion, particularly of the Catholic variety, is a venal enterprise that like tobacco promises satisfaction but ultimately brings death. All three uses of Christian symbols were offensive to many audiences, and surely these scenes contributed to the "C" (Condemned) rating given by the National Catholic Office of Motion Pictures, the then-current incarnation of what had been the Legion of Decency.

The use of these Catholic symbols invites some reflection. Allen's debt to Ingmar Bergman's procession of flagellants in THE SEVENTH SEAL (1957), is clear in the first two instances. The mock commercial in the context of Fielding's trial for being, among other things, Jewish, is not as easily explained. The scene is not particularly funny, and it is tenuous at best to associate it with Bergman's coughing Lutheran pastor in WINTER LIGHT (1962), whose Swedish title is literally translated as THE COMMUNICANTS. The choice of content is especially strange in light of the number of actual television commercials that offer wonderful targets for parody. Perhaps the reason is as vague as a non-Christian's puzzled fascination with Catholic ritual, filtered through unarticulated resentment of what is often perceived as the "Christian" majority culture and the polite but very real anti-Catholicism common among intellectuals and artists. While certainly offensive by today's standards of hypersensitivity, Allen should not be faulted for deliberate blasphemy. As one who was surely familiar with the films of the Spanish iconoclast Luis Buñuel, Allen could have been much nastier in his parody if he had wanted.

Allen does not limit his religious imagery to Catholics. The comic orthodox rabbi makes another appearance in BANANAS. When the dictators feel need for American support, they plan to call in the C.I.A., but they mistakenly call in the U.J.A. (the United Jewish Appeal). The camera shows a regiment of orthodox rabbis heading down a street to pacify the civilian population, much like uniformed soldiers, yet stereotypically comic in their movement and costume. One observation is noteworthy. In the early comedies, when Allen lampoons Jewishness, the targets are cultural and ethnic: families, mothers, customs and, of course, the comic rabbis. He rarely touches on matters of belief. When he turns to Christianity, however, the satire touches the most sacred religious symbols and profound sensitivities. Allen, like many practicing comedians, often seems unaware of the difference.

The Jew in Christian America is the outsider in many Allen films, but in BANANAS the American also is the outsider in San Marcos. Everyone in the "banana" republic speaks English, but Fielding is still culturally out of place. Through the standard food/sex metaphor, Allen shows that Fielding finds gratification elusive in this strange country. The bananas of the film's title are, after all, food. As a guest of the dictator, he faces danger of poisoning at the formal banquet. Later, in the camp of the revolutionary army, he gags at the thought of eating lizard. When ordered to supply food for the army, Fielding responds according to the conventions of his own culture: He finds a lunch counter and orders take-out sandwiches, with side orders of cole slaw. Allen reinforces the notion of Fielding as an outsider during his military training in the rebel camp. As a soldier he is a misfit with grenade and rifle, much as Virgil was with his switchblade knife.

This culture shock is essential for Fielding's redemption as a person. He must leave his familiar surroundings and undertake a journey of growth through a kind of Dantesque underworld. During his time in the jungle, he becomes even more the outsider but in the process he discovers his own intrinsic worth. Away from New York and thus deprived of his usual cultural props, defenses and rituals, he is free to search, to love and to grow, and eventually he is able to establish peace with himself.

Most importantly, Fielding discovers that a sense of alienation is not unique to him, and so his pattern of self-absorption is broken. Once Esposito, the rebel general, has solidified his power in San Marcos, he insists that the national language is now Swedish. With that decree, the citizens of this banana republic become aliens in their own land. Esposito's lunatic orders underline Fielding's realization that all political power has the potential for insanity. Political reform will not solve the world's problems, since all forms of political power hold the potential for repression. This is a lesson he will have to communicate to Nancy as he sheds his Castro beard and passes from extraordinary lover to Fielding Mellish, adequate. Even though they are products of the late 1960's they discover that they do not have to solve the world's problems; they only have to love and support each other.

The opening and closing sequences frame the narrative with a parody of television sports reporting. Before the titles roll, veteran sportscasters Don Dunphy and Howard Cosell, complete with monogrammed blazers and hand-held microphones, invite the television audience to witness the assassination of the president of San Marcos, live and in color. At the end of the film, Howard Cosell alone interviews Nancy and Fielding on their wedding night. All that has intervened in the story, has brought the film and Fielding from taking life to creating life. Perhaps, Allen suggests, politics and love alike are products of the media. In that case, the

Woody character will find happiness within his ordinary nonmedia self and in a loving relationship with an ordinary nonmedia woman like Nancy. The outcome of Fielding Mellish's adventures, then, is not all that bad.

Again with due caution about leaping too quickly to an explicit Christian analysis of Fielding's adventures, it is important that Allen has shown the death of the old, self-absorbed Fielding Mellish, his descent into the purgatory of San Marcos (Saint Mark is, after all, the author of one of the four Gospels of the New Testament). and his rebirth as Fielding Mellish, loving husband and potential giver of life.

EVERYTHING YOU ALWAYS WANTED TO KNOW ABOUT SEX* (*BUT WERE AFRAID TO ASK) (1972) is more an uneven collection of seven sketches than an adaptation of Dr. David Reuben's best selling sex manual of 1969 or a reaction to it. The two-part title reflects the ambiguity of the American media's discovery of public sex in the 1960's: People are endlessly fascinated by the topic, down to its last clinical detail, yet there remains an element of embarrassment as well. To recall Rudolf Otto's terminology, sex is "mysterium fascinans et tremendum." It is a "mystery" that "fascinates" and "terrifies." Successful marketing involves both facets of the mystery: recognition of curiosity and the suggestion that satisfying that curiosity means entering into forbidden territory. Movies and television more frequently than not cheapen sexual material with a wink and a leer as though offering forbidden fruit to a perennially curious adolescent audience. When Allen attempts a parody of the phenomenon, the satire is devastating, even though many of the jokes are as infantile as the audiences he is criticizing.

Producer Jack Brodsky bought the rights to Reuben's book and envisioned Elliott Gould, the comic-neurotic anti-hero of the 1960's, as the central figure in the film. But in the days that Richard Nixon rode the crest of conservative reaction right into the White House, the original concept seemed as dated as bell-bottom jeans and love beads. Gould's popularity declined, and some of the coy and supercilious purveyors of "the new sexuality," once thought daring, began to sound not only dehumanizing but a trifle silly. When the project stalled on Brodsky's desk, Allen jumped in, and the film took off in a very different direction.[13]

EVERYTHING YOU ALWAYS WANTED TO KNOW opens on a pen packed to overflowing with pink-and-white rabbits while the sound track provides a jazzy version of Cole Porter's "Let's Misbehave." The rabbits suggest the natural quality of sex, and the singers imply bawdy fun in forbidden games. Neither group needs the leaden commentary of a sex manual.

Each segment of the film begins with a printed question. The first sketch purports to answer the question, "Do aphrodisiacs work?" Since the film as a whole follows a rough chronological order, the first sketch is set in the Middle Ages and is a parody of swashbuckling costume movies. Felix, the Fool (Woody Allen), no longer amuses the royal household with his jokes, and he is excluded from the banquet while the others eat enthusiastically. The Fool is, however, smitten by the Queen (Lynn Redgrave), and after experiencing a Hamlet-like vision from his dead father, he plans to bring her a love potion in her orange juice. Having taken the draught, the Queen responds to his ardor, but the clanging of iron as the Fool tries to remove her chastity belt awakens the King (Anthony Quayle) and Felix soon finds himself beheaded.

The Fool reverts back to the pattern of the early Allen heroes. He is the outsider, a ridiculous figure unable to join the meal with the others. Food is once again the metaphor for sex. Like Fielding Mellish, he wants neither romance nor companionship, only sex. He feels self-pity at being denied this basic human experience, aims at an impossible goal, the Queen, and resorts to artifice to pursue his quest. Without the drug, the Queen could not endure his presence. Finally, another form of hostile machinery, the uncooperative chastity belt and the devices he uses to try to undo it, frustrate him and lead to his capture and execution. As in the original scenario for Virgil Starkwell, death provides the only escape from failure.

Despite the bawdy humor and grim outcome for Felix, Allen is now able to offer a serious critique of his character. The Fool is in fact a fool. He is self-centered and consumed with his own gratification to the extent that he is willing to drug the ideal woman of his dreams to win her favors. Her desires mean nothing to him. Death finally puts an end to his insane ambition.

The second sketch begins with the question: "What is sodomy?" This parody of romantic melodramas, like THE BLUE ANGEL (Josef Von Sternberg, 1930) or LOLITA (Stanley

Kubrick, 1962), repeats the moral lesson of The Fool's story that inappropriate love can be destructive. It is, however, far less successful than the earlier segment. Dr. Ross (Gene Wilder) has a happy marriage, but when an Albanian shepherd comes into his office with a sheep named Daisy, Ross falls in love with her.

The concept pushes the premise of the earlier films to their absurdist extreme. Professor Unrath (Emil Jannings) in BLUE ANGEL becomes infatuated with a cabaret singer (Marlene Dietrich), and Humbert Humbert (James Mason) with the very young Lolita (Sue Lyon). The Fool, in the first sketch, loved above his class, while Unrath and Humbert stepped down in social class. By his infatuation with a ewe, Dr. Ross becomes the ultimate extension of the other two. In each case, the illicit love brings destruction. After a few painfully contrived comic moments, like Ross's bringing Daisy to a hotel for an afternoon rendezvous—where, of course, he orders food from room service—his life collapses and he becomes a derelict, sitting on the street drinking Woolite.

Ross is as much a fool as the jester. Both are self-centered and try to enter into a relationship where mutual love is impossible. Both receive the rewards of their foolishness. Allen is no longer cynical about frustrated love, nor does he shrug a nihilistic shoulder at the way life is. In these first two episodes, he is capable of offering a critique of a quest for love that is totally self-centered.

The third episode is a spoof on the then-fashionable European art films that explored the ennui of the rich in newly prosperous post-war Europe. Its lead question is: "Why do some women have trouble reaching orgasm?". This question like the others is left unanswered. The sleek design of the film with its sterile white walls and plastic furniture beautifully captures the emptiness of sophisticated Italians as reported by Michelangelo Antonioni. Fabrizio (Woody Allen) wears white suits and speaks sultry Italian. As a reminder of WHAT'S UP, TIGER LILY?, the romantic language is translated into New York Jewish slang in the subtitles. Gina (Louise Lasser), Fabrizio's new bride, does not respond to him with the enthusiasm he thinks appropriate for one of his irresistible charms and inventive technique.

Fabrizio, like the previous heroes, is a fool. He approaches sex as though it consists exclusively of cold, mechanical techniques, much like those described by Dr. Reuben. Fabrizio even tries to stir Gina's ardor with an electric vibrator, but with Allen's usual bad luck with machines, it blows up in his hand. Fabrizio seeks advice, first from a fashion photographer, who because of his work with models is supposedly experienced in "handling" women. He offers more suggestions on technique. Next, he consults a priest, supposedly experienced in affairs of the spirit. The priest tells him to enjoy himself, even if Gina cannot respond to him. Neither the mechanical nor the spiritual advice offer much help, mainly because as men they ignore the perspective of the woman. What all the men have ignored is the element of the spontaneous and unpredictable, which is all important to the more romantic half of the species.

After several experiments, Gina and Fabrizio discover that making love in public places provides the thrill she needs for success. Naturally for Allen, a restaurant is the most fortuitous locale of all, and in the midst of her passion under the table Gina bites the leg of an unsuspecting woman trying to enjoy her dinner, another echo of Allen's and China Lee's last scene in TIGER LILY. Gina discovers the mystery of love on her own, and teaches the men, and Allen's audience, a valuable lesson.

In the fourth episode, Allen turns from films to a style more easily connected to popular television. The question, "Are transvestites homosexuals?" introduces a parody of the family sitcom. Sam and Tess, a stereotypically Jewish couple, are having dinner with the highly refined parents of their son's fiancee. As Sam (Lou Jacobi) feels more and more inferior to his future in-laws, he excuses himself, goes upstairs and changes into his hostess's clothes. Fearing discovery when the host comes up to the bedroom, he lets himself out a window and drops to the street, where a mugger snatches his purse. Police and neighbors sympathize with his plight, believing him a victimized, helpless old woman. Tess and the in-laws arrive and reveal his true identity. At home once again, Tess tells her humiliated husband that she could have forgiven him, if he admitted that he was not fit to live in human society.

Ironically, this silly plot would be more congruent with today's pretentious, "message" sitcoms than with the shows of the 1970's. Today's writers would use the events to denounce the evils of homophobia and the joy of accepting sexually diverse people.

Allen's purposes are more devious. The bride and groom do not appear at the family gathering, yet the norms and expectations of their parents are extremely important for their marriage. In all likelihood, they will become carbon copies of their parents, and it is not altogether clear which side of these incompatible families will surface more prominently in the next generation, or if a reconciliation between the two will be possible. For once, Allen situates love in a context of society and family. It is no longer the frantic quest of one, small, isolated, lonely individual to find love and discover instead failure, frustration and even greater isolation. Love in the context of families is, after all, the lot of most of the world's citizens, and for many of them families, their own or their spouse's, can hold many surprises, not all of them pleasant.

After exploring the lives of Dr. Ross and his ewe and Sam and his garter belt, in the fifth segment Allen addresses the question: "What are sex perverts?" The format is a television game show patterned after "What's My Line?", the popular CBS series that began in 1950 and lasted nearly 20 years. To add to the authentic quality of this segment, Allen called on several well-known television personalities to play approximations of their familiar guest-celebrity roles. Perennial quiz master Robert Q. Lewis acts as host, while the panelists include Pamela Mason, Regis Philbin and Toni Holt. Game shows provide ample material for parody, but it is too easy. Allen's treatment of it is obvious, and the comedy becomes simply embarrassing.

Allen has, for example, raised the question of homosexuality gently with Sam's misadventures. In this segment, the treatment becomes more heavy-handed than comic. During a commercial break for hair tonic, he shows two male athletes in a locker room locked in an amorous embrace. The questions posed by the panelists of a man who exposes himself on the subway are inane, with the kind of predictable double meanings believed original only by the sophomore-class wit.

The program's mystery guest is a rabbi who fantasizes about being tied up and beaten by a *shiksa* (a gentile woman), while his wife sits at his feet eating pork. The odd blending of forbidden sex/forbidden food and religion is striking in the context of Allen's contempt for the media. The parody shows people willing to go on exhibition, cheapening what is most personal: their sexuality and their religion. The marketing of self in exchange for a moment of fame before the cameras is the ultimate perversion, and it is one shared by the leering panelists and their smirking audiences alike, including those watching this portion of Allen's own film.

This notion, only vaguely articulated in this disappointing sketch, provides a key to Allen's "religious" thinking. In EVERYTHING YOU ALWAYS WANTED TO KNOW, he brutally satirizes the hedonistic, self-centered notion of sex provided by the media. He is turning to a more sacred notion of sexuality, one that implies something more, like love, the quest not of self-gratification but of mutual self-giving. In the later films, he will ask if this is possible, and the question will receive religious overtones as he asks whether some force, like God, exists to give meaning to a universe in which love can survive. The religious imagery will appear more frequently in the later films, and it will hold more significance than Allen's early clownish rabbis. At this point, however, the association between love and religion is vague and negative. To cheapen love by reducing it to comic sex is like cheapening religious belief, and to do that is to cheapen the self.

The sixth sketch addresses the question, "Are the Findings of Doctors and Clinics Who Do Sexual Research Accurate?" The style is that of the low-budget horror film, like the cult classic, THE NIGHT OF THE LIVING DEAD (George Romero, 1968). Sexologists and their venal allies in the media have indeed made sex a horror show, according to Allen.

On his way to work on experiments with the famous Dr. Bernardo (John Carradine), Victor Shakopopolos (Woody Allen) picks up Helen Lacey (Heather McRae), a reporter who is also going to the laboratory to interview the Doctor for a Sunday supplement feature. His house is a showroom of stock horror-movie furniture, including a deformed houseboy named Igor (Ref Sanchez). At dinner, (of course!), Bernardo describes his grotesque, thoroughly dehumanizing experiments. He determines to make Helen the object of a multiple rape to measure her respiration and ties up his two visitors to prevent their escape. Victor manages to get free and rescues Helen, but in the process he blows up Bernardo's laboratory. The explosion, however, causes a dangerous mixture of chemicals that in turn creates a 40-foot high silicone breast. Like a classic movie monster it stalks the countryside, leaving a swath of death and destruction by milk inundation. Victor manages to trap the monster in a huge brassiere, that looks like a billowing mainsail on a schooner. Once contained, the breast is no longer a threat and will be sent to an orphanage to provide milk for babies.

Allen's parody of mad scientists and helpless women, the standard fixtures of monster movies is clear enough, as is his lampoon of America's fixation on oversized breasts. Whether he was aware of the fact or not, the sketch represents a critique of his own earlier films. From this point on, he will no longer feature actresses of voluptuous proportions. His women may be neurotic and infuriating—as are many of his male characters, including especially the Woody persona—but they will no longer be simple objects for the randy, adolescent men to pursue and possess. There will be much less of the smirk and leer in his comedy, much less of the sexual innuendo in his dialogue. This represents a real development in his thought. Recognizing a value in the other person is fundamental to the possibility of love and, consequently, the end of loneliness.

The final sketch addresses the question "What Happens During Ejaculation?" The most successful of the seven, this parody of science-fiction provides a futuristic balance to the opening story of Felix the medieval court jester. The action takes place in a sterile white command central, with the language and equipment reminiscent of NASA's Mission Control. Tony Randall is the prim and proper commander, and he is assisted by Burt Reynolds, at the time a popular movie sex symbol. Their control center is located inside the brain of Sidney, the unseen hero, as he prepares to woo and win his date. Each sensation is filtered to the brain and the brain mandates the appropriate response.

The comedy rests on its reducing very personal, human reactions to sterile, objective, scientific concepts that can be manipulated without reference to feelings. The Woody character, for example, is a neurotic sperm cell awaiting ejaculation, and his reflections on his anxieties provide the title for the skit. The digestion room crew is inundated with fettucine and wine and must receive instructions from upstairs on processing the mess. When Sidney fails on his first attempt, the crew blames a priest, who has filled Sidney with guilt, another unflattering reference to Catholic religious belief in the context of a hero named Sidney, a name more commonly associated with Jews than Catholics.

Blaming sexual dysfunction on preoccupation with scientifically explained technique and then on religion echoes the theme of Fabrizio's search for a solution to his problem. Allen wants to assert the primacy of nature and fun over those who contaminate love with mechanics and morality. As the film closes, the couple, finally successful, returns for an encore performance. They have worked through their own problems without the help of a manual, and Allen finds them rewarded for their efforts.

The Woody character, as he appears in the four sketches, shows a progression.[14] As Felix the Fool, he is lecherous, inept and condemned to death. As Fabrizio, the stereotypical Italian superlover, he learns the limits of his sexual arrogance. As Victor, he risks his own life to save Helen, thus winning her affection, and he tames the mammalian monster of his unrealistic fantasy. He is bumbling, but heroic. Finally, as a sperm cell, he is the source of life itself. When sex is stripped down to its basics, pretense has no role. Nature rules in this realm.

SLEEPER (1973) closes out the early cartoon phase of Allen's film making career. It recapitulates the themes of the earlier films, shows his growth as a visual artist and opens the way for the more serious reflections that will preoccupy him in his mature phase.[15]

As a spoof of science fiction, SLEEPER visually echoes the final story of EVERYTHING YOU ALWAYS WANTED TO KNOW and it reprises the narrative line of BANANAS with several interesting thematic twists. Miles Monroe (Woody Allen) is an outsider not only because of his Jewishness or because of his entering a foreign country. A literary descendant of the legendary Rip Van Winkle, Miles has been frozen for two hundred years after a bungled operation for ulcers had led to his death. He awakens in a science fiction world, more precisely in sterile surgical theater, where he has been thawed out by doctors eager to use him, a man with no traceable identity, in their revolution against The Leader. When the Gestapo-like security guards break in, Miles escapes by hiding in a delivery van for robots.

Disguised as a robot, with painted face, metallic mouth and helmet like theirs, but with the dark-rimmed glasses that distinguish him from them, Miles is installed as a butler in the futuristic home of Luna (Diane Keaton). With a mudpack on her face and a towel covering her hair, she looks like a robot herself. At a social gathering, Miles observes that Luna and her vapid friends are creatures of the new utopia, where conformity and happiness are valued above thought and individuality.

Everything in Luna's home is artificial, even to the instant pudding that Miles as an inexperienced domestic robot tries to prepare in the kitchen. The ready-mix dessert becomes a monster out of control, like the breast in EVERYTHING YOU ALWAYS WANTED TO KNOW, and Allen's standard food/sex metaphor implies that artificially contrived sex in this future age holds the potential for destruction. The chic visitors trade silly platitudes about the arts, slip into an electric Orgasmatron for sterile sex and rub a huge chrome ball to achieve what someone of Miles's vintage would call a drug-induced euphoria. Although the Sleeper of the title initially appears to be Miles, it becomes clear that Luna and in fact her whole world are the real sleepers. Miles realizes that to survive in a world designed and ruled by The Leader, he must pretend to be a robot, while Luna and her friends have become spiritual robots. They enjoy their carefree lives; Miles, however, understands what is happening to him, and he wants out.

At this point in his development, Allen has pushed his social criticism to a new level. The target of his satire is no longer limited to America's fascination with a mechanical notion of sex, as in EVERYTHING YOU ALWAYS WANTED TO KNOW or in simplistic political movements of the 1960's, like BANANAS. He now expresses a horror with the dehumanization of life in affluent America. Miles is still the Allen outsider, but he is no longer a passive victim of the majority culture. He is instead its savior. He assumes an active role in saving not only himself, but Luna and eventually the revolutionary movement and humanity itself. Fielding Mellish, it should be remembered, has little interest in the people of San Marcos. In SLEEPER, Miles's escapades are not designed to lure Luna—or anyone else, for that matter—into bed but to rescue her from her antihuman society and from herself.

Miles and Luna begin their relationship with hostility. When his true identity as a human person is discovered, Miles, the ex-robot, kidnaps her as a hostage as he tries to escape from the factory where he has been sent for a robot head transplant. During their flight, Allen works a variation on the food/sex metaphor. Starving in the forest, Miles leaves Luna alone while he searches for food. He discovers a factory for huge artificially developed fruits and vegetables. He slips on the carpet-sized banana peel, but he manages to outrun a monstrous, menacing chicken and bring a slice of banana the size of a manhole cover back to Luna. Once again, food/sex in this future world of artifice has become monstrous. The idea of sex with Luna is surreal, and in fact she rewards Miles for his food-gathering by clubbing him into unconsciousness. Their relationship continues on this note of hostility.

Luna happily turns Miles over to the security guards, but they try to arrest her as well, since she has had too much contact with the alien and must be presumed contaminated. This mindless persecution by the authorities forces them to join forces. They escape together, and like a return to the womb, Miles brings Luna back to the home of the doctors who originally defrosted him. He is about to give her a sense of his old fashioned world by making natural love to her without the Orgasmatron, when the police break in. They arrest Miles, but Luna escapes to the wilderness, where she tries to become a child of nature with the revolutionary forces in the forest. She has a difficult time learning a new life away from her customary luxuries. Like Fielding Mellish in BANANAS, she must abandon her old life and become an alien in the underworld so that she can be reborn as a dedicated revolutionary. The old hedonistic Luna dies so that the new altruistic Luna might live.

Once in the custody of the security agents, Miles the outsider must be altered to "fit in." The Leader's scientists program his brain to be Miss Montana in a Miss America contest. His comments are suitably inane, even though he scarcely "fits in" in the bathing suit competition. Satisfied with his progress, the captors bring him for a computerized fitting of his new depersonalizing uniform. Two robots, Ginsberg and Cohen, have extraordinary neon noses and speak with heavy Jewish accents, like Yiddish-language R2-D2's. The new computer-generated suit does not even approximate Miles's size, but the robots bicker with each other and finally agree to take the jacket in a little. Aside from some very funny lines, the vignette points out that Miles's (and Allen's) Jewish roots will not allow him to fit in to the majority culture. Thanks to the Jewish tailors, he will preserve his individuality while the world becomes uniformed, and by being himself, he can save the world from its own mindless conformity.

The reprogramming of Miles Monroe, however, is successful, at least for the present. He works as a computer operator in The Leader's headquarters, seduces another technician with his previous-life charm but then feels the need to confess his "sin" to an absolution machine. But what is his sin? Surely, it is not a casual and comic dalliance, so common and absolutely amoral in Allen's films, as it is in Roman comedy. Perhaps it is a sense of disloyalty to The Leader, or more likely, he feels remorse for his betrayal of Luna. This is an early suggestion that love and fidelity have values, and to reject them is wrong. At this juncture, Allen is beginning to wonder if there is, in fact, some moral structure in the universe. In the later films, he will add Immanuel Kant's second question: Does such a moral order require a Supreme Being to erect and sustain it?

The revolutionaries rescue Miles and bring him to their camp. His knowledge of The Leader's headquarters will be invaluable to them, but first he must be restored to his original mental state. Luna and the revolutionary commander Erno Windt (John Beck), imitating Miles's very Jewish mother and father, re-enact a Passover seder at their Brooklyn home 10 years before Miles's death. Their accents are forced and their Yiddishisms always a bit off the mark, but their acting does stir Miles's ethnic and religious memories. His true self is beginning to reemerge.

Their work is not yet complete, however. Miles (and Allen) have come a long way from Brooklyn. In a hypnotic trance, Miles becomes Blanche DuBois from Tennessee Williams's A STREETCAR NAMED DESIRE, with Luna responding with a mock imitation of Marlon Brando as Stanley Kowalski. No matter how brainwashed poor Miles is, the legacy of the arts remains deeply imbedded in his personality. Miles (Woody Allen and the human race alike) becomes human and remains human because of the arts.

Especially for Woody Allen, playwright, actor and director, the theater provides a sense of his own humanity and his own individuality. This is an early reference to the arts, but it will not be the last. Before this point, Allen heroes have been failures at the most commonplace of occupations. The Woody characters have been unsuccessful criminals, endangered product testers, unfunny court jesters, inept laboratory technicians, failed lovers or even anxious sperm cells. Miles himself ran The Happy Carrot, a health-food shop in Greenwich Village. In the future films, Allen's heroes will be more often than not men of the arts: television producers, film makers, writers and professors of literature.[16] In the later films, the action will invariably include sophisticated New Yorkers with some degree of involvement in fiction, drama and the other arts. If these characters, played both by Allen and by other actors and actresses, continue to consider themselves losers, it is because they do not live up to the extraordinarily high standards they have set for themselves. The perfect book is never finished; the important film never made.

With Luna's help, Miles finally becomes his old, old self. He and Luna quarrel as they enter the medical center to steal the nose of The Leader, which is all that is left of the dictator after an assassination attempt. Twenty-second century science is about to clone the Leader back to life by duplicating the cells from the nose. After being pummelled by a malevolent computer in the headquarters, another Chaplinesque combat with a machine, Miles and Luna succeed, destroy the nose and escape together.

Since Miles and Luna are real people and no longer robots, they argue just like real-life lovers. Through their love and their quarrels they have deprogrammed each other, or referring to the title, they have awakened each other from a deep sleep. Both have been anesthetized by the hedonism of their respective cultures, yet Miles, having escaped the health-food mania of Manhattan Yuppies in the 1970's, becomes a robot when The Leader's scientists reprogram him. During this period, Miles reverts to a self-centered notion of sex by seducing the computer technician. While she is learning to be a real person in the forest, Luna has an affair with Erno in the revolutionary camp. It is a first experience of natural love for her. During their separation, Luna is naive, Miles is cynical, and both are very human. In any event, when they are reunited, the saving effect of their love is mutual.

After they capture and destroy the nose, Miles and Luna escape, and they argue once more. Miles recites his anti-creed, denying belief in science, politics and God. All he can believe in, he claims, is sex and death. These statements demand a bit of scrutiny. Science has certainly caused trouble for Miles, but it also preserved his life for 200 years, until he could meet Luna. Technology has thus won some grudging approval from Allen. The 200-year old Volkswagen starts with the first touch of the starter, and a back-pack helicopter enables him to escape from The Leader's police.

Erno's involvement with Luna should indeed make Miles skeptical about politics: One politician is as treacherous as the next, a point established forcefully in BANANAS. Still Miles and Luna undertake a dangerous mission to insure that The Leader does not return to power, which is indeed a political objective. At the end of the film they have saved the world from dictatorship and have grown to love each other in the process. Finally, Miles may remain closed to the notion of God, but his discovery of the possibility of mutual love and a moral structure in the universe has opened the curtain of Allen's agnosticism at least a crack.

Miles's professed belief only in sex and death is similarly questionable. Miles has been unable to die for more than 200 years, and the intervening two centuries have given him the time to find Luna. Perhaps Allen has concluded that finding happiness is a project that takes more than one lifetime, but the quest is worth the effort whether it succeeds or not. Life offers possibilities, not guarantees. Finally, with Luna he has found love without sex. He did not pursue her as an object to be possessed, yet in their sharing of the dangers and challenges of postmodern living, they have found love. While Miles Monroe may be an unreconstructed cynic, Allen seems to have raised at least the possibility of belief in life and love. Only later on will he wonder about the possibility of a belief in God.

NOTES

1. Douglas Brode, *The Films of Woody Allen* (New York: Citadel, 1991), p. 31, quoting an interview with Allen in "Boston After Dark."
2. Maurice Yacowar, *Loser Take All: The Comic Art of Woody Allen* (New York: Continuum, 1991), pp. 26–27.
3. Nancy Pogel, *Woody Allen* (Boston: Twayne, 1987), p. 3 and following develops her analysis of Allen's comedy from his "Little Man" persona, which has its roots in the comedies of the silent era, most notably Charlie Chaplin.
4. Brode, p. 46, explains that the Japanese distributor, Toho, had already dubbed the film into English, but the result, A KEG OF POWDER, was so horrible that the would-be thriller had been unwittingly transformed into a comedy. Bringing in a successful humorist and television writer, like Woody Allen, to complete the travesty seemed the only logical way for A.I.P. to salvage the project and protect its investment.
5. Yacowar, p. 114.
6. Graham McCann, *Woody Allen* (Cambridge, Mass.: Polity, 1991), pp. 152–57 presents a catalogue of Nazi references.
7. Brode, p. 48
8. Thomas Schatz, *Hollywood Genres: Formulas, Filmmaking and the Studio System* (New York: Random House, 1981), p. 82 ff.
9. Yacowar, p. 121.
10. Pogel, p. 35, explains that "Virgil" is a "meek" name and "Starkwell" suggests Charles Starkweather, a famous murderer of the 1950's. It is possible, however, that Allen simply found humor in giving his Jewish character (an Allen alter ego) a quintessentially Wasp-sounding name, much as he seemed to revel in naming a Japanese detective Phil Moskowitz.
11. Foster Hirsch, *Love, Sex, Death, and the Meaning of Life: Woody Allen's Comedy* (New York: McGraw-Hill, 1981), p. 150.
12. Pogel, p. 35.
13. Brode, p. 113.
14. Yacowar, p. 150–51, points out the progression of the four Woody characters, but his interpretation is less optimistic than the one presented here. He sees the final character as a failure, who is afraid of the life he will generate.
15. Brode, pp. 126–29, discusses Allen's remarkable transformation in SLEEPER from a film maker who illustrates verbal jokes by his visuals to a genuinely physical comic artist who no longer needs words to achieve his comic goals.
16. McCann, p. 170, notes Allen's use of characters from the world of letters.

CHAPTER III: THE ROMANCES

While SLEEPER marks the close of one period of Allen's work, LOVE AND DEATH (1975) provides the transition to the beginning of the next. Miles Monroe is the last of the bumbling anti-heroes. The transition takes place during the story. He enters the screen as fate's pawn and gradually achieves a status that is both altruistic and redemptive. By putting his own life and comfort at risk, he saves Luna and her world from its suicidal self-anesthesis. No longer merely a self-seeking "Fool," the clown finds a meaningful role in life. Through his adventures the Woody character explores a world that remains threatening, but one that he can change for the better. The universe may be hostile, but it is not meaningless, and thus human actions have a value. Miles can both help shape his own destiny and in the process make the world better through his works.

In LOVE AND DEATH, the Woody character again becomes an accidental hero and revels in the role, taking upon himself ever more dangerous and carefully planned adventures. Similarly THE FRONT (1976), directed by Martin Ritt and written by Walter Bernstein, puts the Woody character through a similar moral progression while reconstructing the chilling atmosphere of the blacklisting days of the McCarthy era. Howard Prince (Woody Allen) is a hack writer of limited talent and reputation. While the more famous are being hounded by anti-Communist vigilantes, no one can bother with him. An anonymous, unsuccessful artist, he allows himself to be drawn into a comic plot to market the scripts of banned writers under his own name. When his friend, the blacklisted comedian Hecky Brown (Zero Mostel), takes his own life Howard becomes aware of the actual danger to freedom and to his country. As a result, in a final sequence he rises to the stature of cultural hero. He defies the House Un-American Activities Committee and chooses going to jail rather than naming names of alleged Communist sympathizers in the entertainment industry.

The Romances

ANNIE HALL (1977) is a paradox. With its four Academy Awards, it brought Woody Allen into the public mainstream as a popular film maker. At the same time, the film is more private. Alvy Singer, the hero, becomes more closely identified with Allen himself. He is funny, but he is neither Fool or Clown. Alvy works as a successful stand-up comedian and writer, like the young Woody Allen. For good or ill, autobiography will remain inextricably tied into the subsequent films. Alvy seeks love, but unlike the characters in the earlier films, the hero fails to keep his beloved. With his help, however, Annie (Diane Keaton) is able to grow from a dependent scatterbrain to a mature woman with her own life and her own career ambitions. This is the theme of SLEEPER restated in contemporary New York. Alvy has awakened Annie and given her a life, but at great personal cost to himself.

INTERIORS (1978) represents another artistic breakthrough for Woody Allen. An obvious *hommage* to Ingmar Bergman, the film not only lacks comedy, but at times its seriousness easily lapses over into the lugubrious. If this film is a failure, and critics may have been too eager to dismiss it, it is a bold experiment.[1] The Woody character does not appear, but his spiritual role is divided among three daughters, Joey (Mary Beth Hurt), Renata (Diane Keaton) and Flyn (Kristen Griffith), who try to save Eve, their suicidal mother (Geraldine Page). Each daughter employs some form of artistic expression, and each is willing to sacrifice herself to rescue her mother from her self-destructive impulses. Love, sacrifice and art become commingled, as though Allen the writer-actor-director tries to define his own relationship to a world that cannot sort out its own problems.

Not only do different facets of his art, in the personae of the three sisters, offer competing solutions, but their own artistic expression is muted because of their own confused status. Renata is a poet with writer's block, Joey is tired of her job as editor and Flyn is dissatisfied with the roles she receives as an actress. Each of the sisters has problems of her own to deal with as she tries to help her mother. In Eve, Allen sees the world as hostile, yes, but not as malicious. Eve is in fact destructive of the lives of those around her, but she is a sick woman, and life has not been gentle with her. In this film the world's intractable hostility is no longer funny; it is profoundly tragic.

In MANHATTAN (1979) Alvy Singer is reincarnated as Isaac Davis, television-comedy writer. The conflicted state of the artist carries over from INTERIORS. Isaac becomes revolted with his program and quits to concentrate on his novel. His love affair with 17-year-old Tracy (Mariel Hemingway) disintegrates, and their separation allows her to mature into an independent woman with a life of her own, much like Annie Hall. The eponymous hero of the film is Manhattan itself, a glorious combination of the beautiful and the grotesque. It is a moral universe where love and loneliness, loyalty and betrayal wander its streets hand-in-hand. In such a milieu, the hero-artist's search for love and authentic art makes life a little more bearable for people, and at times, even adds a few moments of joy to the world.

Allen's exploration of the artist-hero in STARDUST MEMORIES (1980) borrows heavily from Fellini's "8 1/2" (1963) and from Bergman's THE SILENCE (1963). It crosses over the border from autobiography to solipsism and is one of Allen's least appreciated efforts. Sandy Bates (Allen) is a film maker whose talent has apparently waned since the days when he made successful comedies. He has turned to serious films, but has difficulty expressing himself through them. During a retrospective of his work, representatives of several charitable and humanitarian organizations ask for his help. He is overwhelmed by their needs and by the images of evil he sees in the world, but he can do little to help. His ideal lover, the schizophrenic Dorrie (Charlotte Rampling) needs lithium, and his real lover, Isobel (Marie-Christine Barrault) cannot remain with him. Sandy's life and his films become eerily intertwined, and both verge toward disaster. In a final scene, he remembers a moment of tranquility with Dorrie, his "memory" that makes his own life and art worthwhile. Sandy Bates is scarcely a hero. He has lowered his expectations of ideal love and of changing the world, but he is a fragile human being seeking happiness in small pleasures and modest production. It is a tender film despite its self-consciousness.

A MIDSUMMER NIGHT'S SEX COMEDY (1982) is a direct *hommage* to Ingmar Bergman's SMILES OF A SUMMER NIGHT (1955). Three couples gather for a summer holiday at a beautiful cottage in the country, and during the course of their visit, the lovers re-arrange themselves in surprising combinations. Andrew Hobbs (Woody Allen) is an inventor of odd mechanical devices, but he still tries to make people soar (with his odd flying machine, which is oddly reminiscent of his backpack helicopter in SLEEPER), so he may still be called an artist. Amatory chaos reigns around him, yet as artist and lover he manages to restore a semblance of order to this remarkable world. Since the film is a traditional bedroom farce, the relationships are imaginary and the couplings lack a seriousness found in the earlier films. Nonetheless the artist-inventor hero searches for love and eventually rejects his momentary adulterous romance to find happiness with his wife Adrian (Mary Steenburgen). After all the excitement of romantic adventure in this summer paradise, lasting relationships offer the promise of real happiness, while momentary infatuations lead only to disappointment and death.

In summary, in this period of the film maker's development, the snide comic in search of sexual gratification yields ground to a more serious character searching for love. Self-sacrifice as a gift to the other defines the essence of love. Such a surrender of self offers meaning to the universe. The question of "how to live, whether or not there is a God" is resolved by human experience, not philosophic formulation. Giving one's self to another justifies human existence and reveals a purpose to the universe. Moral value involves surrendering the self to the interests of another. Not to love is death, or worse nothingness. The artist is the privileged soul who can point out the meaning of life and love, of death and emptiness.

LOVE AND DEATH (1975), as the title suggests, places some of Allen's philosophical and religious questions at the forefront of his film making. Like Tolstoy's dyad *War and Peace,* which the film parodies, "love" and "death" represent polar opposites. Love is life, and the absence of love, loneliness, is death. Allen has already advanced beyond the notion that love is "getting good sex," so in the present context the idea of love must include self-sacrifice in pursuit of a good for others. While it is true that the first part of the film explores love, as the characters search for satisfactory marital relationships and that the second part deals with a plot to kill Napoleon, the two themes are inseparable.[2] In this film, too, Allen introduces two themes that will occur several times in subsequent films. First, faced with a meaningless universe and no way to prove the existence of God, his character contemplates suicide. Second, moral action also hinges upon the existence of God: If there is no God, why choose the moral option in life?

In the opening voice-over narrative, as clouds billow on the screen, Boris Grushenko (Allen) explains that he has been condemned to death for a crime he has not committed, but that is the fate of all men. The bulk of the film provides the flashback that leads to his condemnation. After introducing his family, the young Boris (Alfred Lutter III) appears hanging on a cross, thus associating himself with the Christian notion of the condemnation of the innocent man, Jesus Christ. This is not an association Allen treats with reverence. The young Boris argues with Father Nikolai about the existence of God, using a parody of the Thomistic argument from causality, but concludes his quasi-serious inquiry by asking if Christ were a carpenter, how much would he charge for bookshelves. Thus fatalism, cynicism and guilt, major themes of the film, are reduced to a joke of dubious taste.

The second part of Boris's youthful quest is revealed in a conversation with Death, a parody of the character in Ingmar Bergman's THE SEVENTH SEAL (1957). Bergman's Death is a serious grim reaper dressed in black; Allen's is played for laughs and dresses in white. Bergman has him lead his new clients in a solemn dance of death; Allen has him lead Boris into the unknown with a bouncy Russian folk dance. After asking Death about the afterlife, Boris wants to know if there are girls there. Both key questions, the existence of God and of an afterlife are reduced to irreverent absurdity in the opening minutes of the film.

Neither Boris nor Allen can laugh away the questions quite so easily. Moments later, Boris contemplates suicide and argues with his beautiful cousin Sonia (Diane Keaton) about the possibility of morality without a God. He cannot pull the trigger, just in case someone eventually discovers "something" up there. Years later, after many adventures and a troubled marriage, Boris once again is attracted to suicide, and again Sonia is there to provide a foil for a stilted discussion of the standard arguments on the meaning of life. Once again, Boris backs away from the brink and decides to become a poet. The decision is comic, but the point made is quite important. If the world is meaningless and there is no convincing argument against suicide, then at least art makes human life bearable and productive. Boris finds meaning in poetry; Allen in film making.

As a member of a good Russian Orthodox family Boris is not the outsider by virtue of Jewishness, but he is an outsider because of his sanity. His family includes various forms of psychological misfits; his father boasts of owning a small piece of land, which, it turns out, is the size of a dinner plate, and his mother makes blini with the help of a geometrical wall chart. The world's insanity becomes obvious when Napoleon invades Russia and both family and village are caught up in a frenzy of war fever. Only Boris has the good sense to look at the issues of life and death and to try to avoid the violence. Even his mother urges him to rush off to battle and possible death for Mother Russia. He eventually leaves for the front, but with his butterfly collection. Boris rivals Fielding Mellish in BANANAS in his ineptitude as a soldier, but after his regiment loses all but 14 of 12,000 soldiers, he accidentally captures the French general staff and becomes a hero.

The madness of war leads Allen to consider the caprice of military victory and the world's folly in rewarding its accidental heroes. Boris finds himself in a universe that has no rationality, and where his deeds are meaningless, a mere comic fiasco. With astonishing speed, life changes for Boris. The beautiful Countess Alexandrovna (Olga Georges-Picot), captivated by the charms of the pseudo-hero, invites him to a passionate tryst, the fulfillment of his every adolescent fantasy. Her lover, Count Anton (Harold Gould) discovers her infidelity and challenges Boris to a duel. For the first time, Boris faces death on a one-to-one basis, and although he gains the advantage over the count, he cannot pull the trigger. For reasons unclear even to himself, Boris cannot take another human life, even as he could not take his own. He has some preverbal intuition of the value and meaning of life.

After the war, Boris returns to Sonia, who promised to marry him when she believed he would die in the duel. While Countess Alexandrovna represents the adolescent fantasy come to life, Sonia mirrors the slow development of mature love. At first she rejects sex altogether. Using his customary food/sex metaphor, Sonia prepares meals of snow and sleet. Their marriage is cold and tasteless. Gradually, their love ripens and they settle into a life of familial bliss. Even during this interlude of happiness, the old questions return, and Boris contemplates suicide. With Sonia's help he decides to live on as a poet. With both love and art, Boris has reached a period of contentment in his life.

The world in its madness cannot endure tranquility. Napoleon begins another invasion, and violence once more intrudes into their lives. This time, at Sonia's urging, Boris reluctantly joins her in planning to assassinate Napoleon before he devastates all of Europe with his insane dreams of empire. When the opportunity arises, Boris once again cannot pull the trigger. He cannot resolve the conflict between greater goods, or greater evils. He cannot kill directly to save thousands of lives indirectly. Although he has chosen to be an active force in this war, instead of a reluctant conscript as in the previous one, in the moment of crisis, moral realities are too complex for him to take decisive action.

Boris's (and Allen's) world is capricious, and thus his moral paralysis is understandable. Chance is the arbiter of morality. Just as he aims the pistol at the unconscious Napoleon, an unidentified assassin does the job for him. The victim, however, is not the Emperor, but an imposter, set up to trap would-be assassins. In the confusion, Boris's gun goes off, and holding the proverbial smoking gun, he is convicted of a crime he never committed. In prison, Boris finally receives the sign from God that he had craved all his life. An angel appears and tells Boris that he will be pardoned at the last minute. Boris now knows that there is a God and that the universe has a meaning. There is one more surprise, however: The angel lied.

And so Boris's problems with God and morality remain unanswered. Allen does, however, offer a moment of hope. In the final scene, as Death leads Boris away, they pass by Sonia's cottage, where Natasha (Jessica Harper) recounts an endless list of romances and infidelities in the village. Sonia fights off sleep during the monotonous, depressing catalogue of human folly. Boris appears at the window, and from the perspective of a dead man, the seductions and conquests seem trivial. Knowledge of death puts life in its proper perspective.

Religion of the non-angelic variety offers little guidance either. The bearded Orthodox priests are comic figures, and with their Russian accents veer very close to Allen's comic Orthodox rabbis who speak with a Yiddish flavor to their English. When Sonia goes to Father Andre for advice, she steps on his beard, he complains and rambles on unintelligibly. When pressed for a solution, he explains the best thing in life is two 12-year-old blond girls. Through Father Andre, the morality proposed by the organized Christian churches is dismissed as both senile and hypocritical.

As Boris dances off with Death, he offers the moral to Sonia and the audience "Life must go on." The phrase is ironic. Motivated by his love for Sonia, Boris embarked on a heroic venture that would have changed the course of world history. He dies for his effort. Sonia has rejected Boris's love continually and she was the one to engineer the plot to kill Napoleon, yet she lives, listening to Natasha's tedious narrative of love and infidelity. Life and love go on, but are they essentially meaningless? His discovery of love has led Boris reluctantly into a plot to kill Napoleon and eventually to his own execution. Thus, his decision to act in a way that would have meaning in the larger universe precipitates his death.

Boris is not bitter about his fate, but he is disappointed. At the close of his adventure, he is still not certain about the existence of God. Such a being, he muses, is not malicious; he is just ineffective in taking care of his own.

Throughout the film, romance itself has functioned as an agent of death. In an early scene, the aged Minskoff drops dead when Sonia announces her intention to marry him. The athletic sexual encounter with Countess Alexandrovna leads Boris directly to a duel that threatens his life or Count Anton's. Sonia's first husband, Voskovec the herring merchant, shoots himself while preparing for a duel with a Turk who had made a disparaging remark about Sonia's honor. Sonia herself and the attending servants giggle at the notion of her chastity, but nonetheless Voskovec dies. Finally, the Napoleon imposter is lured to his death by Sonia's promise of sexual favors.

In each case, the promise of life appears in the usual food/sex metaphor, but ironically the promise of food leads to death. Voskovec, the herring merchant, repels his wife by his smell. Countess Alexandrovna invites Boris to join her for tea, and Sonia, at the deathbed of her husband, laughs off references to her virtue and asks the servants if they know a restaurant that serves good sausage. With a variation on the theme that ties food directly to death, Napoleon urges his bakers to complete the recipe for napoleons before his rival perfects beef wellington. Both men are preparing the carnage that threatens all Europe.

The caper of Boris and Sonia has certain points of similarity to that of Miles and Luna in SLEEPER. In both, the characters embark on an adventure in order to save the world. They believe that their actions hold a meaning for the future, and thus they are willing to risk their own lives to achieve a greater good. In both, too, the Keaton character awakens from a slumber of inanity and dedicates herself to a serious moral and political cause. Sonia, in fact, develops a hard, cynical edge as the catalyst of the action. Boris prefers to flee from the invading army, while Sonia plans to murder Napoleon with the calculating coolness of a hardened assassin. In SLEEPER, their search for the Leader's nose is comic; they succeed in their adventure and go off together happily. In LOVE AND DEATH their plot involves the premeditated murder of an actual person. It fails and leads to death for Boris. Napoleon's war of conquest continues, and Sonia is left to a life that is essentially boring despite its romantic intrigue.

With LOVE AND DEATH Woody Allen begins to explore darker realms of his own artistic universe. He seeks a meaning in life in a context overwhelmed by death. His human actions are futile, even preposterous, since all ends in death. When Boris and Sonia discuss their concerns in philosophic language, the dialogue quickly turns to parody, as though philosophy itself is a joke; it provides a glorious jargon, but no answers. It will takes several years before he achieves an uneasy truce with the world as he perceives it.

ANNIE HALL (1977) returns to the questions of SLEEPER and LOVE AND DEATH, but the answers Allen provides are more nuanced and closer to his own life experience. His characters no longer inhabit a distant future world or nineteenth-century Russia. The questions and their solutions will be probed in a maddeningly complex world much closer to home. Beginning with Alvy Singer, his pilgrim heroes begin to look and sound much more like Woody Allen himself. They are contemporary New Yorkers, successful artists, Jewish, as financially secure as neurotically insecure. If he is to achieve his truce with the world, the Allen hero will have to do it in the here-and-now, not in a distant, imaginary reconstruction of reality. He will have to find peace by savoring life's small pleasures, aware that none of them will last forever.[3]

Furthermore, in ANNIE HALL Allen no longer looks for the perfect philosophical formulation to questions of his own mortality and the meaning of the universe. Living life becomes more important than formulations about life. In the opening monologue, Alvy describes the ambivalence he feels about life: He finds that it provides loneliness and suffering, but at the same time it ends all too quickly.[4] This is no longer a theoretical question for Alvy, since he has just passed his fortieth birthday, a moment when most people are suddenly struck face-to-face with their own mortality. It is also a time when most people become realistic about their life's goals and distance themselves from adolescent fantasies about the world and their role in it.

One indication of his shift in goals is that the cosmic questions, such as those argued by Boris and Sonia, are left only to Alvy Singer the child. In an early scene the boy is depressed and has stopped doing his homework because he read that the universe is expanding. He fears the end of time. The family doctor offers the solution that summarizes Allen's own attempts to reach reconciliation with his hostile world, when he advises him to enjoy life as much as he can while he has it. (5) The words of the chain-smoking doctor to a whining child and his hysterical mother contain the solution that Allen will continue to test throughout his film-making career.

In ANNIE HALL, Allen returns to his Jewishness in a gentile world to describe his sense of personal alienation in a hostile universe. Immediately after the scene in the doctor's office, Alvy, now a television producer, reveals to his friend Rob (Tony Roberts) that he is upset by the anti-Semitism he finds even in New York. He complains that a colleague at NBC, significantly named Tom *Christ*ie, elides the phrases, "Did you eat yet?" and "No, did you?" In both cases Alvy translates the "did you" into "Jew." (9) Rob compounds the problem by addressing Alvy as Max. When Alvy protests, Rob assures him that it is a good name for him. As a sign of Alvy's alienation, his best friend does not even use his proper name.

Two of Alvy's most profound moments of alienation occur in the context of Christian feasts. Alvy joins the Hall family for Easter dinner of ham, prepared by Grammy Hall, whom Alvy quickly categorizes as a classic anti-Semite. (56) Of course, he has been primed for this reaction, since Annie has already warned him that Grammy believes the standard creed that Jews make too much money. (39) He feels so alienated and Jewish at that moment that he imagines himself, as seen by the Hall family, as an Orthodox rabbi, complete with broad brimmed hat, beard and curled sideburns. Not only does he freely eat pork, but when making a joke about his therapy, he says he no longer needs a lobster bib during his sessions, a gratuitous reference to another forbidden food.

During Alvy's visit to Los Angeles, Christmas carols and decorations provide a Christian setting for Alvy's alienation. (83 ff.) He is so clearly out of place in this antiseptic setting so far from New York, that he becomes sick and cannot host the awards show he was scheduled to do. Puzzled by the sudden illness, the doctor asks if he has been violating Kosher dietary laws. (87) Once released from the television contract, the illness vanishes immediately, and as a sign of his recovery, he begins to attack a plate of boiled chicken, a food perfectly acceptable in Kosher kitchens. During the trip, his relationship with Annie begins to disintegrate during a Christmas party, and back in New York, as Annie packs her belongings and prepares to move out of Alvy's apartment, the scene includes a Christmas tree. Christian imagery consistently provides the background for the failures in Alvy's life.

The relationship between food and dietary laws and cultural conditioning is a constant theme throughout the film. Annie and Alvy begin their romance after he listens to her sing in a night club. They go to a quiet delicatessen for a late supper and she commits gustatory blasphemy by ordering pastrami on white bread with mayonnaise. (43) (The joke is repeated in HANNAH AND HER SISTERS [1986], when Mickey Sachs [Allen] buys a loaf of Wonder Bread and a jar of mayonnaise to test his desire to become a Catholic.) In Annie's atrocious selection from the menu, her midwestern, gentile background distances her from his New York Jewish world, where everyone knows with pastrami you have mustard and rye already. His tastes are equally out of place in her world. Their relationship ends in a Los Angeles health-food restaurant, after he has just ordered alfalfa sprouts and mashed yeast. (97) The inept choices of food shows that each is a misfit in the other's world. At the film's bittersweet ending, a lunch together in O'Neil's Balloon, opposite Lincoln Center, shows that their relationship has been transformed. They enjoy a meal in neutral space and the menu is not mentioned. They reminisce about the good times they enjoyed together, and after the meal the camera peers through the window of the restaurant to watch Annie and Alvy parting, no longer lovers but as fellow pilgrims. Their romance is gone, but their friendship and their memories remain.

Food frequently carries more than its obvious meaning. Lobsters, for example, make three appearances in the film. In the first,

Annie and Alvy are preparing a meal in a beach house, when the live lobsters get loose and roam around the kitchen. (22) Alvy is terrified of them. Their attempts to corral dinner are very funny, but also a reminder that Alvy is tasting forbidden food and forming a relationship with a *shiksa*. No matter. This transgression of law and custom brings both of them enormous joy. In the final moments of the film, the scene is reprised when Alvy remembers several of the wonderful moments he shared with Annie. He recalls the comic lobster hunt with great affection. (104) Finally, during Alvy's temporary separation from Annie, the scene is reenacted almost identically with one of Alvy's interim romances, but the joy is gone. This attractive but humorless woman lacks the excitement and zest for life that Annie had. Scarcely amused by Alvy's terror of the escaped lobsters, she seems a bit annoyed at the silliness of it all. (96)

Having set the theme of mortality and the meaninglessness of life in the early scene with the young Alvy in the doctor's office, Allen tries to discover a purpose in life. Such an office frequently provides the setting for confronting life and death, in life and in Allen films. In fact, death is rarely far from Allen's thoughts or images. Alvy, it seems, always buys Annie books that have the word "death" in them, as Annie reminds him during their final break-up. (98) Annie's younger brother Duane (Christopher Walken) confides in Alvy his desire to drive his car into oncoming traffic, and thus after the famous Easter dinner a simple trip to the airport with Duane at the wheel and Alvy cringing in the front seat puts Alvy once more in confrontation with death. The suicide theme, now transferred to Duane, still implicates the Woody character. In its denial of death the California culture appears lunatic, from the healthfood menu to Rob's donning a foil helmet to protect his head from alpha rays. (101) Duane's driving presents a realistic confrontation with death; alpha rays do not.

Even though relationships with their promise of life-giving fade, Allen concludes they enrich the moments of life a person has before death. Alvy has been married twice, first to Allison (Carol Kane), a stage manager for a television variety show (18), and then to Robin (Janet Margolin), a rising member of the New York intellectual and literary elite. (26) In addition, he has a meaningless fling with a reporter for "Rolling Stone" (Shelley Duvall), who significantly remains nameless in the script. (65) Nothing comes of these relationships, and the three women pass quietly out of Alvy's life, and he from theirs.

Annie, however, is different. Coming from Chippewa Falls, Wisc., she is a misfit in New York. Her driving in city traffic terrifies Alvy, her clothes are eccentric even by the standards of the 1970's, and she keeps half-eaten sandwiches in her purse, a hint of her half-hearted affairs with Dennis from Chippewa Falls and Jerry the New York actor. When she tries to sing "It Had to Be You" in a night club, the audience rudely ignores her. (41) Nothing seems to work for her, but Alvy continues to encourage her both as a person and as an artist.[5] He buys her books and encourages her to take courses. Later, after being with Alvy for some time, she gains confidence as a performer. Annie does a marvelous rendition of "Seems Like Old Times," and the audience is mesmerized. (77) In fact, after hearing her sing, Tony Lacey (Paul Simon), a record producer, is interested in furthering her career.

Other pieces of Annie's life begin to come together for her, as well. After a short separation, Annie calls Alvy in the midst of his sexual dalliance with the nameless reporter and begs him to come to her apartment immediately. The reason, he discovers, is a spider in her bathroom. (67) She confesses her need for him and their reconciliation begins with a visit to Alvy's old neighborhood, during which she learns a great deal about his family and its Jewish-American culture. They spend the night together, and since it is her birthday, he gives her a romantic gift of lingerie and a watch, a sign that time is passing for their relationships and their lives.

As she gains independence, however, Annie, who has received her life from Alvy, gradually seems to outgrow him. She moves to Los Angeles, hostile territory to Alvy, to further her own career, lives with Tony Lacey and makes the definitive decision that this time her relationship with Alvy is over. Later, without any influence from Alvy, she decides on her own to leave Tony and return to New York, where she will be a friend to Alvy without being his companion. During their separation scene in the health-food restaurant, Annie acknowledges her debt to Alvy by reminding him that he was influential in helping her to grow emotionally and continue with her singing career. (99) His love leads to giving rather than acquiring.

The gift, however, is mutual. Because of Annie, Alvy has gotten over his severe case of "anhedonia," the inability to enjoy life, which was the original title of the film.[6] In the final monologue he recounts the moments with her that he will cherish forever. After their lunch he recalls how much he enjoyed simply knowing her. (105) He no longer needs intellectual solutions to the problem of the "expanding universe" as he did while a child, nor does he need pleasures that will last beyond death. The transient, simple joys of life are enough to keep him going. But even more, Alvy as a playwright has been able to translate his experiences into art. In a rehearsal, young actors closely resembling Annie and Alvy discuss their break-up (102). They allude to books with death in the title and the health-food restaurant where they ended their relationship. Alvy interrupts the scene to explain that it is only his first play. Life has made its way into Alvy's art and pushed back his limits of being a clever one-line comedian. Loving Annie has made Alvy a richer artist; loving Alvy has made Annie a richer person.

A critic whose responses are influenced by traditional religious beliefs might be understandably negative about the casual nature of sexual relationships among Allen's characters. Such a view would be an unfortunate limitation on an appreciation of Allen's complex but profoundly moral statement. He can be faulted in seeing human love as ephemeral, it is true, but at the same time, his notion of love as mutual self-sacrifice to enable the other to grow is a deeply religious notion in the Judaeo-Christian tradition.[7] Allen is not a theologian or a homilist. He is an artist, and his presentation of the human condition can help people of many religious traditions, or of none, to understand their loving relationship with their God and with one another.

INTERIORS (1978) so defies the normal expectations of a Woody Allen film that it seems made by someone else, like a clever film-school student trying to do a parody of Ingmar Bergman.[8] Under its austere surface, however, float many of the questions that have been slowly developing in the mind of the artist. Unlikely as it seems, this solemn drama, without jokes and without the Woody hero, fits comfortably in the mainstream of Allen's works. Thematically, it is a most "Allen" film.

Although Allen does not appear in person, his personal preoccupations as an artist surface in almost all the characters of the very comfortable Wasp family at the center of the story. The "interiors" of the title refer primarily to the interiors of the houses which serve as habitat and prison for the families, but clearly the architectural interiors serve as a metaphor for Allen's own artistic and spiritual life in its maddening self-enclosure as he looks outward to a world that threatens and fascinates him. In this film, Allen's characters continually gaze through windows at a foreign, outside universe. They smart at the separation, but at times eagerly seal them to shut out the outside world even more completely.

Eve, the matriarch (Geraldine Page), constantly tries to rearrange the interior spaces of her life and her homes and those of her children, but nothing satisfies her. Like any artist, and perhaps like Allen, she attempts a kind of ideal artistic order that is unattainable. Her search for perfection leads her to suicide, and her family to desperation. In her quest of perfect controlled order, she prefers neutral colors. Her hair is combed into a tight bun, and she wears a suit referred to as "ice" blue.[9] Of all flowers, she prefers white roses. Nothing, no sensation, color or sound, may intrude upon the placid, perfect world she strives to create.

Eve has a history of suicidal depression. Through this character, Allen continues to ask if the only reasonable response to the world's hostility and artistic frustration is self-inflicted death, but her option is not set in a context of comedy, as it was with Boris in LOVE AND DEATH. Her self-destructive impulse involves others, as did Duane's in ANNIE HALL. Since Eve never attains her artistic perfection, her personal demons torment her, and her husband Arthur (E. G. Marshall) finally decides he must leave her if he is to make anything of his own life. He eventually decides to remarry. Allen presents him as a most ambivalent character. Allen is uneasy about his abandoning his sick wife, but after all those years of loyalty, he rather approves of Arthur's ability to make the decision to begin a new life.

Each of her daughters, facets of Allen's own artistic life, is powerless to help Eve find a solution to the hostility of her universe. Like Allen in his self-image, the daughters look out from their respective interiors not as pure artist-perfectionists like their mother Eve, but as people of limited talents struggling for authenticity and craving recognition. Although she has published poetry in *The New Yorker*, Renata (Diane Keaton) fights writer's block with the help of a psychiatrist. In one chilling, Bergmanesque scene, she struggles with a new poem, and as she looks out the window of her studio, she is terrified by a tree, which seems to grow larger and more menacing as she contemplates it. She explains to her husband Frederick (Richard Jordan) that she reached a state of panic when she realized the world, as represented by the tree, and she were two separate entities and she could not put them together. (140) Eve's illness may represent the presence of inexplicable evil in the world, while Renata's vision captures the brute indifference of a vaguely menacing external world. Both concepts are horrifying.

Renata has had a child, Cory, thus her life is as fruitful as her art, yet the child seems distant, a peripheral presence in her life. There is little affection shown between mother and child, as though the remoteness of Renata from her mother Eve is being carried over to the next generation. Renata's husband Frederick is an aspiring novelist who receives terrible reviews for his work. In his anger, he lashes out with withering reviews of other novelists as a means to prove to himself that he is protecting his own drive toward for excellence. (164) He fears, as does every artist including Woody Allen, that his work is incomplete, but he is not sure if he has a talent that he lost or whether the talent never existed in the first place. (142) He tries to flee this uncomfortable question by drinking heavily.

Joey (Mary Beth Hurt) is restless as an artist and as a person, but she is also a realist. Alone in the family, she realizes that Arthur, her father, will never return to Eve, and she refuses to encourage her mother with false hopes. Joey also understands the limits of her own talent. In the past she tried acting and then photography, but neither worked out for her. She tells her husband Mike that her need for self-expression is matched by confusion about what she wants to express. (125) She is rapidly growing bored with her job as a reader for a publisher. In her restlessness, she dreads a time when her mediocre talent will confine her to the life of copy writer at some advertising agency. (146) Her fear of routine is reinforced when she discovers that she is pregnant and expresses the fear that motherhood will further limit her career aspirations.

While Joey is actually capable of producing life, she refuses to settle down with Mike (Sam Waterston), and despite his mild protests she is determined to get an abortion. (144) Mike makes socially relevant documentary films, but Joey lacks the sense of political commitment to enable her to join him. Her self-absorption puts her in a state of paralysis. She wears glasses with thin oversized frames, as though her own myopia insulates her and keeps her from making any kind of commitment to the outside world.

Flyn (Kristin Griffith), the youngest daughter, is the least complex. She is an actress whose sensual good looks keep her constantly involved in making television movies and commercials. She has no illusions of artistic achievement, but rather she seems content with her financial success. Her conversation lacks depth, and since her visit to her family is brief, she never becomes engaged with the family tragedies around her. She flirts mildly with Frederick, and later, quite drunk, he attempts to rape her. (171) Flyn, as a superficial artist without a husband or present male companion, bears no promise of life. Her sexuality is limited to her appearance and the illusion of availability she creates in others, a misperception as she proves by rejecting Frederick's violent advances. An artist confined to commercial work like Flyn's risks sterility, surely a fear of Allen, then known only as a successful funny man.

Since none of the four women artists in the film show any promise of dealing with the world that exists outside her "interior," has Allen succumbed to hopelessness? Not quite. Pearl (Maureen Stapleton) provides a solution to his apparent despair. Appearing more than half-way through the film, twice-widowed Pearl arrives as Arthur's fiancée. She is a creature of the senses and of simple pleasures. The couple met in Greece, a warm sunny climate compared to the wintery beaches of Long Island and the confined spaces of the family's New York apartments. She wears red, dances and does card tricks. As the family discusses the complexity of a modern play, she is content with a simplistic interpretation. While Arthur visited temples and churches in Greece, Pearl preferred to lie in the sun. And although little is made of it, she appears to be Jewish, as out of place in this family as Alvy Singer was among the Halls.[10]

Pearl is the antitype of Eve. In a bit of heavy-handed symbolism Allen focuses attention on flower vases, perhaps with some vague allusion to Keats's "Ode on a Grecian Urn," a reminder of timeless beauty created through art. For her part, Pearl likes to collect ebony fertility images from Trinidad, and she calls attention to their exaggerated physical characteristics. (151) In an opening scene, Eve brings a $400 vase to Mike and Joey, and although they cannot afford it, she discusses the shape and texture as though it were an absolute necessity for their apartment. After her wedding to Arthur, Pearl dances energetically and knocks over a similar vase, smashing it and spilling the white roses on the floor. In anger, Joey calls her an animal. (170) Quite properly so. Pearl radiates a healthy animal vitality in contrast to Eve's purely spiritual morbidity. By shattering the vase and spilling the flowers, she asserts the triumph of body over spirit.

Pearl has simple appetites, revealed in her taste in foods. In Greece she could eat lamb every day and likes her steak blood red. (149–50) The hors-d'oeuvres she prepares are plebeian meatballs and little hot dogs, which seem oddly out of place in the elegant setting of the Southampton beach house. She encourages Arthur to take gravy for his meat, and offers him a second piece of cheesecake. When he takes it, he licks the excess from her fingers. (153) In contrast, the only time Eve appears at a table it is to receive two blouses from her daughters as birthday presents, which she obliquely criticizes because they are similar. (129) She appears never to eat.

Through Pearl's physicality, Allen is scarcely reverting to an earlier notion that one survives a grim existence through abundant noncommittal sex. Pearl represents life and its enjoyment. As mother of two sons, she is a giver of life, while Eve embodies death. Eve uses a black tape to seal her windows as she turns on the gas jets during her nearly successful suicide attempt. By her act, she shuts out life and the outside world. After the wedding of Pearl and Arthur, Eve mysteriously appears to Joey. Curious about the voices she hears, Pearl enters the scene and Joey mistakenly calls her Mother. (172) Eve vanishes and walks into the surf to complete her suicidal urge. Joey rushes after her to try to save her and nearly drowns herself, but when she is pulled from the waves, Pearl, her new mother, breathes life into her with mouth-to-mouth resuscitation.

Although Pearl offers life, Allen doubts whether the artistic daughters or he himself as an artist can accept it. After Eve's funeral, the three daughters return to the beach house and once again encased in its interior they stare out through the glass. Through Joey's diary they recall several memories of their mother, especially as she decorated the Christmas tree. As in ANNIE HALL the Christian symbol alienates the Jewish Allen from this idealized and very distant world. Pearl is not present at this post-funeral scene, and thus the family lacks the life-giving joy and simple pleasure she represents.

The remoteness of the alien, gentile world appears in another context. After Eve's first suicide attempt, she watches religious television programs. An evangelical preacher brings to the stage a convert named Roy Schwartz, who identifies himself as Jewish. (143) The preacher asks Schwartz an unintelligible question about the role of the Jewish people in God's plans today. A parody of Christianity challenges the Jewish outsider to justify his role in history. The television program is interrupted at this point, but later on Renata remarks that Joey believes that her mother's interest in Christian television may actually help her, even if it is all ridiculous. (161) While Eve in her desperation clings to an exaggerated form of her own Christianity, the artistic daughters remain as alienated from Christianity as the Jewish Allen. They are troubled, but not desperate enough to reach for nonsense.

The foolishness of Christianity provided a fragile refuge for Eve, an unrealistic source of hope that her daughters could not share. Still believing reconciliation possible, Eve invites Arthur to meet her in a Christian church, St. Ignatius Catholic church on Park Avenue, ostensibly to look at the mosaics. (158) When Arthur tells her of his intention to finalize the divorce and remarry, Eve smashes a bank of vigil candles. Placed in the context of human realities, Christianity, even in these sacred precincts, cannot offer much consolation.[11] The artistic person may initially find aesthetic value in Christianity, as in the mosaics, but deceived and angered by the trials of real life, such a person must reject it.

In INTERIORS Allen once again presents the quandary of the outsider in a menacing world, seeking love and life, and able to find neither. Suicide remains an option, but it is rejected. Art offers a way to deal with life, but it offers no guarantees. God and religion, previously only an occasion to present comic priests and rabbis, now is a serious option, if only in the mind of a disturbed, tragic woman. The characters, husband, daughters and sons-in-law struggle with their desire to act morally and lovingly in the face of Eve's inexplicable illness, but without any external guidance they are locked in their "interiors." They simply do not know what to do. Eve's illness has forced them to rearrange their ethical furniture, as Eve's art forced them to redecorate their apartments. The questions are sharpened, but answers remain as elusive as ever.

MANHATTAN (1979) initially seemed a weak attempt by authors Woody Allen and Marshall Brickman to recreate the success of ANNIE HALL. As the years pass, however, ANNIE HALL seems merely a rough draft for the much stronger MANHATTAN.

The shift in titles points to a subtle but significant shift in emphasis. In the earlier film, Allen explores the characters, like Annie Hall, who try to cope with a puzzling world, discover love and continue building lives for themselves. They never quite fit in, never fulfill all their plans and in the end must be happy with memories of small pleasures. In MANHATTAN, the central figure is the island itself, the world of contradictions and ambiguities that drives people into frantic, desperate and often very funny situations as they look for stability, companionship and meaning in their lives. This island-universe provokes ambivalent feelings in Allen. He has grown to appreciate its simple pleasures, thus his "anhedonia" fades into the background, but at the same time he realizes the world will never grant him the peace and security he longs for. In ANNIE HALL Allen presents the pilgrim; in MANHATTAN the world the pilgrim must journey through.

MANHATTAN begins and ends with shots of famous nighttime scenes in New York, shot in magnificent black-and-white by Gordon Willis. This universe is the constant, and people merely drift in and out of its confines like passing shadows. Accompanied by the ebullient theme of Gershwin's "Rhapsody in Blue" performed by the New York Philharmonic Orchestra, the City glows in a radiant, but brute, impersonal beauty. Isaac Davis (Woody Allen), in his opening monologue, tries to capture the alien loveliness of the setting through a book he is beginning to dictate as he writes that his character adored the City.[12] A few lines later, he presents the other side of his feelings, when he says that the City represented the decline of modern culture. (182) And still later, Isaac comments that it is difficult to live in an environment dominated by the crudeness and violence of the modern city. (182)

Isaac, known as Ike, can find no safe refuge or stable home in such a world. When he leaves his very well-paying job with the television program, he must find a smaller apartment, and with its rusty water and noisy neighbors, he finds it far from satisfactory

(230–31). The City itself is in constant motion. Ike watches a demolition site, and regrets that the authorities have not been more successful in having old buildings declared landmarks (252).

In the final scene, as he rushes toward Tracy (Mariel Hemingway), the woman he thinks he loves, he runs through varied, identifiable neighborhoods along the length of the East Side, from Yorkville to Gramercy Park, as though the City itself were keeping them apart. Tracy, he discovers, has decided that she must go to London, far away from the madness of New York and its dizzying whirl of relationships, if she is to have any chance of growing into a mature person and accomplished artist. In fact and fiction, young people traditionally come *to* New York to find themselves and begin a life in the theater. In Allen's metaphorical use of the City, Tracy, herself a metaphor of innocence, must gain some distance from it if she is to survive.

As the story line begins, Ike shares a late evening supper with Tracy, and his friends Yale Pollack (Michael Murphy) and his wife Emily (Anne Byrne). Almost immediately, the notion of mortality is introduced, when Ike discloses that Tracy is 17 and he is 42. (Days later, in the intimacy of his apartment, Ike and Tracy watch a television talk show and mock the toupee and face-lifts of a man and woman trying to mask their aging processes.) Later in their conversation at the restaurant, Ike asks about moral options by wondering which of the four of them would have the courage to jump into an icy river to save a drowning man. (182) Thus in the opening minutes of the film, the perennial Allen questions arise: "What is the meaning of life, if it ends only in death? How do I best live my numbered days in this chaotic and vaguely hostile planet?" Tracy, with her odd mixture of youthful naivete and sophistication, represents a future of unlimited possibilities.

Ike's other love in the film is Mary Wilke (Diane Keaton), who is the logical and unpleasant outcome of the transformation of Annie Hall from country girl to New Yorker. Annie came from Chippewa Falls, overcame her insecurities, took control of her life and moved first to Los Angeles and then back to New York to further her career. Mary comes from Philadelphia and settled into the New York literary scene. Her opinionated self-assurance as a critic makes her more than a trifle obnoxious. Annie gradually found the freedom to move from one relationship to another, while Mary has already gotten used to the idea of easily changing partners. She has no anchor; she merely drifts in and out of men's lives with little thought of the consequences. She spent time as Yale's mistress, then moved to Ike, and on an apparent whim, went back to Yale.

Mary is attracted to intelligent men, and seems eager to use the word genius. Yale is a handsome professor of literature, but he is a failed writer. Ike is scarcely physically attractive, but he has been a successful writer for television and holds further promise with his book. Mary finds talent sensual. She holds an idealized memory of her former husband Jeremiah (Wallace Shawn), a professor of linguistics. She remembers him as brilliant and comments that other women found him irresistible. (222) When Ike finally meets Jeremiah, he gasps in disbelief at his rival, who is short, balding, chubby and speaks with a slight lisp. In her confusion, Mary keeps Jeremiah as the ideal she can never replace with any of her casual partners.

Mary remains attractive, like Annie, with her stammering speech and ready smile, but her needs for affirmation are destructive. She has talent, but flits from one project to the next as easily as she moves from one lover to another. Mary is an empty woman, a victim of Manhattan's sophisticated decadence, a burnt-out Annie Hall.

Yale Pollack, too, has been swallowed by the chaos of Manhattan. With his combination Ivy League and Jewish name, he is a man searching for an identity and purpose in life. A once promising professor of literature, he cannot finish his book on Eugene O'Neill, nor can he get around to founding his prospective literary journal. On blind impulse he uses the money saved for these ventures for the purchase of a Porsche convertible. His affair with Mary begins while he still pretends to have an ideal marriage with Emily. When he leaves Mary, he urges Ike to take his place, and finally without apparent forethought, he decides he prefers Mary to Emily and reclaims Mary.

Furious at Yale's betrayal and dishonesty, Ike rushes into the university while classes are in session, interrupts Yale's lecture and insists that he leave his class and talk it out. They enter a classroom used for physical anthropology. As Yale lies, contradicts himself, admits his duplicity and professes seeing no problem with his action, he is photographed in front of a chart of evolving primate skulls. He angrily excuses his actions by declaring that he is not saintly. (265) During the exchange, Ike shares the screen with the skeleton of an ape, and using it as sign of his own mortality, Ike remarks that one day they will both be skeletons. Before that time, he maintains, one must have a kind of personal morality. Yale rebukes him for being self-righteous and believing that he is God. Ike does not deny the charge, and his response relates the possibility of a moral order in the universe to the existence of God, a theme that Allen will revisit frequently in the later films.

In theory, Ike recognizes the need for personal integrity, whether or not it is based on God, but in practice it comes no more easily to him than to Yale. His relationship to Tracy is extremely ambiguous. She is a delightful, loving companion, who shows him the beautiful side of New York by taking him on a hansom-cab ride through Central Park. (227) He longs to usher her toward maturity, as Alvy did for Annie Hall, but he is troubled by her age. When Mary comes into his life, he drops Tracy completely, not even answering her phone calls. When he learns that Mary has returned to Yale, he remembers the good times with Tracy and rushes off to reclaim her. In his own self-interest and with very little concern for her well-being, he even tries to disrupt her arrangements to go to London. Looking very mature in her traveling suit, she declines his invitation and enunciates the theme of the film, maintaining that corruption is not universal, even in New York. She admonishes Ike to have faith in people. (271) Manhattan, then, may be a hostile, corrupting universe, but it is possible for some people to preserve personal integrity.

Ike's response to her line demonstrates the kind of wonderful ambiguity that is possible only in film. He smiles, but the meaning of the smile is magnificently ambiguous. Has Ike (Allen himself) finally understood that it is possible for human integrity and moral living to exist in the chaotic universe he has imaged in to Manhattan? And does that thought make him happy? Or does he smile because Tracy has the wisdom to leave this jumbled universe with its twisted relationships to try to make some sense out of her world through art in London? Or finally is the smile a kind of cynical comment on her youthful naivete? Does he believe that one day she will be as corrupt as everyone else in his spiritual Manhattan? Or is it all of these?

The arts in Manhattan are no guarantee of integrity and, in fact, they offer their own potential for corruption. Ike is successful as a writer for the television comedy series "Human Beings Wow!" a program he despises. In his own estimation, his successful writing diminishes him as an artist and as a person. As he watches an episode from the control booth, he becomes disgusted with his work and quits. It is the beginning of a long process that may lead to his regeneration.

The others are not so fortunate. Yale fails with both his book and his literary journal. Mary turns from magazine pieces to a novelization of a film script because of the easy money. The most successful author is Jill (Meryl Streep), Ike's second wife, who writes a tell-all story of their marriage and divorce. Her book draws attention from movie producers. Yale and Ike dismiss this kind of self-revealing work as gossip and new pornography. (184) Her accounts of their sex life add a certain validity to the allegation.

In this world of pseudo-art, true artists are at risk. Yale and Mary meet Ike and Tracy in the Guggenheim Museum, where the secretly adulterous couple sneer at the exhibits and dismiss those who enjoy them, like Ike and Tracy. In their arrogance they compile a membership list for the Academy of the Overrated: Gustav Mahler, Isak Dinesen, Carl Jung, F. Scott Fitzgerald, Lenny Bruce and others. Ike expresses amazement at their selection, but when they include Ingmar Bergman, Ike reacts heatedly that Bergman is one of the truly brilliant directors in cinema today. (194) The reaction should not be surprising since Allen's previous film "Interiors" was an obvious tribute to and imitation of Bergman.

Ike finally receives word that Viking Press liked the first four chapters of his book. With this news he has begun to find peace and productivity in this corrupt universe, but the work is not yet complete. There are chapters yet to be written and relationships yet to be sorted out. Yet in contrast to the Academy of the Overrated, Ike finds that art has a purpose and composes his own lists of people who make life worth living: Groucho Marx, Willie Mays, Louie Armstrong, Flaubert and others. For one striving for authenticity, as Ike is at this point, art does have a purpose in Ike's cruel world.

At their separation, Tracy gives Isaac a small harmonica, which Ike cannot play at all. Tracy explains that she is trying to reach new talents in him. (244) In context, these talents are many: artistic, loving, and spontaneous. His love for her will "redeem" him morally and artistically. The scene is a direct counterpoint to Mary's separation from Yale. Tracy's separation comes in a soda fountain; Mary's in the Stanhope Hotel. Tracy gives a simple musical instrument as a parting gift, which Ike will keep and cherish, even though he shows no immediate interest in learning to play it. Mary angrily offers Yale tickets to a concert by Jean Pierre Rampal, which she then tears to shreds. Mary's notion of art is sophisticated and professional. She and Yale are cast as spectators, not participants, and at the end it comes to nothing. The tickets fail to form a bond between them, nor do they provide enjoyment for either.

Although Ike cannot imagine Tracy as opening him up, and thus doing for him what Alvy had done for Annie Hall, he does at one point describe her in religious terms, which offer a hint of his realizing that she may be his salvation. (Again, she must not be considered a Messiah figure; neither Ike nor Allen is thinking in those terms.) Ike tells Tracy that she would have settled Job's argument with God. Job, it is remembered, could not understand why God allowed evil to come into his life in such abundance. Ike tells her that in the midst of Job's laments God would have pointed to her and explained that despite all the terrible things he does or allows, God could also make someone as lovely as Tracy. (207) Ike, like Job, continues to try to comprehend the evil he finds in Manhattan, and he admits that Tracy makes the effort worthwhile.

During his struggle, frustration with his world does not lead Ike to a contemplation of suicide, a common theme in the earlier films, but to attempted murder. His destructive wrath turns outward. Jill, his second wife, is bisexual, but after bearing Ike's son, she decides to leave Ike and take her son to live with Connie (Karen Ludwig). A cruel turn of fate has robbed him of his search for human love. Enraged and humiliated, he nearly runs her and her companion over with a car. It is unclear, even to him, whether it was an accident, as he claims at times, or deliberate, as the women believe and as Ike admits openly to Mary, when he admits that he tried to run both of them over with his car. (207) The conceit offers comic possibilities, but comic murder is still murder, just as comic suicide is still suicide. Murder adds another level of seriousness to the corruption already established through lies, adultery, exploitative, self-serving relationships, pretension and fraudulent art.

The food/sex metaphor remains throughout the film. At the height of their romance, Tracy and Ike shop for food at a super-market and share Chinese food in bed together. She tells him about her desire to go to London while they are eating pizza. His is served plain, but she has all the fixings, as though she wants variety in her life while he is settling in to basics. He accuses her of forgetting to add coconut. (226) In a later scene, he tells her of his relationship with Mary while they have ice-cream sodas, and she responds that she feels a bit ill. (245) Their food/sex has upset her life. His final, self-serving argument to keep her from going to London is the prediction that she will meet people and have lunch a lot, suggesting possible relationships with other men (271), a development he previously encouraged as he urged her to turn her attention away from him and toward boys her own age (246).

Similarly, Ike and Mary begin their romance when they order take-out hamburgers. Their evening together ends near dawn under the 59th Street Bridge, with the structure suggesting a bridge forming between them. Their relationship is cemented after a dinner in Brooklyn and a taxi ride back to Manhattan. Yale and Mary end their relationship for the first time in the Stanhope Hotel, but food is scarcely in evidence. They have come to the table of love and found it empty.

As in the case of ANNIE HALL, critics from a religious tradition with clearly defined moral teachings on fidelity will surely find the casual relationships in MANHATTAN difficult to appreciate. Doubly difficult is the suggestion that Ike finds a form of redemption through a relationship with a 17-year-old girl. Clearly, Allen allows Ike to exploit her innocence for his own personal salvation, and in most religious traditions, this is clearly unacceptable.[13] To reduce the characters to realism is to misconstrue Allen's point. Tracy represents beauty, purity and hope in Ike's tortured world; she is the opposite of Mary Wilke. Ike has failed with two wives, one a drug addict and the other a lesbian, and his affair with Mary, who is self-absorbed and irresponsible, has led only to frustration.

Paradoxically, Tracy for all her apparent promiscuity is an innocent. Her sexuality is natural and uncomplicated, like that of the rabbits in the introduction to EVERYTHING YOU ALWAYS WANTED TO KNOW ABOUT SEX. Contact with love in its purest form, with an "innocent" girl who teaches him how to enter love as a giving relationship, holds a profoundly moral meaning for Allen and his audience. Ike, and Allen, may not be able to accept this kind of love as a norm for personal behavior, but they find it highly attractive as a goal to be striven for. A theologically-minded critic can see in this model of love, this growth through altruism, a theological model for the human relationship with others and ultimately for the human person's relationship with God.

STARDUST MEMORIES (1980) is an intensely personal film, even though its borrowings from Bergman and Fellini are obvious. In an interview session at a mock film festival, one film buff in the audience asks if a scene in the film they had just screened was an *hommage* to Vincent Price's THE HOUSE OF WAX. From the stage, Tony (Tony Roberts) responds: "An *hommage*? Not exactly. We stole the idea outright".[14] STARDUST MEMORIES is an exercise in grand larceny. In this instance, unlike INTERIORS, the parody is deliberate and frequently very funny. Part of the enjoyment for audiences comes from recognizing the allusions to earlier films, especially Fellini's 8 1/2 and Bergman's THE SILENCE, both released in 1963 and accorded the dubious distinction of "classics." Thus these films became open to constant reinterpretation by pretentious, symbol-hunting critics. Film students and critics also receive their richly deserved share of the parody. Many of Allen's darts strike embarrassingly close to home for anyone who writes and teaches about films.

Like Guido (Marcello Mastroianni) in 8 1/2, Sandy Bates (Woody Allen) is a once successful film director who cannot bring his current project to a conclusion. Like its predecessor, 8 1/2, the bulk of the Allen film takes place in the director's head, a mixture of fact and fantasy in which even "reality" appears in highly subjective form, filtered through the perceptions of a director under terrible stress. As a fragile artist experiencing strain in his personal and creative lives, Sandy perceives reality through images that are grossly distorted and often very funny. These images then become incorporated into the film he is trying to complete.

Several of Allen's key themes appear in the opening dream sequence, which turns out to be a scene from Sandy's uncompleted film. Borrowing sound effects and the eerie over-exposed black-and-white photography from the opening of THE SILENCE, Sandy pictures his character as finding himself trapped in a train populated by black-clad, grim, unsmiling people, including a priest. A ticking clock reminds him that time is running out on his journey of life, and the destination is not yet clear. Looking through the window, he notices another train headed in the opposite direction. Its passengers are dressed in white and enjoy a party atmosphere. A very young, pre-BASIC INSTINCT Sharon Stone, smiles and seductively kisses the window as she looks across the siding at Sandy. Wanting to join the other train, Sandy discovers that he is locked in with his funereal fellow passengers. As he pounds on the windows, his suitcase, the burden he carries through life, opens and spills sand on Sandy, as a visual and verbal association indicating the sterility of his life. Its spilling may also suggest the passage of time like sand through an hourglass.

The trains leave the station in opposite directions. Sandy and his dark companions next appear at their destination: a huge garbage dump near the sea. Much to his surprise, he sees the revelers from the other train approaching the same dump from the opposite direction. In Sandy's view then, whether people are happy or morose, rubbish is the universal outcome of human life. The film cuts to a projection room, where the producers have just viewed this scene as the conclusion to Sandy's latest film. Little wonder they find its grim message unacceptable for commercial release. They complain that Sandy and his films are no longer funny (282), a criticism that Allen must have heard many times when he tried to promote "serious" film ideas.

In this sequence many of the constant Allen themes converge: anhedonia, mortality, the passage of time, and the futility of art in a world destined for annihilation. When the scene cuts back to Sandy in present time, he is trapped in traffic, caged in the back seat of his Rolls Royce. The dream he presents on film, then, arises directly from his own experience of life. He is hemmed in on all sides.

Despite the problems with his current film project, Sandy has a reputation for making successful comedy films, and his producers urge him to attend a weekend retrospective of his films at a seaside resort, called the Stardust Hotel. The name suggests not only the nostalgia of the wonderful Hoagy Carmichael song but the notion of stardom turned to dust. The review of the films allows Sandy to take a look at his life as well. The distinction is not easily maintained; the films are his life.

Through his heightened subjective perspective, Sandy finds himself under attack from every direction. His secretary scrambles his appointments. Aspiring actors and performers force themselves on him, looking for a chance to use him to further their own careers. One celebrity-smitten young woman, Shelley (Amy Wright), bribes a doorman to give her access to his suite. She waits in his bed to have sex with him. Sandy expresses outrage, but she explains that she believes meaningless sex is preferable to no sex at all. (312) At the ambiguous end of the scene, Sandy apparently complies with her request. Autograph seekers intrude on his private moments, interrupt his telephone calls and conversations, and one young woman wants him to autograph her left breast. People make claims on him because they come from the same neighborhood in Brooklyn or because their mothers shop at the same butcher shop. The inconveniences of celebrity are beginning to get to him.

Most insistent of all the grotesque guests of the hotel are representatives of various charities: cancer, the blind, architectural landmarks, scientists imprisoned in the Soviet Union, the Jews. How can Sandy possibly respond to so many needs? His penthouse apartment is decorated with a blown up copy of the famous image of the Vietnamese prisoner being executed by a bullet to the temple. Sandy can do nothing in the face of such evil. As a child, he longed to be God in plays presented in Hebrew school, but in the real world, he is aware that he is not God and cannot solve the world's problems. In fact, he is an impotent creator; he cannot even finish his own film.

Faced with a universe presenting such demands and so many faces of evil, and finding himself incapable of addressing its problems through art, Sandy longs for companionship to help him continue his journey through life, but he is no more in control of his relationships with women than he is of his art. His ideal is Dorrie (Charlotte Rampling), who is beautiful and interesting, but schizophrenic. For two days each month she is wonderful, but the rest of the time she is a loonie, according to Sandy's friend Tony. (340) She stops taking her lithium because it makes her feel fat. Near the end of the film, when Sandy is trying to remember reasons for living, he pictures Dorrie dressed in white and reading the Sunday *New York Times* on a perfect spring day. The camera reproduces Sandy's point of view and lingers on this peaceful image. Dorrie a metaphor of Sandy's life: these brief moments of joy make endurance of the rest worth the effort. By the time of the film festival, Dorrie has passed out of Sandy's life. She is married and living in Hawaii, but Sandy cannot forget her.

Isobel (Marie-Christine Barrault) introduces the opposite pole in Sandy's life. At Sandy's suggestion, she leaves her husband, who was having an affair, and joins Sandy at the festival. Her two children meet them later, and their presence offers Sandy the possibility of family and stability. At the mention of her separation from her husband, Sandy faces a decision about Isobel and immediately becomes nauseous. (316) He loves her, but he is afraid of the commitment. He tells his sister that he likes the fact that she is French, because that makes their relationship romantic, but he cannot deal with the prospect of suddenly having two children. (327) After a fainting spell, Sandy calls out from his hospital bed for Dorrie. Isobel, who had been at his bedside, is furious, takes her children and runs toward the train station. His close brush with death—he thought he was dying—helps him to reconsider his life through a series of dreams he experiences during his moments of unconsciousness. He joins Isobel on the train, and as it leaves the station, they kiss, reminding audiences of the "joyful train" in the opening dream sequence. With Isobel and her children, he has discovered the possibility of joy in life's journey.

The happy ending is deceptive, however. As the film ends, Allen reminds his audience that the neat solution to Sandy's loneliness is only an illusion, just another movie happy ending demanded by the front office. The film ends with Daisy and Isobel, now revealed as actresses in Sandy's now completed film, complaining about his open-mouth kissing during the shooting. Sandy, it seems, is not quite ready for the quiet life of domestic bliss.

The third woman enters Sandy's life during the film festival. Daisy (Jessica Harper) continually stirs up memories of Dorrie. They meet when Sandy is besieged by fans, and Daisy and her boyfriend Jack offer to take him out for a quiet beer. Like Sandy, Daisy is an artist, so they have a great deal in common. She is a violinist with the Philharmonic orchestra. She and Sandy see THE BICYCLE THIEF (Vittorio De Sica, 1948) together and discuss its social implications. When Daisy asks Sandy to explain why she reminds him of Dorrie, he stutters in confusion and comes up with little more than noting that they are both seductive and attractive. (356) He proposes to her, and she declines. The act is irrational; Dorrie is the elusive ideal of permanent love that he tries to recapture through Daisy.

In Allen's world love is ever irrational. Sandy explains during an interview that he believes that relationships exist as a matter of luck rather than any rational pattern of maturity or compromise. (338) In a comic sketch in one of the movies at the festival, Sandy plays a mad surgeon who transplants the ideal personality from a plain woman into a woman of extraordinary physical beauty, who happens to be Dorrie. In exchange, he transplants the difficult personality into the body of the plain woman. The operation is a success, the personality switch is achieved, but the doctor then falls in love with the wrong patient, who is both unattractive and difficult. (338) Like his comic doctor, Sandy makes disastrous choices in love. This is evident even to a Martian he meets later in the film who steps off his space ship and says that even with his superintelligence he cannot understand what Sandy ever hoped to accomplish in his relationship with Dorrie. (366)

Living in a frantic, demanding world with love difficult to find, Sandy resurrects the childhood fears of the young Alvy Singer. Early in the film, Sandy complains that the entire universe is decomposing and soon everything will be destroyed (286). Near the end of the film, Sandy is desperate enough to engage in a dialogue with extraterrestrials at a UFO landing site. The conversation, it is soon clear, is part of the movie Sandy is making. He asks the usual Allen questions about evil in the world and the passage of time, wondering why he bothers to make films if the entire universe is passing away. (366) Og, the visitor, offers a word of encouragement by reminding Sandy that he enjoys the films, and then adds the barb that he particularly enjoyed the earlier funny movies. The answer doesn't satisfy Sandy, who insists that he still needs to have meaning. (367)

Faced with these unanswerable questions, Sandy does not contemplate suicide, as have several of Allen's earlier characters. He explains to Dorrie that no one in his family had taken his own life, since middle-class people did not view this as a possible option. (308) Nor does he threaten to murder anyone in his frustration, as did Ike in MANHATTAN. In this film, however, an irate fan shoots Sandy. The murder is a fantasy triggered by hostile questions, and the scene is merely another part of Sandy's movie, but it gives the director the opportunity to review his life from the vantage point of death. During one of his recollections, his analyst tells him that Sandy saw reality too clearly and did not deny the terrifying truths of reality. (370) As the dream continues, Sandy gives an acceptance speech for his posthumous award, and reveals that his memory of the Sunday morning with Dorrie made life endurable. (372)

Other images of death intrude into Sandy's world as he continues his artistic enterprise. In the opening minutes of the film he admits that he is depressed by remembering the death of a boyhood friend, Nat Bernstein, who at 30 succumbed to Lou Gehrig's disease. (286) Later, Sandy reminds an obnoxious fan from the old neighborhood of Nat's death, telling him to be satisfied with his own lot in life. Finally, during Sandy's "death" scene, a nurse eats an apple and comments that for all Sandy's skill he could not save the life of Nat Bernstein. (364) Yet people continue to struggle against the inevitable finality of aging and death. Charlotte Ames, an actress who once played Sandy's mother in a movie, is all but unrecognizable because of the extensive plastic surgery she has undergone to delay the relentless impact of the years on her body. (352) Sandy's sister Debbie does yoga to keep young, while his brother-in-law Sam spends hours on the exercise bicycle after his two heart attacks, but he has had two more attacks after he began his regimen. (324)

Thoughts of mortality torture Sandy. With all his talent and concern for people, Sandy feels that he cannot begin to heal the world's evil, and even more, since the world is doomed to end, his efforts are meaningless. Dorrie brings these themes together with a series of gifts she gives Sandy for his birthday: a flute to encourage his pursuit of art; a book on Zen to give him peace in a hostile world, and a watch to indicate the passage of time.

Art is not really enough for Sandy. He wants to be God. In a Hebrew school play, he starts a fight with another boy because he wants to play the part of God himself. (326) During the posthumous tributes he receives, a critic reminds the audience that Sandy once won an Academy Award nomination for playing the part of God, even though they had to have another actor supply the voice. Sandy admits that he does not have a voice appropriate to play the role of God. (371) As a child, he dresses in a Superman costume and tries to fly, but of course he cannot. When a questioner calls him Narcissistic, he rejects association with Narcissus and asserts his preference for Zeus, a Greek version of the Judaeo-Christian Yahweh. (313) After his "resurrection from the dead" in the hospital, he finds himself as powerless as ever. He nearly loses Isobel by calling out the name Dorrie in his coma, and when he tells a trooper that he need not go to jail because he is a celebrity, the officer is not impressed. (374) Sandy is not God, and he is not even an effective celebrity. He has little control over his own life, let alone the external universe. Only as a director can he assume the role of creator God, and even there his power is limited by the team from the home office, who insist on a more marketable happy ending.

In keeping with the Allen pattern, Sandy's Jewishness underlines his alienation from his universe. Jerry, the boyhood friend from Flatbush, refers to him as Sandy Brockman. (314) The adopted name Bates is quintessentially Wasp, although some critics believe it suggests Bates Motel in PSYCHO (Alfred Hitchcock, 1960), or even an autoerotic allusion to the young Master Bates, whose mother discovers pornographic pictures in her son's bedroom (303).[15] His childhood friends from Flatbush have clearly Jewish names, like Jerry Abraham and Nat Bernstein. To keep the notion of alienation from the majority culture, one of the producers, a woman with the obviously Irish, and thus supposedly Catholic, name of Walsh objects that Sandy's film is too grim for an Easter release. (334) The dominant gentile culture once again is at cross-purposes with his art.

The food/sex metaphor remains constant. In a ribald exchange in his apartment, Sandy and Dorrie have just completed an evening meal and presumably a sexual encounter. As she dries her hair, she tells him that the spaghetti should have been cooked another 20 minutes, and he asks her if she would have preferred a limp noodle. (307) His meeting with Isobel in the ice-cream parlor is interrupted by the presence of her children, whose rowdy behavior spoils their relationship and sends Sandy into a reverie of Dorrie. A woman gives the visiting celebrity a salami, which he refers to as a suggestive item of food (298), and the young woman who plans to share his bed offers him brownies with hashish on the side. (311)

In STARDUST MEMORIES Allen once more presents the world as a rather inhospitable arena of human activity. Human persons are compared to characters in some film that God views in his own private screening room. (361) Sandy, however, is able to see himself as something more than an actor in some celestial farce staged for the entertainment of the Divinity. He eventually gathers the courage to risk a relationship with Isobel, and in this, along with the recollection of happy moments with Dorrie, he is able to find enough joy to continue life's journey, almost as though he had discovered a meaning in the enterprise.

Doubts remain, however. STARDUST MEMORIES reveals an Allen much less satisfied with the recollections of happy memories than he was in ANNIE HALL or MANHATTAN. The final dialogue between Daisy and Isobel reminds the audience that this is only a movie, and it suggests that real life may be quite different. More disturbing is his reversion to a form of self-seeking that had been absent from the earlier romances. Sandy has little interest in doing anything for any of the women in his life. He is exclusively concerned about what they can do for him. None of the three is any richer for having dealt with Sandy, and he has taken advantage of his role as director to engage in unwelcome kissing on the set. Theologically, this is a step backward, and his later films will reveal whether this regression is permanent, or a mere aberration in his constant growth as an artist.

A MIDSUMMER NIGHT'S SEX COMEDY (1982) is the Woody Allen recasting of Ingmar Bergman's SMILES OF A SUMMER NIGHT (1955). It is a self-conscious borrowing, but without the elements of parody found in STARDUST MEMORIES. A second consecutive film based on earlier familiar classics indicates that Allen had reached a plateau in his creative life. In this second borrowing, the grand larceny of STARDUST MEMORIES was becoming a deeply entrenched kleptomania, a cover for waning originality. This film, like the previous one, was not well received by the public or by critics.[16] Not since his early comedies had he been so dependent on other films for his material. In this film, too, he abandoned his contemporary world for the first time since LOVE AND DEATH (1975) and distanced himself from his materials by setting the action on a country estate in the early 1900's. His characters are not Manhattan literati but Wasp aristocracy.

In his two previous films, MANHATTAN and STARDUST MEMORIES, Allen had set his characters in a swirling vortex of action. People and events intruded on all sides, and in a claustrophobic atmosphere, like the island or the hotel, the characters were left to sort out their own lives. In A MIDSUMMER NIGHT'S SEX COMEDY, Allen gives his people room to breathe fresh air, relax and walk in the sunlight. They leave behind classroom, hospital and brokerage house respectively for a sojourn in the country. The setting is one of breath-taking beauty, highlighted by the lovely color photography of Gordon Willis and the lush music of Felix Mendelssohn.

In this rural paradise Allen makes little attempt to cite his Jewishness as sign of his alienation from his surroundings. Andrew Hobbs (Allen) has a distinctly Wasp name, owns the estate and works on Wall Street. The farm represents a return to Eden after a life in the city. In comparison with other Allen worlds, this universe is scarcely hostile. His persona, Andrew, is at home in the country. Allen discovers, however, that regardless of the setting human nature remains confused and love is as difficult to find as ever.

While this film extends his stay on the creative plateau, Allen adds a few new dimensions to his characteristic questions about the meaning of life. One of the few truly odious people Allen has ever created is Leopold Sturgis (José Ferrer), a pompous self-centered professor of philosophy and expert on just about everything else. In an opening scene, Leopold lectures his class about his belief in absolute empiricism, humiliating students who suggest that there might be something in the universe beyond sense perception. One temerarious student voices Allen's own concern by suggesting that Sturgis's purely materialistic view of the universe leaves many basic human needs unanswered. Leopold's reply is withering, when he retorts that he did not create the universe, but merely tries to understand it.

Dr. Maxwell Jordan (Tony Roberts) is a physician of such uncontrollable sexual appetites that in today's climate he could scarcely hold a medical license for a week. In his office, he helps an agreeable female patient button up and invites her to join him for a weekend in the country. When she declines this particular invitation, even though their affair is well established, he politely returns her to her husband and turns his attention to his nurse, Dulcy Ford (Julie Hagerty), who as a liberated young woman accepts without hesitation or scruple. As Max, Tony Roberts reprises the modern, self-centered oily character he created with Rob in ANNIE HALL and brought to its nadir with Tony in STARDUST

MEMORIES. In that film, Tony gives Sandy his philosophy of life: One must provide for golf, women, and drugs. That is the purpose of life. (339) The same self-seeking, exploitative type of character also appeared as Yale in MANHATTAN, played by Michael Murphy, an actor with a strong physical resemblance to Roberts.

Neither Leopold's intellectualism nor Max's carnality hold much promise for Andrew. He is an inventor of flying machines and an investment broker; thus he is rooted in terrestrial matters while he longs to soar. A gentle man, he desires only a happy , mutually fulfilling marriage with Adrian (Mary Steenburgen), but for the past year she has been rejecting his sexual advances. He has many of the things most men want in life, but because of his isolation from Adrian, he cannot enjoy them as he thinks he should.

The three men come together with their companions at Andrew's summer estate to celebrate Leopold's wedding to Ariel Weymouth (Mia Farrow). Max brings Dulcy. Ariel and Dulcy are both extraordinarily free spirits. Once she left the convent school, Ariel seems to have slept with an incredible number of men, including the entire infield of the Chicago Cubs. Dulcy, the nurse, knows how all the organs work and seems equally uninhibited. She brings contraceptives along in case Max forgot, puts on a bathing suit for the afternoon but tells Max she would prefer to swim naked in the mountain streams. She even offers advice on sexual technique to Adrian, who as the only married woman in the group remains the most reserved and paradoxically asexual. Adrian even expresses some reservations about having these two unmarried couples share their bedrooms in her home.

While the men seek sexual fulfillment as a way to find peace with their universe, the women become the objects of their desire. Leopold looks forward to showing off Ariel to his friends on the faculty, as though she were a new possession. On the eve of his wedding, however, he is smitten by Dulcy and longs to make savage love to her, as though he were a Neanderthal and she were his prey. Dulcy does little to discourage his attentions. Max similarly falls in love with Ariel, despite Dulcy, but his plans are shattered when Andrew, denied fulfillment with Adrian, rekindles his old love for Ariel. The two friends become competitors. None of the women gains anything for herself in this round-robin mating, and in keeping with the conventions of the bedroom farce, Allen seems little concerned about their well-being. They exist as goals for the men to achieve.

Their desperate search for companionship in this idyllic world leads the guests only to disappointment. Ariel rejects Max, but her love-making with Andrew proves unsatisfying to both of them. Their sexual relationship is forecasted in a comic scene when Andrew takes her for a ride in one of his flying machines. They soar for a moment of delirious glee and then plummet into the icy waters of a stream. Such is their love: short and sweet but ultimately chilling. For his part, Leopold literally dies in the arms of Dulcy "at the height of ecstasy." Ariel is left with her third choice, Max, who will undoubtedly wander off to some other woman, and Dulcy, the uninhibited child of nature, is left with no one. Her plight is sad, but as a hollow person who does not distinguish love and lust, she will find another partner just as meaningless to her as Max was.

In contrast, after witnessing the frantic liaisons around them, Andrew and Adrian admit their infidelities to each other (Once, a long time ago, she had yielded to Max's passionate advances, and Andrew acknowledges his past and present infatuation with Ariel.) and their mutual candor opens the way for them to renew the sexual element in their marriage. Andrew calls their love-making a religious experience. Their reconciliation restates a constant Allen theme: Enjoy the pleasures at hand and don't become frustrated in the search for an unattainable and illusory ideal. Adrian offers love here and now; Ariel is a dream.

Their search for love in this unloving world becomes frantic because of the passage of time. Ariel justifies her decision to marry Leopold, an unpleasant, older man, because of her need for security and stability. She muses that the time slips by quickly for a woman. Max, in turn, justifies his womanizing to Andrew by telling him that one lives only once and thus it is important to seize the opportunities that present themselves. As Ariel and Adrian talk quietly on a covered glider, Adrian mentions that the beautiful summer light does not last forever. Andrew and Ariel speak about their lost opportunities, believing that love comes so rarely that they must leap at it whenever and wherever it appears; their lives would be different now, they feel, if they had grasped the moment of love that came to them years ago. They do not want to make the same mistake again, but as they part after their disappointing try at love-making, Ariel mentions that Andrew's hair has thinned over the years since they first met. Time passes, and the allotted share of opportunities irrevocably diminishes.

Allen again examines death as a solution to loneliness and frustration in this hostile universe, and in A MIDSUMMER NIGHT'S SEX COMEDY both suicide and murder are possible answers. Rejected in his quest for Ariel, Max leaves the dinner table in tears, perhaps a bit drunk. In Allen's metaphorical vocabulary of food and sex, Max feels himself excluded from the meal and from sex with Ariel. Moments later, a shot is heard. Max has found an old revolver in the barn, loaded it and fired a glancing shot to his forehead. There is bloodshed, but the wound is superficial. Later in the evening, when Andrew first discovers Adrian's sexual experience with Max in the previous year and traces their own marital dysfunction to her resultant guilt, he puts the same gun to his own temple. Adrian stops him, confesses her guilt and tells Andrew that a burden has been lifted from her. Her desire for Andrew has returned, as she will demonstrate moments later.

Attempted murder also adds a surprising twist to the story. Realizing that Andrew has been with Ariel, his fiancée, Leopold takes an archery set from the porch and runs into the night to kill Andrew. Several arrows come dangerously close to Andrew, but one strikes Max, who has rushed out to warn him. Max believes the wound in his chest is fatal and says he has been mortally struck by Cupid's arrow. Ariel finds him, and her tenderness in trying to comfort him in his final moments leads to their reconciliation. The wound is less serious than he thinks, and their love indeed has a future. In a bizarre twist of fate, the sight of the blood he has drawn stirs up the animal passion in the stuffy Leopold. He sees himself as a primitive hunter and rushes off to Dulcy. His violent, clothes-ripping onslaught leads to an apparent heart attack and his own death. In passion, she shrieks that she wants him to bite harder, but he demurs, saying that his teeth are not his own. Neanderthal hunter or not, Leopold is too old for Dulcy's energetic love-making.

None of these acts of violence has its intended result. The two failed suicides live, and because they live they find a resolution to their loneliness.[17] Their gestures, futile though they are, show a willingness to die rather than face life separated from their beloved, and their self-discovery in this moment is rewarded with both life and love. The failed murderer dies himself, yet he enters a form of afterlife not punished for his violence, but rewarded for his discovery of passion. Leopold's life of the intellect counts for very little in the world of love.

Art offers more insight into affairs of the heart than intellect alone. Andrew calls himself a crackpot inventor, and his strangest invention is the spirit ball. This device, looking very much like the CBS eye, reacts to the presence of spirits in the area. When activated, presumably by the spirits, the eye becomes a form of movie projector. As a film maker, Allen appreciates the power of the eye to observe and the projector to reproduce the observation as art. When Andrew arranges a demonstration of the ball for his house guests and the spirits call it to life, the eye projects images of a man and woman meeting, but who is meeting whom? Each of the six lovers watching the shadows sees them differently and according to their own memories or expectations of romantic bliss. Such is the ambiguity and power of art that it touches each one in a personal and moving way.

The intellectual formulations, proposed with pompous certitude by Leopold in the opening scene, are by the end of the film as dead as Leopold himself. In this transitory universe, where death is the only certitude, love provides the only reason to continue living. In affairs of the heart, art offers more satisfactory explanations than does the intellect. These are standard Allen themes, but A MIDSUMMER NIGHT'S SEX COMEDY shows another step in the director's thinking. Rejecting rational empiricism as definitively as he does, he has opened up the question of a world beyond the senses.

To be sure, Allen has not yet resolved the problem of the God/Creator, which he sees as needed to uphold meaning and a moral structure in the universe. In a light and playful way, however, in this film he suggests the possibility of life after death and of reward or punishment based on one's moral actions in time. He will continue this exploration for years. The search is fascinating, as theological inquiries are, and it becomes doubly fascinating as he develops ever more varied ways to pursue his quest through his art.

NOTES

1. Douglas Brode, *The Films of Woody Allen* (Citadel: New York, 1991), p.169, summarizes critical reaction to the film.
2. Nancy Pogel, *Woody Allen* (Boston: Twayne, 1987), p. 75, sets up the division between two halves of the film.
3. Graham McCann, *Woody Allen* (London: Polity, 1991), p. 84, discusses the contemporary Allen's fixation with mortality.
4. Woody Allen (and Marshall Brickman), "Annie Hall," in *Four Films of Woody Allen* (New York: Random House, 1982), p. 4. Page numbers in the text refer to this edition of the film script.
5. Maurice Yacowar, *Loser Take All, The Comic Art of Woody Allen* (New York: Continuum, 1991), p. 173, discusses the significance of the two songs in Annie's development.
6. Brode, p. 156.
7. For a theologian's treatment of the phenomenon of love, see Anders Nygren, trans. Philip S. Watson, *Agape and Eros* (New York: Harper Row, 1969), a classic study first published in Sweden in 1930. *Agape,* self-giving love, is spontaneous, unmotivated and creates value in the beloved, pp. 75–80. *Eros,* by distinction, responds to values the lover discovers as already present in the beloved. The author places this Christian notion in its proper Jewish context, showing that it is common to both traditions, pp. 62–63. For a theologian, God's *agape* for the human person creates value and thus redemption; for Woody Allen, Alvy's love "creates" a new person in Annie, thus "redeeming" her personally and artistically. To go beyond this interesting point of comparison by, for example, making Alvy a God-figure clearly works violence on the text of the film.
8. Brode, p. 169, relates that some critics actually believed that Allen intended a comic parody of Bergman.
9. Woody Allen, "Interiors" in *Four Films of Woody Allen,* p. 117. Page numbers in the text refer to this edition of the script.
10. Yacowar catalogues the small touches that would lead him to believe Allen created Pearl as a Jewish character, p. 191.
11. Pogel, p. 103, sees this act of iconoclasm as another sign of the collapse of Eve's carefully and artificially structured world.
12. Woody Allen (with Marshall Brickman), MANHATTAN in *Four Films of Woody Allen,* p. 181. Page numbers in the text refer to this edition of the script.
13. Brode, p. 184, quotes the outrage of John Simon and Pauline Kael at Allen's having Ike sexually exploit a young girl as a means to discovering true moral values. The point is well made, but Brode perceptively points out that Tracy is not a real figure but an allegorical representation of innocence.

14. Woody Allen, STARDUST MEMORIES, in *Four Films of Woody Allen,* p. 339. Subsequent page numbers in the text refer to this edition of the script.
15. Yacowar, p. 228.
16. Brode, p. 210, quotes critical reaction to the film and adds that Allen now had "two failures in a row."
17. Pogel, p. 158, explains that the awareness of death provides "moments of enlightenment." The point is valid, even though it is weighted toward an experience that is intellectual. It might be more congenial to Allen's intent to think of these confrontations with death as reorienting the affections toward their proper object. It is more a question of passion than intellect.

CHAPTER IV: THE EXPERIMENTS

Woody Allen's sojourn on his creative plateau was happily very brief. The characteristic spiritual and philosophic questions defy simple solution, as they must for artist and theologian alike, but Allen's versatility in restating his concerns becomes astonishing. In the years that follow A MIDSUMMER NIGHT'S SEX COMEDY, Allen grows into absolute mastery of his medium. He pushes back the frontiers of cinematic technique and narrative complexity. During this period, it is no longer possible to predict what to expect in a Woody Allen film. During the next few years, he appears as an actor less frequently, no longer relying on the familiar Woody character to provide the jokes as a safety net for his films, as though failing all else a few one-liners could save him. Woody Allen, director and writer, has become a true innovator in the medium.

ZELIG (1983) is a cinematic tour-de-force. Allen returns to the documentary format, last used in TAKE THE MONEY AND RUN (1969), but his second visitation of the medium demonstrates his growth as an artist. In the earlier film, he employs a parody of the television documentary to present the life of Virgil Starkwell, failed gangster. In ZELIG, his technique is more complex. Through the wizardry of the modern photographic laboratories, he inserts the character of Leonard Zelig (Woody Allen) into actual newsreels of the late 1920's and early 1930's. He recreates the era as well as the character, even though the subject matter is not life in America during the Depression, but human life anytime, anywhere. The blending is seamless.

In a style that owes more to Orson Welles's CITIZEN KANE (1941) than to Movietone News, Allen weaves the authentic newsreel footage, with Zelig photographically inserted, into the narrative of Leonard Zelig.[1] While the importance of art has been a constant theme in his work since ANNIE HALL (1977), with ZELIG Allen begins to explore the relationship between art and reality. The question assumes autobiographical urgency in this particular film, when Allen uses Zelig to unmask the artificial nature of celebrity. The media have robbed Zelig (and Allen) of his privacy and made him a public figure. Everybody may profit financially from the arrangement, but is there any persona left? The question, of course, goes beyond Allen and his well-known desire for privacy. Have modern people become "The Hollow Men" that T. S. Eliot warned about a half-century ago, and has the process of conformity been accelerated by the media? Are modern people merely a collection of traits that others expect of them?

For human beings with no interior life and no personality of their own, is it possible to find a meaning in life? Zelig was in turn beloved, reviled and restored by a fickle public, manipulated by the media, but his fluid public status means little for him or for the world. Popularity is fleeting. In this whirlwind, true love of another individual person, not the amorphous public, is essential if Zelig is to be saved from his own emptiness. And if finding this kind of love with another human person is difficult, how much more difficult is the human capacity to find a loving, saving God. This unresolved possibility continues to lurk in the shadows for Allen.

BROADWAY DANNY ROSE (1984) lacks the technical virtuosity of ZELIG, but it continues to probe the question of love in an unloving universe. Continuing the documentary artifice begun in ZELIG film, Allen unfolds his story through the narration of a comedian (Sandy Baron), who tells the story to his cronies at the Carnegie Delicatessen on Seventh Avenue. On several occasions the comics comment on the story like a Greek chorus, and Sandy's voice-over explanations effectively compress the action. The straightforward photographic technique may mask the brilliant complexity and economy of the script.

Like Leonard Zelig, Danny Rose (Woody Allen) would like to be a celebrity, but he lacks both talent and good luck. A failed stand-up comedian now self-employed as a talent agent, Rose represents show-business acts destined to fail as he has. These are flawed artists: a blind xylophone player, a one-legged tap dancer and an overweight, alcoholic crooner. The world has not been kind to Danny, and he in turn has little to offer to win the esteem and love of others. He is, frankly, a loser. With it all, however, Danny is a *mensch* and a gentleman. While Allen might not have had in mind the medieval epic "Romance of the Rose," his Danny Rose character is a knight in shining polyester plaid armor on his quest for an ideal love. Betrayed, scorned and belittled by those closest to him, he continues to sacrifice himself for others. In the end, he finds a love that is far from ideal, but one that seems to make him extraordinarily happy, if only for a short time.

Woody Allen does not appear on screen in THE PURPLE ROSE OF CAIRO (1985), but his Zelig-Danny character is reincarnated as Cecilia (Mia Farrow). In this brilliant film, thought to be Allen's own favorite, he returns to Zelig's Depression America.[2] Like Danny, Cecilia is a loser, trapped in a sputtering economy and in a horrible marriage to Monk (Danny Aiello), a gambling, brutish, philandering husband. Bitterness could easily suffocate such a woman, but she continues to hope for better days to come, working in a diner and taking in laundry to keep her loveless marriage afloat. Like Danny, too, she is on the verge of rescue by a handsome fantasy come to life, only to be betrayed by life once more. It is more than anyone should be asked to face in life.

Cecilia's only relief comes through the movies, a few minutes of fantasy that allow her to escape the horrors of her most inhospitable world. Allen's film itself is a fantasy, and part of the fantasy he creates involves ability of Cecilia's imagination to break down the barriers between her day dreams and reality. Allen allows a romantic hero in an adventure film to leave the screen and become a reality for Cecilia. When forced to distinguish between a fictional lover and a real-life suitor, she knows that the illusion cannot last and opts for reality. Her living suitor, however, is no more faithful than Monk. Cruelly abandoned by her cynical but real suitor, she has no recourse but to return to the movies for another 15-cent illusion before she must return to her apartment and Monk.

A sad ending? Perhaps, but not necessarily. Watching Fred Astaire and Ginger Rogers dance, Cecilia finds a few moments of true happiness. What is more real, Allen asks, the misery she will have to face after the house lights come on and she returns to her dreary marriage or a delightful escape into the world of the imagination? This is the most poignant setting yet for Allen's on-going search for reasons to continue living a possibly meaningless life in a manifestly hostile world. If real love cannot be found, then imagination and the arts, particularly the cinema, must supply the need.

Woody Allen populates his next film HANNAH AND HER SISTERS (1986) with many different kinds of artists, all, like Cecilia, searching for love and for a meaning in their lives. In this splendid ensemble cast, the Allen character, Mickey Sachs, could be considered a minor figure, but through his own neurotic and very funny concerns with his health and his nearly successful suicide, Allen places the members of this affluent, successful band of sophisticated New Yorkers securely in the context of their own mortality. Each strives for an ideal love to put meaning in life, and each falls short of perfection.

Like Cecilia, at the movies Mickey finds a reason for living, but his solution to the problems he faces in a world without meaning is more satisfactory than hers. Cecilia's world remains dichotomized; she commutes between reality and fantasy with little connection between the two. Her real world becomes no less painful because of her visits to the world of the imagination. For Mickey, the exuberant joy of the celluloid Marx Brothers opens him to the possibility of here-and-now happiness and love with Holly (Diane Wiest), a real flesh-and-blood woman. Art then not merely offers a refuge from life, as it does for Cecilia, but it gives Mickey's life a fresh meaning.

The world does not oppress Mickey Sachs with a burden of cruelty and betrayal, as it had Danny Rose, Cecilia and to a certain extent Leonard Zelig. Mickey's problems arise not from external reality but from his own soul. He has wealth, talent, security, friends and at one time a marriage to Hannah (Mia Farrow), portrayed as an ideal woman. In the midst of all his success, however, his quest for a meaning in his life torments him. In several very funny sequences, he even looks for answers in various religious traditions, but he ultimately finds them as useless as Eve does in INTERIORS, when she smashes the vigil candles in St. Ignatius Church.

While the milieu and the characters of HANNAH AND HER SISTERS obviously suggest kinship with ANNIE HALL (1977) and MANHATTAN (1979) in a kind of "New York Trilogy," Allen's thinking has progressed remarkably. Both Annie and Tracy function as ideals of love, pursued and lost, but cherished as lovely memories of what might have been. Recollecting happy but fleeting moments with them helps ease the pain of loneliness and meaninglessness that Alvy and Ike experience. In contrast,

Holly, hypersensitive, fickle, irascible and occasionally cocaine dependent, scarcely represents an ideal. In fact, in divorcing Hannah, Mickey has rejected the ideal. In Holly, however, imperfect as she is, Mickey finds happiness that is lasting and earth-bound. The universe Allen creates for Mickey is far less antagonistic than those in earlier films. Allen seems to have solved Cecilia's dichotomy. With the assistance of the arts, one can have happiness in the real world by choosing something that is less than ideal.

Investigating this very personal conclusion at its roots, Allen probes his own childhood in the lovely RADIO DAYS (1987), set in the late-1930's through 1944. Here the art form of choice is not the movies but the radio programs of the day. Woody Allen does not appear on the screen, but his voice-over narrative provides the strong suggestion of autobiography. The extended Jewish family living in cramped quarters in the Rockaway Beach section of Queens does not present the ideal of family life or of love. Theirs is hard Depression-shaped life, much like Cecilia's, but beneath the bickering and competition lies genuine affection. The three adult women in the family compete, but they also support one another. The three-woman family structure echoes both INTERIORS and HANNAH AND HER SISTERS, but the fragility is gone. Tess, Ceil and Bea are tough with one another, but they do not bruise easily. They give as good as they get, and they bounce back.

Joe (Seth Green), the Allen persona as a boy, is too young to face Allen's questions of meaning and love. He takes these things for granted. In the end, Allen the adult narrator expresses a longing for those simpler days that remain a part of him, even as they grow gradually dimmer with each passing year. The dimming is not altogether bad. Joe's childhood recollections of Judaism are either comic or harsh, as are most childhood memories of religion. Although memories of the Yom Kippur fast and Rabbi Baumel continue to mellow for him, the adult Joe (Woody Allen's voice-over narration) still does not look to his childhood religious experience to supply answers to his grown-up life. Fair enough. As the memories soften, however, he may yet find something helpful in his religious tradition. Since this is a look back in time, the questions have not yet become as poignant as they would later on.

ZELIG (1983) is the story of Leonard Zelig (Woody Allen), one of the great phenomena of the Jazz Age. As the country stupefies itself with a concoction of bootleg whiskey, flappers, movie stars, stock market speculation and instant heroes, Leonard Zelig develops the ability to adapt to his environment like a human chameleon. He has no personality of his own. In turn a socialite and a commoner, a New York Yankee, a Chicago gangster, a black musician and a Chinese opium addict, Zelig becomes what he has to be to survive. His problems began, it turns out, when in school he had to pretend to have read *Moby Dick* in order to fit in with his erudite companions. Later, he wandered into an Irish bar on St. Patrick's Day and for self-preservation had to become Irish.[3]

Zelig's world is not malicious but it is overpowering. Irish, Italians, African-Americans, Greeks, Native American and Chinese do not force Zelig to become one of them, but the weight of their presence irresistibly transforms him. Neither do musicians, ball players, psychiatrists, dentists or aviators demand that he adapt their skills and mannerisms, but around them he must. He has to be someone, but oddly not an individual in his own right but one of the crowd. In one pathetic scene, Zelig sits alone in a hotel corridor, slowly eating a roll, while the voice-over narrator describes him as an empty person who only wants to fit in to his context of the minute. (56)

Resurrecting the theme of the Jewish outsider in a gentile world, Allen presents a mock commentary by Irving Howe explaining that Zelig's story embodies much of the familiar Jewish drive to push in and stake out a place in American society. (97) The *goyim* are not terribly hospitable to Jews who are trying to move in on their territory. In a world of such animosity Zelig develops a disconcerting habit of becoming invisible; he simply vanishes into his surroundings.

Zelig loses his cover after his first disappearance when as a member of the papal retinue of Pope Pius XI, he causes a disturbance on the balcony of St. Peter's Basilica in Rome. The Pope swats him with a papal edict. Zelig is arrested, identified and deported to the United States. The event takes place on Easter Sunday, a date on the Christian calendar that since ANNIE HALL Allen uses to underline his Jewish-outsider status. Years later, when Zelig, now recognized as a celebrity, had fallen into disgrace with his public, Prof. John Morton Blum comments that the Catholic Church still bore a grudge because of his indecorous encounter with the Pope. (97) During this nadir in his life, a woman commentator for The Holy Family League on a Christian radio program ends her remarks with the proposal that those who would preserve a pure society in the United States should hang Zelig, whom she calls a little hebe (109). In Paris, during the height of his popularity, he talks to two orthodox rabbis on stage and gradually grows a beard and side locks like theirs. A voice-over narrator wryly explains that his sudden incarnation as a rabbi was so convincing that many of the French people want him exiled to Devil's Island. (53)

The hostility that Zelig experiences in this gentile world, from Catholic Rome to fundamentalist America, remains a painful mystery to him, just as Allen continues to puzzle over his own place in a secularized but equally malevolent universe. Zelig's Jewish tradition offers little help. When he was 12, he asked a rabbi to explain the meaning of life, but the rabbi offers the explanation in Hebrew, which Zelig does not know, and then wants to charge him $600 for Hebrew lessons. (77) Even as a child, when anti-Semitic bullies beat him up, Zelig remembers that his parents sided with the anti-Semites. (20) The world's hostility assumes a more cosmic dimension when Leonard's father tells the boy that life will offer him nothing but misery. (20)

Alone in this alien territory, Zelig becomes a ready victim of the world's exploitation. His sister Ruth (Mary Louise Wilson) and her boyfriend Martin Geist (Sol Lomita), a sometime carnival impresario, take Zelig from the hospital and discontinue his treatment. In Zelig they see an opportunity for personal gain. They begin a world-wide tour with The Human Chameleon. Through their management, Zelig becomes an international celebrity. He endorses products like cigarettes and underwear and becomes the basis of an industry of schlock souvenirs, popular songs and dances. Even his doctor, the brilliant and beautiful Eudora Fletcher (Mia Farrow), devotes herself to the case solely for the learned papers she can present and the prestige she will gain among her professional peers. (80) Later, she realizes that this kind of prestige is merely a hollow, childish daydream and she renounces her earlier ambitions for recognition. (98)

So used and abused by others, it is little wonder that Zelig wants to escape once more into anonymity, even if it means becoming a Nazi at a Munich rally. On screen, novelist Saul Bellow explains this strange phenomenon. Zelig, Bellow maintains, longed for affection with such intensity that he wanted to be swallowed up in the crowds around him. (115) In Zelig's pathetic longing for acceptance, Zelig's ability to transform himself into a Jewish Nazi makes perfect sense.

Those who enter Zelig's life cannot remain untouched by him. Dr. Fletcher goes through the most dramatic conversion, and thus she becomes the thematic center of the film, a counterpoint to Zelig himself. As Zelig is the victim outsider, Dr. Fletcher is a child of the majority establishment. During an interview, her mother reveals that the Fletchers of Philadelphia are a family of such wealth that it had no problem sending Eudora through medical school. (90) Yet these two opposites—wealthy gentile and poor Jew, insider and outsider—complement each other. Initially an exploiter, she gradually becomes a healer and finally learns to love Zelig. In their final adventure together, Dr. Fletcher rescues Zelig from his Nazi persona and arranges his escape from Germany in an airplane stolen from the Luftwaffe. An accomplished aviatrix, she faints as they flee the Nazi fighter planes, and Zelig, ever the chameleon, becomes a pilot by being close to her. He flies the plane to safety, albeit upside-down.

The reciprocal nature of their relationship appears throughout the film. During their first interview, Zelig adapts the style of the professional psychiatrist when he talks with her. (16) Later, they go through a role reversal when as part of her therapeutic strategy, Dr. Fletcher pretends to be a patient with Zelig's symptoms and she asks Zelig to cure her. (74) In a very real sense, while she, the physician, cures him of his emptiness, it is Zelig who heals Dr. Fletcher and rescues her from her loneliness and self-centeredness, much as Miles saves Luna and Alvy Annie Hall.

Their love and healing thus becomes mutual, and both become cured of their respective illnesses. This transfer comes as a bit of a surprise, since during his testing at the psychiatric hospital, a radio news announcer assures his audience that Zelig's transformations do not occur with women, and noting this limitation in Zelig's power, the doctors are about to experiment with a midget and a chicken. (29) In fact, Eudora Fletcher, psychiatrist and aviatrix, is the exception, since Zelig borrows those occupational roles from her quite easily.

Because they never achieve altruistic love, healing never comes to Ruth Zelig and Martin Geist. During a Zelig tour in Spain, Ruth falls in love with an inept matador. In a jealous frenzy, Geist kills Ruth and her lover and then turns the gun on himself. Once more, and in particularly stark terms, Allen proposes murder and suicide as a possible response to a world without love or meaning. Without his managers, Zelig again is nothing, a cipher, and in depression he vanishes into Europe.

Zelig himself is not altogether innocent of the sin of exploitation, yet Allen's script manages to distance Leonard Zelig from the evil he generates. It seems Zelig has been exploiting others on a fairly regular basis. Zelig's fall from popular adulation begins with the allegation of Lita Fox, a showgirl, that Zelig, then appearing to be an actor, had married her and fathered her child. (103) Other charges soon follow. As a fur trapper, he fathered the twins of another woman. (105) Soon, as the narrator explains, he is being sued for all manner of crimes and misdemeanors, from his multiple marriages to his practicing dentistry and pulling teeth without due cause. (105) In a particularly ghastly admission of guilt at a press conference, Zelig admits his ineptitude as a bogus doctor when he apologizes to a Michigan family for trying to deliver their baby with the help of ice tongs. (107) The deeds are horrible, but Zelig excuses himself by maintaining that it was some other personality that acted and that this other person must assume responsibility.

In an earlier scene, Allen provides Zelig with another instance of his moral distancing of himself from his acts. As his cure advances with the help of Dr. Fletcher's therapy, Zelig becomes more confident in his own opinions and less desperate to please others. The progress appears innocent enough when Zelig tells Dr. Fletcher that he hates her cooking and her house in the country and that he wants to have sex with her. His new-found independence becomes more troublesome when a board of examiners visits Fletcher and Zelig to check on their progress. Zelig argues with one of the doctors about the weather and attacks the entire group with a rake. The violent behavior in this very funny scene is excused by Dr. Fletcher who switches the blame from Zelig to herself because of her failure as a psychiatrist. (85) According to Allen's script, then, the blame lies not on Zelig but on a defective form of therapy.

For one who has been so long obsessed with morality in a meaningless world, Allen's reluctance to assign personal responsibility for immoral acts represents a step backward. Under hypnosis Zelig offers an expression of his own moral philosophy when he defends the importance of making courageous moral decisions, since without them one is merely an automaton. (83) This connection between morality and courage echoes the opening conversation in MANHATTAN, when Ike wonders if anyone would jump into an icy river to save a drowning man.[4] The linkage of moral action and courage, stated so clearly by the script, never functions in Zelig's life. Leonard Zelig is a moral cipher. He rarely takes decisive steps in any moral situation. Things merely happen to him and he copes as well as he can, assuming no responsibility for the outcomes of his action or inaction.

In ZELIG, Allen begins a systematic exploration of art, in particular the cinema, as a means of reshaping the world into a more congenial arena of human activity. By its very nature, film distorts reality even when it is trying to be most objective. Dr. Fletcher hires her cousin Paul Deghuee (John Rothmann) to film her sessions with Zelig in the White Room. She tells Deghuee that film will provide an important record of Zelig's miraculous changes. Describing these events in words would be clearly inadequate, she believes. As a secondary motive she admits that the filming will record her contribution to medical history. (65) Installing the hidden camera also demands setting up huge stage lights in the office, which Zelig notes immediately during his first session. As Dr. Fletcher explains the cameras, Paul opens the one-way mirror and waves. It is clear that from this moment on Zelig will be performing for the camera and that objectivity has thus been lost.

The laboratory's brilliance in altering the archival newsreel footage used in ZELIG also raises doubts about the authenticity of the film medium. If Leonard Zelig's image can be inserted into footage of Herbert Hoover and Calvin Coolidge, then even newsreels can lie, even though they are proposed as unbiased, objective records of reality, like Dr. Fletcher's films. The scratchy sounds of the recorded therapy sessions and the grainy texture of the newsreels, films made to seem old through very modern technology, include contemporary actors in authentic period costume. The technique blurs the distinction between artifice and reality. Finally, according to the script, Warner Bros. released the story of Zelig's life entitled THE CHANGING MAN in 1935. Clips from the imaginary film demonstrate just how much the action has been changed to fit the demands of Hollywood. Finally, their adventures ended, Leonard Zelig and Eudora Fletcher are happily married and pose for home movies with all the stagy awkwardness generally found in that medium.

In this extensive and complex use of the films-within-the-film, artistic and theological questions converge. Allen seems to suggest that human beings can never capture reality as it actually is, even through the most "realistic" of the media. The reason for this lies not only in the limitations of the medium, but in the human capability to perceive. Perhaps the real problem rests not with Leonard Zelig, but with the outside world that perceived him in drastically different guises. The sad fact is that there *is* no real Leonard Zelig; he is merely the sum of the impressions he makes on the varied others who form their own perception of him, and who of course shape him into their own subjective image. Not even the motion picture camera can grasp the reality of Leonard Zelig, and if the camera and its director are inadequate to the task, the audience watching the film is similarly frustrated.

If this is the case with Zelig and his films, then on the wider horizon, it is quite likely that one can never achieve objective knowledge of the world, and the search for certitude in this inhospitable universe is futile. What then becomes important for Allen, after all these years of searching, is the meaning that he, the maturing artist, can impose on events and persons. After all, by manipulating newsreels he has even rewritten history. Death then, rather than exposing human action as meaningless, may in fact signify merely the cessation of artistic activity, the re-creation of reality. On his deathbed, Zelig notes that his only regret is failing to finish *Moby Dick,* because he was curious to find out how it ended. (129) As a final consequence of Allen's reliance on art to put meaning in his universe, the need for a personal God to provide a moral structure in the universe becomes irrelevant. Art provides meaning and value, not God. The God-question will enter into a temporary sabbatical.

Despite this venture into a form of romantic subjectivity in an unknowable universe, Allen's norms for moral action remain consistent with his earlier works. Morality consists in surrendering selfishness and pursuing the good for another, a pattern of moral behavior that stretches back to SLEEPER (1973). The doctors at the psychiatric hospital, for example, are essentially amoral when they experiment with Zelig in hopes of testing their theories and furthering science. They have little apparent concern about their patient. Chiropractors turn his legs backward and wonder drugs make him walk the walls like an insect. (27) Although Allen does not make the point directly himself, the appearance of Nazis at the end of the film does suggest an association with the medical experiments in the prison camps. Dr. Fletcher's conversion comes when she separates herself from her medical colleagues, acknowledges her ambition for what it is and risks her own reputation, security and safety to bring Zelig back from Germany. Their escape together and their marriage introduce a notion of mutual love that will bring both of them a life of happiness. Her surrender of self brings her own redemption along with his.[5]

Allen has refined some of his earlier ideas and introduced new ones with ZELIG. The search will continue throughout the next several years.

BROADWAY DANNY ROSE (1984) revisits ZELIG's themes of healing love and moral conversion. Once again the Woody character sacrifices himself for his beloved, a theme consistent with SLEEPER, ANNIE HALL and MANHATTAN. Although the narrative center of the story remains the eponymous hero Danny Rose (Woody Allen), the change takes place in Tina Valente (Mia Farrow), the tough-talking Mafia moll who functions as the thematic core of the film.

The other word of the title, Broadway, is significant as the geographic center of the film. The story begins and ends at the Carnegie Delicatessen (actually a venerable eating establishment on Seventh Avenue, not Broadway) the heart of the legendary theatrical district known popularly and generically as Broadway. The slight shift in geography is understandable. No one sings "Give my regards to Seventh Avenue, remember me to 53rd Street." The film also begins and ends with a meal, Allen's ordinary device for providing the image of friendship and love. The seven comedians sitting around the table provide a comfortable ethos of easy companionship. They have had similar show business experiences, and they even steal jokes from one another. They wonder why some sure-fire routines fail in some circumstances, as must every comic, including Woody Allen. With all their problems, they have each other, and that camaraderie brings a kind of rough-hewn joy into their lives. Danny Rose never appears at this table. He is once again the outsider, this time not by virtue of his Jewishness, since most of the comedians appear to be Jewish as well, but because of his obvious lack of success either as a comedian or as a theatrical manager (156).[6]

Danny's knightly *gestes* will end at the Carnegie Delicatessen, his Camelot, where he will have achieved acceptance and immortality at the Round Table by having a sandwich named after him. His quest begins when out of devotion to his worn-out Italian crooner, Lou Canova (Nick Apollo Forte) he travels to New Jersey to bring Lou's girlfriend, the Mafia widow called Tina (Mia Farrow), back to New York to attend Lou's opening at the Waldorf-Astoria Hotel. Arthur and Guinevere these two are not. Danny's adventures just as appropriately recall Xenophon's *Anabasis,* the story of a Persian hero who led his stranded army safely home through enemy territory. Like Lancelot and Xenophon, Danny wants to come home, but crossing the Hudson is a task more challenging than he might have imagined since he also has to bring Tina with him.

Danny may be too naive, too gentle for this formidable deed. He lives for others, a giant of self-sacrifice in a universe of greed, a model of altruism in an industry propelled by ego. When Lou complains about being unable to meet his alimony payments to two ex-wives, Danny offers to forgo his commission to see him through. (170) On the verge of splitting with his third wife Teresa (Sandy Richman), Lou insists that Danny protect him from Teresa's wrath by pretending that Tina is his own girlfriend. Danny has his own standard of ethics, and it is grounded in the religious tradition of belief in a Creator, even though his own belief remains questionable. When Lou takes him into a florist shop to arrange for the customary daily white rose to be sent to Tina, Danny reminds him that some day he will be called to account by the big guy, (174) a recollection of elusive Mr. Big who functions as the goal of Kaiser Lupowitz's quest in Allen's short story of the same name. The white rose, used as a sign of Eve's cold, passionless existence in INTERIORS, is an ironic comment on the tumultuous relationship between Tina and Lou.

The extreme long shot of Danny's crossing the George Washington Bridge to New Jersey makes it clear that he is entering foreign territory, where Danny's ethical standards are a minority opinion at best. For Danny, New Jersey is an alien land in every possible sense. The flat, open landscapes of meadowland (or swampland depending on one's point of view) provide a terrain far different from the murky canyons of mid-town Manhattan. Danny finds himself a Jew among the Italian-American Mafia, and a gentle man who first meets Tina, a shrieking harridan, as she screams into the phone at Lou that she wants to stab him in the heart with an ice pick. (188)

Violent death is more than an idle threat on the left bank of the Hudson. Tina's husband, a Mafia soldier, has been shot in the eyes, and the grieving widow tearlessly comments that he deserved it. (219) When Tina's infidelity to her current boyfriend Johnny Rispoli (Edwin Bordo) becomes known, Johnny attempts suicide by drinking a safely inadequate amount of iodine. The hysterical family immediately suspects Danny, the outsider, of staining the family name and swears a vendetta to avenge Johnny's honor. Once again in comic fashion, Allen examines suicide and murder as strategies to deal with a loveless universe. The chase is on, and Danny longs for a return to the apparent safety of Manhattan.

Having escaped Johnny's brothers by a timely exit through a restaurant kitchen, Tina and Danny wander on foot through the swamplands searching for a way back to New York. Their car has been abandoned and will soon feel the sting of Mafia baseball bats on fender and windshield. At this point the narrative takes a biblical turn. Danny refers to himself as Moses in the bullrushes. (234) They are in despair about being able to reach the Promised Land in Manhattan, when Ray Webb (Craig Vandenburgh), an actor in a Superman type of costume filming a commercial nearby, appears like the voice of God in the wilderness and tells them about a boat that will lead them across the waters to Manhattan. The Hudson River is scarcely the Red Sea or the River Jordan, but the dirty tug does part the waters for them, and they leave their tormentors trapped, if only for a while, on the other side.

The hitmen follow them into the Promised Land, capture Tina and Danny and threaten to dismember them with an axe. The captives are tightly bound together, face to face, as though now their fates are united as tightly as their bodies. To establish his own innocence and to gain time, Danny gives his captors the name of Barney Dunn, an inept ventriloquist he thinks is out of town, as Tina's real boyfriend. Barney's plans have changed, however. He is still in town. The hitmen find him and nearly beat this innocent man to death. As Danny and Tina escape, another Mafia soldier opens fire on them, and violent death threatens them once more. The violence is muted, however, because in their flight, Tina and Danny enter a vast storeroom for the huge helium-filled balloons of the Macy's Thanksgiving Day parade. As the guard fires at them, he releases the helium. Inhaling the gas raises his voice to a comic pitch, thus making a joke out of standard gangster lines threatening violent death if they keep running. (274) To say that the gentle Danny feels himself an outsider in this violent world is an understatement.

Far more lethal is the moral violence Danny encounters in his journey. When Tina and Danny escape from Johnny and his brothers for a momentary pause in a New Jersey diner, Danny complains that as soon as his acts begin to get attention they leave him without any guilt. Tina does not understand his complaint, because according to her value system, it makes perfect sense for people to go with the best deal they can find, regardless of who gets hurt. (223) Danny is astonished. He tells her that it is important to feel guilty, even if one has done nothing wrong, otherwise one is capable of doing terrible things. He quotes Rabbi Perlstein, who taught that everyone appears guilty in the eyes of God. (224) "The eyes of God" is a notion he will probe at greater depth in CRIMES AND MISDEMEANORS (1989). Danny admits, however, that he does not really believe in God. As he did with Lou in the florist shop, he has invoked God as the basis of morality, even though he cannot believe himself.

Tina and Danny resume their conversation in his apartment as they continue their flight. Danny feels that life involves a balance of good times and suffering, but Tina offers an alternate philosophy of life. She holds the philosophy of "eat, drink and be merry." She sees no point in bothering with the concerns of other people, since everyone is out for number one. She is determined to be a taker rather than a victim. (254) Danny is shocked and replies that she talks like dialogue from *Murder Incorporated*.[7] He offers his own alternative philosophy of life, quoting his Uncle Sidney: Acceptance, forgiveness, and love. (255) These words will return to haunt Danny in the final scene.

Danny could scarcely imagine the treachery that Tina had planned for him. Days before they even met, Tina had arranged a meeting between Lou and Sid Bacharach (Gerald Schoenfeld), a theatrical agent who can open more doors for Lou than Danny now that his career is beginning to take off on the winds of a nostalgia craze for Italian novelty songs of the 1950's. In an extremely long shot after Lou's successful show at the Waldorf, after Danny has risked his life to deliver Tina, the three walk together toward the camera. They calmly discuss dumping Teresa, and as the stationary camera captures Danny in close-up, he finally realizes that they intend to dump him, too. When Danny protests in amazement that Lou owes him everything (287), Tina coldly ends the discussion by telling Lou to go ahead with his plan and let Danny figure out the situation for himself and learn to live with it. (288)

The theme of the victimized innocent echoes Boris's lament in the opening scene of LOVE AND DEATH as he awaits execution for a crime he did not commit. As Danny and Tina work their way through the Jersey swamps, Danny admits to being angry because he is forced to flee for his life even though he's done nothing except try to do a favor for a friend. (231) Danny is mistaken. He is not altogether innocent. He has been an accomplice, however unwilling, in betraying Teresa and destroying her marriage. Later, when the hitmen threaten him and Tina, Danny names names and turns in the perfectly innocent Barney Dunn, who nearly dies because of Danny's self-serving ploy. Writers like Woody Allen who lived through the era of blacklisting rank this kind of cowardice high on the list of personal crimes. Danny sees clearly the evil of Lou's betrayal of his wife and children, yet he helps him further his plan by bringing Tina to New York. After Lou's successful show at the Waldorf as he talks calmly about leaving Teresa for Tina, Danny offers not one word of protest until the treachery turns on him personally. At the close of MANHATTAN Tracy commented that corruption need not touch everyone, but now Allen may be questioning that premise. Danny may be beginning to show signs of corruption by complicity in evil.

Despite his lapse, Danny Rose is not really evil. He is at heart a profoundly moral man, but in this environment he does make mistakes. Crushed after his conversation with Lou, Danny sits alone in the Carnegie Delicatessen, and the counterman tells him about Barney's brush with death, which Danny's lie has precipitated. It is a moment of conversion for Danny. He goes immediately to Roosevelt Hospital and offers to pay Barney's medical expenses. (291) Whether or not he feels that he has been seen by "the eye of God," Danny recognizes his sin and takes responsibility for his actions in a way that Zelig could not. His generosity toward Barney is his act of atonement.

Despite her chilling "philosophy of life," Tina, too, is capable of a moment of conversion. She moves in with Lou, but she has bad dreams and cannot sleep. Irritable and depressed, she visits Angelina (Olga Barbato), her favorite fortune teller. Displayed prominently above Angelina's bed is a large crucifix. Spurred by Angelina's questions she admits that she has done wrong, but it was only an insignificant matter. (295) Angelina tells her that she sees a vision of Tina staring at herself in a mirror, and asks what she is looking for. Tina replies that she simply wants to be able to sleep again. (295) Later that night, Tina stands before her bathroom mirror, staring into her own face. From behind the shower curtain, Lou tells her of his plans to go to California, which for Allen traditionally signifies selling out. Tina refuses to go with him. Lou will continue his own self-centered existence, trying to salvage his precarious career, but Tina has at last had her long-overdue moment of moral insight. She wants no part of him.

As time passes, Danny's true personality reasserts itself. He hosts a Thanksgiving dinner for his friends and clients, among them Barney, the stuttering ventriloquist and victim of Danny's lie, a woman who plays water-filled glasses, a lady with a trained parrot and the blind xylophonist. His friends are not the ideal friends he might have wanted, but they do enjoy one another. The dinner too is not the ideal; Danny serves frozen turkey TV dinners. Danny, too, realizes that he himself is far from perfect. He is morally flawed but repentant, and that is the best any human being can hope for.

Still, this is a happy party. Allen has no longer situated the Jewish outsider at the Easter feast, but he has chosen as his setting Thanksgiving, a secularized American feast celebrated with equal enthusiasm by members of all religious traditions. At Danny's table there are no outsiders. Since Allen had confronted his anhedonia, his characters have learned to take great enjoyment in simple pleasures in a clearly imperfect world. In contrast, during her stay with Lou, Tina becomes upset and rude when a waiter delivers the wrong drink to her during Lou's act in a night club. (292)

One wonders if Tina could ever enjoy the company of this nondescript band of so-called losers. She has left Lou and is currently living with Ray Webb, the Superman of the Swamps. As they watch Macy's Thanksgiving Day parade, she remembers the flight with Danny among the giant, helium-filled balloons in their warehouse prison. It is a moment of insight for her, and she pushes past Ray and disappears into the crowd.

Driven as much by love for this good man as by remorse for her treachery, Tina tries to crash Danny's party. As his guests share their modest banquet, Danny meets her at the door, hesitates and does not invite her in. He ignores the curiosity of his dinner guests. Tina reminds him of Uncle Sidney's triad of acceptance, forgiveness and love. (306) Unable to forgive, he turns his back on her, and she silently vanishes. Realizing his great mistake and perhaps that he has sinned once again, Danny has another conversion and rushes after her, catching her in front of the Carnegie Delicatessen. They must have lived happily ever after, since one of the comics describes the Danny Rose sandwich as a combination of a Jewish bagel and Italian marinara sauce. (309)

Allen is too much of a realist to leave his audience with a perfectly happy storybook ending. The camera remains on the outside of the Carnegie Delicatessen, and the comedians continue their chatter. For them the story is a joke. Living as they do in a harsh world, where survival is a full-time job, they have missed the point of this fable of moral regeneration. They laugh about the Danny Rose sandwich and his frozen turkey dinners on Thanksgiving. They plan to meet again tomorrow to tell more stories and have more laughs. In the final exchange, however, one comic, Corbett Monica, offers to pick up the check for all of them. Through this gesture of altruism, Allen asks whether Danny Rose's story has had its impact on them after all.[8]

THE PURPLE ROSE OF CAIRO (1985) stands out as the most innovative single film during this period of startling originality. In ZELIG Allen explored the relationship between art, especially film, and reality by challenging the medium's capacity for documenting events in the real world. In THE PURPLE ROSE OF CAIRO he turns from the documentary to the commercial entertainment film. Rather than examine the nature of the medium, as he had in ZELIG, he looks at the imagination of the consumer and asks how people use movies to alter their understanding of reality?

In a daring change of pace, Allen absents himself totally from this film, the first time he has ever done this with a comedy. The Woody character, however, appears as Cecilia (Mia Farrow), who like her male counterpart traditionally played by Woody Allen himself, stutters and stumbles her way through life, insecure, threatened and desperately unhappy. Her hostile universe is dominated by her husband Monk (Danny Aiello), who drinks, gambles, womanizes, refuses to look for work and who excuses his violence toward her by explaining that he only hits her when she deserves it and, besides, he always warns her first.[9] (342). This dreary Depression marriage provides the image of the world of loneliness and suffering that continually gnaws at Allen and his characters.

Cecilia's refuge, however, is the movies. The local Jewel Theater provides an escape from her daily routine of waitressing in a diner, taking in laundry and enduring Monk. One day, when she has lost her job, partially because chatting with her sister Jane (Stephanie Farrow) about movie stars has distracted her from her work, she sits through THE PURPLE ROSE OF CAIRO again and again and again. On the third screening of the day, her fifth altogether, one of the movie characters, Tom Baxter (Jeff Daniels), leaves the screen and enters the theater telling Cecilia that he has left the movie forever because he is in love with her. (354) For Cecilia it is a dream come to life: a handsome, aristocratic, gentle man loves her. The other actors would like to join him in the real world but cannot imagine how he did it. (355) Later in the film-within-the-film, another character, Larry (Van Johnson), cries out in a desperate plea for freedom. (393)

Through Cecilia, Allen allows his audience to make a shocking discovery. The ideal world of the imagination, with witty, wealthy, sophisticated people, who visit night clubs, fly off to Cairo on whim and apparently have not the slightest care in the world, are also trapped in an existence they cannot control.[10] The sparkling, well-lighted sets of the movie are an image of heaven compared to the drab brown-and-maroon world of Cecilia's reality. Yet in both cases, the very fact of being human, whether poor like Cecilia and the other dream seekers in the audience or wealthy like Tom and Larry (and Allen himself), condemns one to vulnerability and ultimately mortality. Allen has raised this economic commentary on the Great Depression to the level of philosophic investigation.

The movie characters insist that they are not human, yet they dread the suggestion that the manager may end the on-screen rebellion of movie characters simply by turning off the projector. Henry (Edward Herrmann) shouts in terror at the prospect of death by darkness. He is afraid that if the arc dims, he will be reduced to nothingness, much as a real person without belief in an afterlife might fear death. (359) Perhaps living in Cecilia's drab universe, an option that Tom has deliberately chosen for himself, is better than ceasing to exist. These threatened characters on the screen have no control over their destiny no matter how much they worry about their existence. Their fate rests in the hands of the projectionist, of the theater manager and ultimately of the studio head Raoul Hirsch (Alexander Cohen), whose advisers want to darken the theater and destroy all the prints and the negative of the film. (439) Whether the cinematic world of the movie characters ever ends in apocalypic fire or not is never revealed, but at the end of the story THE PURPLE ROSE OF CAIRO has finished its run at the Jewel and is replaced by another feature: TOP HAT, with Fred Astaire and Ginger Rogers. Tom and his fictional friends, mere shadows on the screen of life, have simply outlived their usefulness and passed quietly away.

While Raoul Hirsch, a not terribly sympathetic god-figure, holds the power to annihilate their universe with the flip of a switch and a match to a negative, the role of the creator is not his alone. He has several co-creators. When Gil Shepherd (also Jeff Daniels), the actor who plays Tom Baxter appears on the screen, he tells Cecilia he is responsible for creating Tom. (399) Cecilia rebukes him for his claim, reminding him of the writer's role. In a later comic scene, when the celluloid Tom Baxter innocently visits the town bordello, he tells his hostesses about his own theological reflections. He used to imagine God in conversation with the two writers of the film script, as though all three shared the role of creator. (424) Having placed his own creators in the role of God, Tom continues his reverie about the meaning of life and death, which he paradoxically finds magical in the real world when compared to the make-believe world of the movies.

Thus while Cecilia sees beauty in the elegant world of movie make-believe, the movie character reminds the women in this rather sordid setting of the magic of this present world. In Tom's speech Allen echoes the theme of Leopold in A MIDSUMMER NIGHT'S SEX COMEDY, when he asks his companions at dinner why they need spirits and insist on having something more than the wonderful world that they can perceive with their senses and that surrounds them in the present.

Creation, all kinds of creation, bind together these worlds of reality and illusion. As Tom and Cecilia walk past a shoe-repair shop, a magnificently pregnant woman with a little boy passes them. Tom is baffled by this phenomenon, since in his production-code experience love making always ends with a fade-out. Cecilia cheerfully explains the facts of life to him, and he seems duly impressed by this human process of pro-creation. As an in-joke and yet one more connection between real life and movie illusion, the shop window is decorated with a decal advertising O'Sullivan soles and heels, a comic recognition of Maureen O'Sullivan, the mother of Mia Farrow. Later in the film, as Tom lounges in the living room of the bordello, he romanticizes the notion of childbirth, which fuses the notions of life and pathos. (425) Through Tom's comments, Allen reminds his audience that art, especially the movies, may be rooted in reality, but creative artists reconstruct human experience to serve their own ends. They are not devious (Tom in fact is naive), but this is just what artists do.

Cecilia herself is torn between the two worlds, as illustrated by her involvement in two romantic triangles. In the first, she faces the stark contrast between Tom and Monk, pure illusion and sordid reality. Allen uses his customary meal imagery to sharpen the conflict. When they first meet, Cecilia offers Tom movie food, popcorn and a Milky Way bar, forming a union in movie terms. As their relationship deepens, Tom takes Cecilia to a comfortable restaurant for dinner and champagne. This is not the Copacabana that Tom and his friends visit in their movie, but it is certainly more elegant than anything in Cecilia's present life. It is, in its modest way, a movie fantasy come to life for her. After an evening of romantic movie talk, Tom tries to pay the bill in stage money, and when they are forced to run away from the angry waiters, he tries to start the getaway car without a key, scarcely aware that the car belongs to someone else. Real life is not like his movies. Safe at last from their pursuers, he continues his romantic dialogue by offering to take her away with him to exotic places where they will only have each other. She reminds him that he is only speaking lines from a movie. (387)

At the other pole of Cecilia's life is Monk, an image of brute, cruel reality. They are never shown eating together. After Cecilia comes upon Monk with another woman in her own home, she packs her suitcase and threatens to leave him. Monk claims he needs her and orders her to stay home and warm some left-over meatloaf for his supper, as though a command could rekindle the lackluster love they once felt for each other. (343) Their marriage has become cold meatloaf, and this is not much of a step down from yesterday's hot meatloaf. In another scene, after Cecilia has agreed to meet Tom later that evening, Monk complains that she has ruined the spaghetti by putting too much pepper in the sauce. (368) Tom has added spice to her life, but Monk is not capable of enjoying it. This is Cecilia's reality, and it is not very pleasant.

The conflict in the triangle reaches its peak when Cecilia leads Tom into a church. The scene begins with a close up of a large wooden crucifix. She asks Tom if he believes in God, whom she describes as giving a meaning to everything. If it were not for God and his designs the whole world would be like a pointless movie, and there would be no happy endings. (408) Cecilia, like Allen, wants to believe in a purpose in life validated by a God, but her hopes for a happy ending are dashed when Monk appears at the back of the church. Brutality reasserts itself in her universe when Monk threatens her, then fights with Tom, flattening him with a cruel knee to the groin and while he is down punching him repeatedly in the face. Cecilia rebukes him for his violence and the harm he might have done to Tom. Apparently triumphant, Monk storms away, but Cecilia remains with Tom. Cruel reality has ruined her dreams once more.

As Monk leaves, however, Tom rises from the floor in front of the altar, unbruised, unrumpled, not a hair out of place. He is after all a movie hero, not a real man. In these ecclesial surroundings, it would not be too far afield to say that he was resurrected from the dead—again Allen's Easter imagery—to offer the prospect that good will ultimately triumph over evil, hope over despair, life over death. It would be all too wonderful for Cecilia (and for Allen) if this were reality and not a movie or a religious myth. Cecilia may be ready to make the assent for dreams over reality, but it is doubtful that Allen is. He remains secular Jewish outsider to Christian belief in the resurrection of Jesus and the redemption of the world.

The poles between reality and fantasy narrow somewhat for Cecilia as she deals with her second triangle. Monk is now temporarily out of the picture, and the two competing suitors are Tom and Gil, both of course played by Jeff Daniels. Again relying on his food imagery, Allen has Cecilia buy donuts and coffee for Tom, the movie character, but when she meets Gil, the actor, at the drug store, she mistakes him for Tom and then gives the food to Gil. Her allegiance becomes ambivalent, and she is confused, being attracted at the same time to the fictional hero and the actor who plays him. Predictably, Gil in turn invites her to lunch. As a real-life movie star, Gil inhabits the territory midway between Tom and Monk: part Hollywood myth, part flesh-and-blood reality. To further his romantic intentions, Tom takes Cecilia into the movie with him for a mad fling with his fashionable friends at the Copa. In a classic montage they are superimposed against the lights of Broadway.

In this world of the imagination, limits to human aspiration are unknown. Arturo, the maitre'd at the Copa, learns that the set plot of the movie has been disrupted. He tells the band to start playing, and breaks into a lively tap dance because he has always wanted to dance in the movies. (449) Arturo's Copa stands a bit above Cecilia's diner, but in this night-club fantasy world his dreams come true, while Cecilia's day dreams are buried in greasy dishes. At the end, Cecilia must choose between Tom and his world of pure fantasy, or Gil and his wildly improbable promise to take her to Hollywood to live with real movie stars. Cecilia chooses Gil, telling Tom that she has to opt for the real world for the simple reason that she is real herself. She has no choice. (459)

Once more Cecilia prepares to leave Monk, but she discovers that once Tom, disappointed in love, went back into the movie, Gil and all the other movie people left town immediately, relieved that the danger to their investment was past. Gil, it seems, had merely been using Cecilia to get to Tom. As an actor he knew all the right lines and how to deliver them. As he flies back to California, the camera lingers on him alone in the plane. He is perplexed, it seems. He may feel a bit of regret for his cynical actions, or perhaps he even finds a bit of love for Cecilia. In any case, he is returning to begin work on a film about Lindbergh, not realizing that he too is a lone eagle, flying through life as a loner and concerned only about his own career.

Those few hours or days with Gil have, however, left another kind of memory for Cecilia. During one of their meetings, Gil buys a ukulele for her, and in an exuberant moment together she energetically plays "I'm Alabamy Bound" while he sings. As an encore, the elderly proprietress joins them on the piano. Tracy in MANHATTAN gave Ike a harmonica, and in STARDUST MEMORIES Dorrie gave Sandy a flute. The gift of a musical instrument invites one to make art out of remembered love. Though no artist herself, Cecilia clings to her ukulele, as heartbroken once more, she retreats into the theater. She has a happy memory that unites her movie fantasies with her real world. She will eventually leave the theater and return to Monk, but with her ukulele firmly in hand. The movies and movie stars have given her a reason to continue living. For those few moments in the theater, she forgets her pain and disappointment. She can almost believe Fred as he dances with Ginger and sings, "Heaven, I'm in heaven." (466)

As is often the case with Allen's heroes, Cecilia finds that she can endure life because of her memories and because of the movies. On occasion she flirts with other escapes from her dreary life. After leaving Monk the first time she watches Emma (Dianne Wiest) and her girlfriend, two prostitutes, enter a local bar. Cecilia hesitates for a moment, as though to follow them, and then returns to Monk. She does then have a sense of morality, sin and guilt. There are limits to what she will do to escape from Monk.

At the same time, Cecilia is quite capable of introducing a certain degree of moral ambiguity into her life, just like Danny Rose. Alone with Monk after she has promised to meet Tom, she drops a glass as a sign of her guilt, just as Andrew did in A MIDSUMMER NIGHT'S SEX COMEDY when he hears that Ariel, his former love, is coming to visit him and his wife Adrian. She lies continually to her husband about her meeting Tom, but she is not very convincing. At the end of the film, she even plans to run away to Hollywood with Gil, even though she has told him that she is married. (457)

The moral question Allen poses here is not one of adultery, for as in many of his films the human relationships have a symbolic rather than a realistic content. In the context of this dramatic event, marital fidelity is not the issue, since it is clear that Monk is a worthless bully and Cecilia should find some way to leave him. Allen is after bigger fish than this. He is asking about the value of human actions in a world created and controlled by forces that lie beyond human capability to understand or modify. The universe can be hostile and unloving, for reasons that defy reason. Raoul Hirsch, God, Monk and the Depression economy made Cecilia's world; she did not. Cecilia cannot escape from the universe that was given to her, and she certainly cannot even begin to solve the mystery of her life. Her actions, even those of dubious morality, cannot change her own lot, let alone her disagreeable world. She can, however, with the help of the imagination (her movies and her ukulele) endure it, and even find a few moments of peace and happiness.

Audiences may be misty eyed as they witness Cecilia's final betrayal, but at its heart THE PURPLE ROSE OF CAIRO stands as a splendid, optimistic testimony to the resilience of the human spirit. Cecilia is a blood sister to Gelsomina the dull-witted but lovable heroine in Fellini's LA STRADA (1954) or Cabiria, the indefatigable prostitute in his NIGHTS OF CABIRIA (1956). These women have seen first hand the cruelty of the world and yet they have found the means not only to endure but to transcend the bitter cruelty they have tasted. Fellini's triumph is signaled in Nino Rota's lively music; Allen's in Fred Astaire's "Heaven."

HANNAH AND HER SISTERS (1986) returns the Woody Allen character to the familiar setting of contemporary Manhattan. He and his comfortable, talented friends hover around the edges of the world of the arts.[11] Like Isaac Davis in MANHATTAN, Mickey Sachs (Woody Allen) is once again a successful writer for television comedy who is able to take a year off to sort things out without much apparent financial sacrifice. Mickey is only part of the story, however. Allen uses the ensemble cast with its tumultuous personal relationships to explore his usual themes, and although the territory is familiar, he seems to become less an alien and more a peaceful resident of a world that remains challenging but far less hostile than it had been.

Structurally, HANNAH AND HER SISTERS repeats many of the elements of INTERIORS. The characters of the two films are mirror images of each other. Each film is the story of three talented sisters and their troubled parents. Hannah (Mia Farrow) resembles Renata (Diane Keaton), the successful artist and mother whose steady leadership provides stability for the entire family. Holly (Dianne Wiest) is a livelier version of Joey (Marybeth Hurt), the sensitive but talented daughter who continually struggles to find herself. Lee (Barbara Hershey) recalls Flyn (Kristin Griffith), the least complicated woman whose sensuous beauty brings as many problems as rewards. The parents are similar as well. Eve (Geraldine Page) is depressed and suicidal, while Norma (Maureen O'Sullivan) is alcoholic; both have had some early success in the arts that they cannot duplicate at this stage in their lives. Both fathers, Arthur (E. G. Marshall) and Evan (Lloyd Nolan) are attractive and successful, while they cope with their difficult wives by a series of affairs.

The differences are significant, however, and point out the development in Allen's thinking. INTERIORS ends with death and silence; HANNAH AND HER SISTERS ends with life and a noisy Thanksgiving Day party. More importantly, Allen shifts his introspective focus from the women, who reflected different aspects of his personality in INTERIORS, to the men, each of whom represents a facet of Allen's thought that he holds up to scrutiny. The women in HANNAH, strong characters in their own right, help the men discover a meaning in their lives.

Again, one must be cautious about reading the film as a clever, thinly veiled autobiography. Allen is exploring the human condition and the role of the artist in discovering love and meaning for himself and others. He may be excused for quoting his own life to illustrate these reflections. Aware of this difficulty, Allen has Holly turn to playwrighting as a career, and her first script infuriates her family because it strikes so close to home. Once she has learned her technique and begun to process her feelings into words, she is able to move away from her own and her family's own private experiences.

The film opens with Elliot (Michael Caine) in a voice-over monologue. He is a successful stockbroker who has been happily married to Hannah, but unfortunately, he becomes infatuated with her younger sister Lee, who is currently living with a dour artist. Not content with the ideal wife he has, he chases a romantic but elusive ideal. Elliot's pursuit has both its comic and pathetic moments. He stalks Lee as she leaves her loft apartment and runs after her, nearly precipitating a heart attack for himself, to arrange his "accidental" meeting. He buys her a book of e. e. cummings's poetry, and tells her to look at page 112, a romantic poem that expresses sentiments he cannot voice himself. He arranges a meeting between Frederick (Max Von Sydow), her artist lover, and Dusty Frye (Daniel Stern), a semiliterate, multimillionaire rock singer who wants to decorate his Southampton mansion with something big, because he wants to fill up all the wall space he has.[12] (78) While singer and artist look at the collection of oils in the basement and begin to detest each other, Elliot puts romantic music on the stereo, warns himself not to move too quickly, and then impulsively pounces upon her, placing a passionate kiss on her lips. (81) In his fumbling he scratches the record. So much for discretion. All the time she has been trying to distance herself from him by talking about having her teeth cleaned.

Elliot and Lee eventually begin their affair in a hotel room at the St. Regis, and after they make love, Lee tells him that his lovemaking was so passionate that she could never love anyone else again. Elliot replies that he would not want her to. (100) Their relationship eventually enables Lee to leave Frederick, but both have their moments of guilt. Lee is queasy about seeing her sister's husband, and she realizes that Elliot is not free to marry her. (146) Besides, after leaving Frederick she begins taking courses at Columbia and grows quite close to Doug, a professor of literature. For his part, Elliot nearly tells Hannah of his infidelity, but he does not want to hurt her. As they embrace at the end of the scene, he realizes how foolish he was to jeopardize his marriage to a woman he scarcely deserves. (121)

At one point, Elliot tries to sort out his life with the help of a psychiatrist. During a therapy session, he acknowledges his many gifts, but despite his intelligence and success, he still cannot understand the movements of his own heart. (144) After Lee has ended their relationship and told him about Doug, Elliot and Hannah finally discuss their marriage. Because of Hannah's achievements and self-sufficiency, Elliot feels unneeded. Later, in bed together, shaken by the fear that her marriage may be ending, Hannah admits to Elliot that she feels lost in the dark of the night, and he simply reaffirms his love for her. (158) In the darkness they discover that, much like Zelig and Dr. Fletcher, they need each other. Later on, he admits his feelings of foolishness to Lee. He admits that his folly put Hannah and himself through a great deal of pain, and he reminds Lee that she was right when she once told him that he really loved Hannah more than he ever knew. (176)

Throughout the story Elliot is searching for an ideal love so frantically that he fails to appreciate the wonderful, loving wife he has.[13] In previous films, the Allen hero searches for love, finds an incomplete woman, like Luna the sleeper, Annie the insecure, Tracy the child or Tina the moral monster. His love helps them to develop a fullness as persons, even though it involves great cost to himself. In Hannah, Elliot has a complete woman, but she is too complete; he has no need to help her grow and she certainly does not need him for that role. Allen has his character appreciate the mutuality of love, and the strong woman helps Elliot realize his foolishness and his immaturity for what it is.

Allen's earlier characters existed in loveless or even hostile worlds. Elliot's world is filled with love, even though he cannot recognize it. One indication of his blindness to love is his reluctance to have children, as though he cannot trust his love for Hannah to last. (Hannah has four children, two by adoption and two by artificial insemination while she was married to Mickey, who was diagnosed as sterile.) As Elliot reaches his moment of enlightenment, Allen reveals himself as enlightened and much more at peace with his world. Elliot's desperate quest for love is frustrated not so much by a hostile, unloving universe, but from his own blindness. Allen does not hold Elliot morally responsible for his failure of vision, however. Elliot truly cannot understand why he acts the way he does. The world may not be harsh, but in matters of the heart, for both Elliot and Allen, it remains very mysterious. It does not yield its secrets to the mind alone.

The intellectual search for certitude, so common in Allen's earlier films, is embodied in Frederick, a humorless, joyless painter who lives with Lee. The character restates many of Allen's earlier concerns, but without the slightest touch of wit. Frederick was also the name of the angry, acerbic aspiring novelist married to Joey in INTERIORS. Like Eve in INTERIORS Frederick is the pure artist, even if the search for his ideal limits his sales and destroys the people who try to love him. Like the earlier Allen heroes, he wants to complete the perfect woman. Frederick defines his relationship to Lee as a five-year attempt to educate her. (103) He needs to keep her as a living work of his art, and he tells her that she is all that binds him to the real world. (105) Lee wants none of this. She will be neither artifact nor lifeline for him; she wants to be her own person, and without hesitation she leaves him for Elliot.

Like the earlier Allen, Frederick holds a bitter view of the world, which the Woody character makes palatable with his jokes. Frederick is utterly without humor. He speaks with withering sarcasm about television, complains about the mentality of people who watch wrestling and the television evangelists who continually dun the gullible for contributions in the hope that they will find God. (102) These were the very preachers Eve watched in the hospital after her suicide attempt. With an edge of cynicism he belittles a television panel of intellectuals who discuss the horror of the Holocaust, observing that they have failed to recognize the fact that people are so evil that there should have been many other Holocausts. (101)

Frederick, as the dark side of Allen's vision of the world, quietly slips out of the narrative after Lee leaves him. As Frederick disappears, Allen has put this grim outlook on the world behind him. Frederick embodies Allen's unrelieved pessimism, and unlike many of his other characters, he cannot be changed even by a loving woman like Lee. He has been reduced to a cartoon figure, a living parody best ridiculed and forgotten.

While Allen uses Elliot to offer his reflections on love and Frederick his views on art, he creates Mickey Sachs to explore the meaning of life in the context of death and uncertainty. Mickey is successful, but the pace in commercial television is killing him spiritually as well as physically. He complains that the network people from Standards and Practices have pulled his sketch about child molesting, while as producer he infuriates a writer by cutting out jokes about the PLO.[14] His associate producer suggests replacing the offensive material with a homosexual dance number featuring Ronald Reagan and Cardinal Spellman. (31) In a world of television, what are the standards of taste, or are there any? How is Mickey to decide the right thing to do? And if the television studio is a microcosm of the world, as it surely is in this film, how can a sane person decide what is unacceptable and what is the moral thing to do? Are there any norms for morality, and if there are, how does one discover them? The evidence is contradictory.

In a scene reminiscent of Danny Rose's attempt to sober up Lou Canova minutes before his show, Mickey finds his star high on

Quaaludes. The actor has found one way to deal with his fluctuating, frantic universe, but his solution does not appeal to Mickey. In a complaint that echoes Boris's proclamation of innocence before his execution in LOVE AND DEATH and Danny Rose's admission of anger because he has done nothing to deserve his fate, Mickey looks at the chaos around him and repeats Job's lament: Why does God allow this to happen to him? (29)

The solution Mickey is forced to explore is far more radical. Ever the hypochondriac, Mickey visits a doctor because of a slight hearing loss and other complications. These are so minor he cannot identify them with any precision. (38) The doctor advises additional tests, and the results of these are ambiguous enough to warrant a full CAT scan. By this time, Mickey's imagination has been activated, and he is convinced that he has an inoperable brain tumor.

Facing what he believes is imminent death, Mickey discovers the beauty of life. He tells Gail (Julie Kavner), his associate producer, about his imminent death. He tells her that earlier in the day, before his fatal but imagined diagnosis, he was a happy man, but she reminds him that his professional and personal life made him miserable. Mickey denies this, maintaining that he was really happy, but simply not aware of the fact. (43–44) Like Elliot, he discovers that even in the midst of his furious activity and maddening frustration in the studio, he was a happy man, if only he had the good sense to recognize it. His world was miserable, but he had life.

During the worst part of his ordeal, Mickey tells Gail that he bought a gun and contemplated suicide rather than face a prolonged illness. After thinking about the customary way Allen characters try to solve their problems, Mickey chooses not to go ahead with his plan, since he is afraid that he would devastate his parents. After he receives the good news that he is perfectly well, he skips ecstatically down Fifth Avenue, but his joy is short-lived. His face-to-face encounter with death has left its mark on him. The lesson of life's fragility stays with him. He tells Gail of his realization that even though he is not going to die today or tomorrow, he will die someday, and because of that he will not be able to enjoy anything again. (97) Death, remote as it is for him, makes all his human activity meaningless. The Allen conundrum of trying to live productively in a universe without meaning reasserts itself with renewed urgency for Mickey, and he decides to leave the show to search for answers to life's great questions. For him, the search has become desperate. (98)

The answers are hard to come by. On the Columbia campus Mickey muses about Socrates, Nietzsche and Freud, who offer little. He scorns the joggers in Central Park, who live with the illusion of immortality through fitness. (109) He becomes obsessed with the approach of death, and wonders if love might not be the only fitting antidote to death (109), but Mickey is currently without love in his life. As she listens to his troubles, Gail even suggests that a fling of meaningless sex may cure his ills. (98)

Religious faith provides one obvious means for people to address the question of death. For a time, Mickey finds himself trying to become a Roman Catholic, but the project seems doomed from its inception. He tells Father Flynn (Ken Costigan) that he is particularly interested in the liberal anti-establishment wing of the Church. (30) This is a wing hard to find in the official Catholic Church. He has one other problem: He does not believe in God, but he offers to dye Easter eggs, if it will help him find the answers and proof he needs. In his desperation Mickey admits that if he cannot discover a God to believe in, then life is meaningless for him. Allen here restates his Easter theme, a sign of his Jewish alienation from Christian optimism, which is rooted ultimately in the resurrection of Jesus. In addition, he repeats an idea from THE PURPLE ROSE OF CAIRO. When the action in the film-within-the-film falls into chaos after Tom leaves the story, the sophisticated Manhattanites on the screen agree immediately to summon a priest (Milo O'Shea), even though the appearance of a clergyman as a character as a moral force in such a plot is highly unlikely. A "priest-figure" is brought in because its presence invariably suggests some form of notional or moral order in a very confusing world.

Mickey and Catholicism make a poor fit. He buys a crucifix, a New Testament and a picture of Jesus with moving eyes. In the same paper bag he has a loaf of white bread and a jar of mayonnaise, foods he thinks will be appropriate for him as a Christian. The horror of this culinary prospect recalls Annie Hall's ordering pastrami on white with mayo as Alvy looks on in disbelief. Mickey's mother is hysterical at the prospect of his conversion to Christianity. His father cannot be concerned about an afterlife, since he has enough problems with the present one. Mickey restates his problem with the existence of God, and asks if there is a God, why is there evil in the world; how could there be Nazis. His father confesses his own puzzlement about Nazis but his inability to answer the question does not surprise him because he cannot even figure out the workings of a can opener. (133)

Not finding his answer in the Catholic Church, Mickey later wonders if Hare Krishna with its belief in reincarnation may be the answer, but the thought of shaving his head and dancing around in airports repels him. (145)

Mickey eventually tells the story of his actual suicide attempt to Holly. He tells her that the thought of living in a godless universe so depressed him that he felt he had to take his own life. (169) As he continues the narrative in flashback, a clock ticks in the background, indicating the passage of life's time. He fires the rifle, misses his forehead and shatters a mirror, thus breaking through his incestuous self-absorption. Walking through the city in a daze he wanders in to a screening of DUCK SOUP, and while watching the Marx Brothers, he realizes that he should stop his futile quest for answers about God and the meaning of the universe. Even if his days are numbered, he resolves to try to enjoy life while he still draws breath. (172) The joy and energy of the Marx Brothers have given him a reason to live, and more, to enjoy life.

Mickey goes beyond Cecilia in his discovery. Cecilia found a moment of escape that would allow her to endure another dose of hard reality with Monk. Mickey's moment of awareness allows him to transform his reality and find love and a meaningful purpose in his life.

This change in Mickey's life is underlined in a subplot. While Mickey is waiting for the results of his medical tests, he recalls a similar instance in a doctor's office, when he and Hannah learn that Mickey's sterility explains their inability to have children. As they leave the office, Hannah asks Mickey if he might have ruined himself by self-abuse. (69) The crude sexual allusion points to Mickey's excessive self-absorption. Like his life, his marriage to Hannah is sterile, even though she manages to have two children without him through artificial insemination. Their marriage soon ends in divorce. In the final scenes of the film, however, after Mickey has faced death, left television and taken a genuine interest in Holly, both as a person and as a writer, he and Holly marry.

At the final Thanksgiving Dinner, where Mickey again is welcome as a member of the family, Holly tells him she is pregnant. His openness to life and happiness has led to a near miraculous healing. His life is no longer sterile but productive in a most meaningful and joyful way. Love between these two very imperfect people in a very imperfect world has made both of them fertile and very happy. They have become creative together.

The model for all these relationships is the older couple, Evan and Norma. Initially, they appear as the loving couple at the first Thanksgiving Day dinner. Later, when Norma is drunk and abusive of her husband, Hannah is called in to try to ease the situation, while they trade vicious, personal insults (88). Time works its healing power, however, and at the final Thanksgiving dinner, they are again a loving couple. Having endured all the real pain they have inflicted on each other, they remain very much in love, and the result of their love is a household filled with children and grandchildren. Their lives reflect Mickey's comment about the human condition. Like the human heart, people who love can survive episodes of pain that had been thought fatal. (180)

Like Mickey, Holly is a model of resiliency herself. A former cocaine addict deeply in debt to Hannah, she begins a catering service with her friend April (Carrie Fisher). David Tolchin (Sam Waterston), a handsome architect shows some interest, but soon switches his attention to April. Holly continues to audition for parts in plays, but never makes the call-back. She is a bit jealous of Hannah's successful career, which continues when she is chosen to do Desdemona on television. Holly's first script is unusable because of her family's outrage at its personal revelations, and Hannah's initial attempt to act as matchmaker for her and her former husband Mickey is a disaster. Like the television actor in Mickey's studio, Holly tries to escape her problems through drugs, and Hannah has lent her money to support her habit. Holly, however, is a survivor. Eventually and against all expectations, she writes the successful script and finds a congenial companion in Mickey. Both have taken the world's cruelest blows and have overcome them.

The final Thanksgiving feast celebrates life and a resolution of all their conflicts, if only for a time. Hannah and Elliot are reunited; Evan and Norma sing around the piano together; Lee brings her new husband Doug to meet the family, and thanks to

Holly, Mickey, excluded from the last two Thanksgivings after his divorce from Hannah as well as from their Christmas gathering, is finally admitted to the table as an insider and generator of new life. Allen has allowed his hero to find peace both through the world of art and in a loving but very fragile human family. His world has become a less inhospitable place, and love in here-and-now circumstances makes survival not only possible but enjoyable.

RADIO DAYS (1987) consolidates Allen's gains in HANNAH AND HER SISTERS. His own first-person, voice-over narrative identifies the film as another personal reflection, but he never appears on the screen. Joe (Seth Green) is the Allen character as a 10-year-old, and the story is told from his point of view, even though the narrator's commentary adds suitable touches of nostalgia from a mature man remembering the past. As in INTERIORS and HANNAH AND HER SISTERS, the central family includes three sisters: Joe's mother Tess (Julie Kavner), Aunt Ceil (Rene Lippen) and Aunt Bea (Dianne Wiest). Unlike their predecessors, however, these women are too busy cleaning fish, raising families and trying to make ends meet to worry about finding themselves as artists.

Allen situates this family in the Rockaway Beach section of Queens, New York City. No longer is Joe, the Allen surrogate, portrayed as Jewish alien in an inhospitable environment. On the contrary, gentiles would need a tourist visa to enter Allen's version of Rockaway. This exclusively Jewish enclave, as beautifully designed by Santo Loquasto and photographed by Carlo Di Palma, provides a sense of confinement with its long alleys, narrow sidewalks and high fences. The houses sit crammed close together on tiny lots, and no family argument escapes notice of the neighbors. With so many relatives living together in Joe's house, privacy does not exist. Only once do the characters reflect on their isolation from the majority culture because of their Jewishness. As Aunt Ceil listens to celebrity chatter broadcast from the Stork Club, she complains that Uncle Abe (Josh Mostel) never takes her there. Abe replies that Jews and colored aren't allowed in.

For the most part, however, Joe remembers a happy, loving childhood in this far-from-perfect world, where bickering is the vernacular of the inhabitants. In one of his day dreams, the mature Joe imagines his parents appearing as guests on a radio program called "The Court of Human Emotions." Tess attacks her husband for failing to earn enough money to buy their own house, and he calls her side of the family "a tribe of Huns." The moderator gives up and tells them they deserve each other, and Tess replies: "I love him, but what did I do to deserve him?" Months later, now gloriously pregnant like the unnamed woman in THE PURPLE ROSE OF CAIRO, Tess advises her sister Bea to stop looking for the perfect man to marry. She tells her that waiting for the perfect man may make her grow old without becoming a mother, which is the ultimate value in their lives. The themes of enjoying and creating life in an imperfect world have become constant elements in Allen's thought.

For young Joe, opportunities for opening himself to wider horizons in this closed world are few. On occasion, Joe wanders down to the seemingly endless beach for an adventure. There, under the boardwalk, he remembers stealing a kiss from Evelyn Garwitz, and when he and his friends take their binoculars to a rooftop to watch for invading Japanese planes, just as Biff Baxter (Jeff Daniels) had instructed them on his radio program, they look into an apartment across the street and spot Miss Gordon (Sydney Blake), alone and naked, dancing in front of a mirror. Some days later Miss Gordon takes over Joe's class as substitute teacher, much to the delight of the young plane spotters. Alone on the beach one day Joe sees a real Nazi submarine, just as Biff Baxter had described it, but he keeps quiet about it for fear that no one would believe him. Does the narrator believe any of these incidents, or are they the boyish memories lingering through the years, perhaps somewhat embellished by his imagination? It is indelicate to ask. At any rate, without leaving his confining neighborhood, Joe is able to gain some experience of the world.

On other memorable occasions, Joe crosses the East River to make a pilgrimage to the distant mysterious island of Manhattan. In one lovely sequence Aunt Bea (Dianne Wiest) and her current boyfriend take Joe to a movie at the Radio City Music Hall, and the warm gold interiors suggest to him an image of paradise. On the screen, he sees James Stewart and Katharine Hepburn kissing in a scene from PHILADELPHIA STORY (George Cukor, 1940). These are handsome, wealthy gentiles from the distant city that produced Mary Wilke (Diane Keaton) in MANHATTAN and the Fletcher family in ZELIG, complete anti-types to Ike's and

Zelig's Jewish culture. With another boyfriend, Aunt Bea takes Joe to a radio quiz program, where she wins money by identifying fish. Aunt Bea and her escort buy Joe a chemistry set and go dancing, while Joe watches, drinking his soft drink. The narrator remembers this as an exciting memory from his childhood.

Despite these occasional adventures abroad, Joe's childhood universe, however, is Rockaway, Queens, just as Allen's was Flatbush, Brooklyn. His true escape from his constricted world is the radio, where like Cecilia in THE PURPLE ROSE OF CAIRO, he and the other members of his family can imagine a world of unspeakable wonders. Joe's favorite program is "The Masked Avenger," a crime fighter reminiscent of "Captain Midnight." Joe wears the Avenger goggles, and perhaps these open up sights to him far beyond his neighborhood. He longs for the Avenger ring with the secret compartment, but the 15 cents is hard to find.

Sight through the magic of radio and imagination becomes a constant theme throughout the film. In the opening sequence burglars robbing the Needlemans' home next door fumble around in the dark. They receive a phone call from "Guess That Tune," and without turning on a light or seeing a thing, they enter into the game. They leave with $50 and some silverware, but the next day a truckload of prizes arrives for the stunned Needlemans. Who needs visual images in 1940, since sound alone creates a world of miracles?

Joe's mother Tess survives the morning and her mountains of dirty dishes by listening to "Breakfast with Irene and Roger," a reminder of the once popular shows "Dorothy and Dick" and "Tex and Jinx." In a setting probably enriched somewhat by Tess's imagination, Irene (Julie Kurnitz) and Roger (David Warrilow) sit in a sumptuous art-deco restaurant, eating breakfast and chatting about all the exciting events and witty people of the previous evening on the town. Again, the two-layered world of reality and imagination—one cramped and dark, the other spacious and bathed in light—recalls the contrast between Cecilia's world and the penthouse apartment on the screen of the Jewel Theater in THE PURPLE ROSE OF CAIRO. Allen's script treats the dichotomy differently, however. Cecilia wanted her ideal world so badly that it became real for her. It was an escape from her grim reality and gave her the spiritual energy to endure life. Joe's family has no such needs or illusions. They are modestly happy in their own little world, as limited as it is. Tess is amused to listen to the radio and imagine how the other half lives. She never thinks of joining her sophisticated radio friends.

Allen sharpens the distinction between worlds of reality and dream by contrasting the lives of the two principal female characters. Aunt Bea desperately wants to marry and have children, but her bad luck is legendary. One suitor is depressed at the death of his financée, who, she discovers, is named Leonard. Another is married and promises to leave his wife but he never does. After a night of roller skating and beer at Coney Island, still another abandons her in terror when the car radio broadcasts the frightening news of Martians landing in New Jersey.[15] When he tries to call her a week later, she leaves word that she has married a Martian. Bea sings all the new songs and learns all the new dance steps. She wears all the latest styles, daubs perfume behind her knees, and when the War creates a shortage of hosiery, she paints her legs and adds seams with an eyebrow pencil. Despite her ingenuity and enthusiasm in making herself attractive, nothing seems to work for her. She comments that she has a knack for picking losers, but she will never admit that she is a loser herself. Bea is right. A woman of such unshakable optimism, good humor, generosity and spirit should never be considered a loser.

Bea's opposite number is Sally White (Mia Farrow), a cigarette girl of easy virtue who aspires to rise from the sheets of her various protectors to radio stardom. She appears first at work in the fashionable supper club where Roger and Irene meet their elegant friends. Sally and Roger are scarcely strangers, and once again he promises to use his connections to further her career in exchange for a quick tryst on the roof. They leave the elegant ballroom for a gritty rooftop overlooking Broadway. Her cigarette tray, a sign of their class difference, momentarily stands between them, but not for long. When they complete their task at hand and try to restore their clothing to its ordinary function, they discover that the fire door leading back to the ballroom has locked behind them. Irene discovers the lovers. Sally is fired, and Irene, ever liberal minded and scandalously daring (at least in the minds of Joe's family) is believed to have taken both Roger and her new Latin lover to her hotel suite in Havana for a week of unbridled double-duty passion. Like super-market tabloids today, radio in pre-War America provided the grist for lurid fantasies to brighten the lives of ordinary, more conventionally inhibited people.

Put out of work for moral turpitude while her accusers enjoy their Cuban adventure, Sally finds life as unfair as Bea does. Sally's luck changes, however, when she finds her next job. Working as a hat check girl in a gangster-owned night club, she witnesses a murder right in the dining room. Rocco (Danny Aiello), the hitman, tries to eliminate her as well, but he runs out of bullets. He drags the screaming Sally to his car so that he can drive home and reload. Rocco's mother (Gina De Angelis) passes the ammunition and advises her son to bury his victim in Red Hook (Brooklyn) rather than taking her to the customary site in New Jersey. Before they go, however, she insists on filling Sally with a good Italian meal, the standard Allen image of fellowship. As she eats, they discover that, like them, Sally comes from the Canarsie section of Brooklyn. They know the same restaurants. It would be like killing one of the family. Their alternate plan is to arrange Sally's big break on radio, by calling in a few favors and twisting—or breaking—a few arms.

Sally's luck changes again, however. Moments before her radio debut, the program is interrupted for a special announcement, and the cruelly disappointed Sally asks in her frustration: "Who is Pearl Harbor?" Sally tries to do a singing commercial for Relax, a laxative, but when the sponsor shows some interest in her career, undoubtedly because of her obvious good looks, his wife orders her fired. The War brings the opportunity to sing at U.S.O. shows, and Sally gains both poise and the realization that her high thin voice is an obstacle to her radio career. After voice lessons, Canarsie vanishes from her accent, her vocal tone drops an octave, and she inexplicably becomes a famous radio star, doing reports on the lives of celebrities.

Both Sally and Bea scheme to get what they want. Sally succeeds, where Bea fails. Bea has never crossed over from grim reality into the world of radio fantasy, but Sally has. Allen asks which one is happier. On New Year's Eve, as the world hopes that 1944 will bring better news about the War, Sally is back on the roof of her supper club with her wealthy friends, showing them the sights of the city. Their sophisticated chatter is just as loveless as her meeting with Roger several years earlier. She travels in a group, having lost even that experience of physical intimacy that she once shared with Roger on that rooftop. Her dreams of radio stardom came true, but in fact, that night she is very much alone.

Bea's career in radio lasted only a few minutes. She identified a few fish and won $50, which she immediately spent on Joe and her boyfriend. Without a date on New Year's Eve, she awaits the dawn of 1944 playing solitaire not alone but with her family surrounding her. As they open their single bottle of champagne, Bea awakens Joe so that he can witness the celebration. Sally has entered the world of her fantasies, and at the end she has nothing. Bea doesn't need her fantasy world to be happy. Cheap champagne, a noisy family and Joe are her reality, and it is quite enough for her. Allen has finally discovered the secret of happiness in this world. This is a remarkable turn-around for Woody Allen.

Although he has reached a resolution of sorts in his search for human happiness, Allen remains uncertain about the presence of God in his universe. In RADIO DAYS he looks at Judaism again, but this time not so much as a collection of comic Orthodox rabbis, but as a possible path to follow in his quest for God, whom Allen needs to provide the ground for ultimate meaning and morality.

In a comic but gentle episode, young Joe's desperation for his Avenger ring leads him to raid the collection boxes that Rabbi Baumel (Kenneth Mars), his teacher in Hebrew school, had distributed to support the foundation of a new state in Palestine. Embarrassed and furious, Joe's parents take the boy to the rabbi, who tries to explain to the boy that he has done wrong. Joe answers the rabbi with a line from his radio hero "The Lone Ranger" and addresses the rabbi as his faithful Indian companion. Stunned at his impertinence, the rabbi swats Joe, and then both parents swing away claiming their own right to discipline the boy. Where, Allen asks, does one gain a sense of morality and guilt, from one's parents, or from religion? Danny Rose, it may be remembered, found guilt essential in establishing a moral order, for without guilt, he reasons, one is capable of doing horrible things. (224)

Before Joe is beaten into a blintz, the Rabbi cautions the parents to desist lest they hurt the boy. Allen seems to feel that religion moderates the harmful effects of guilt, here the specific form of Jewish guilt that Allen and dozens of other comedians have habitually associated with the family in countless Jewish-mother jokes. With the creation of Rabbi Baumel, as a sensitive and wise man, Allen steps away from his collection of comic rabbis and in his new perspective sees Judaism as a moral force rather than merely a cultural phenomenon.

Jewish religious practice leaves Allen as puzzled as he is about the religious foundations of morality. During the Yom Kippur fast the family surrounds Uncle Abe, who squelches the children's complaints about hunger and boredom by telling them they're supposed to sit around all day fasting and praying. He doesn't know why, but this is what they do. Next door the Waldbaums, avowed atheists and Communists, play their radio at top volume and use the holiday to catch up on household chores. Furious at their disregard for their Jewish traditions, Uncle Abe says that he would like to burn their house down, but because of the law he is not supposed to strike a match.

In desperation, Abe charges across the back yard to confront the Waldbaums with their Jewish heritage. After an inexplicably long absence, Abe returns thoroughly converted to Communism. Why, he asks, should he fast for his sins, since he hasn't done anything wrong. In this question he echoes Job's complaint with Boris, Danny Rose and Mickey Sachs. The real quarrel, he maintains, is not between man and some superbeing, but between workers and capitalists. He admits that he had joined the Waldbaums for a dinner of pork chops and clams, in violation of Kosher restrictions as well as the holy day fast. At the peak of his wrath, Abe suddenly clutches his chest in pain and collapses. Is it merely indigestion, or is God getting even with him for his loss of faith? Allen is not sure, but at least he is not yet ready to dismiss the notion of a God who must be taken into account. Abe, he seems to say, would have been better off keeping the law, just in case.

Many of these religious notions are restated in purely naturalistic terms. Again, it would be rash to reduce these scenes to a symbolic function, as though Allen were introducing theological parables into his story. These episodes do, however, illustrate Allen's thought patterns as he approaches his key philosophic questions.

Allen looks at the idea of sin, guilt and punishment in a lovely encounter between Joe and his father (Michael Tucker). Joe has used his new chemistry set, the gift from Aunt Bea, to create a purple dye, with which he ruins his mother's new fur-trimmed coat, a gift for their anniversary from her husband. The sin is certainly serious and the avenging father fully intends to use his belt to punish the boy. After a few blows, however, a radio newscaster announces that Polly Phelps, a little girl trapped in a well, has been found dead. Near tears, the father clasps his son tightly to his chest, so grateful for his life that he cannot punish his beloved. Is this an image of God's dealing with his bumptious human family, as though God permits evil to exist unpunished in the world because he loves his creation too much to loose his wrath upon it? Perhaps this is what Allen intends and perhaps not, but aware of the context of Allen's linkage between God and morality, a believer could be excused for reading the scene in this way. At any rate, it is clear that Allen assigns an important role to love in overcoming and forgiving evil.

Forgiveness of actual evil is essential, since God sees everything. The notion of "the eyes of God" first enters the Allen vocabulary through Danny Rose's quoting of Rabbi Perlstein (224). It will become the central theme in CRIMES AND MISDEMEANORS (1989). In RADIO DAYS Allen proposes in naturalistic terms the notion that evil does not escape scrutiny. Joe's cousin Ruthie routinely eavesdrops on the party line, and she hears Mrs. Waldbaum say that she found a purse on the subway and does not intend to return it to the owner. Ruthie broadcasts the news to her family with great relish.

The optical imagery, so crucial in CRIMES AND MISDEMEANORS, begins to appear in comic fashion in RADIO DAYS. Aunt Bea wears terribly strong glasses, much to her embarrassment, and these suggest her ability to see the flaws in her parade of suitors. Joe himself wears the goggles of the Masked Avenger, whose sign-off line at the end of each program is "Beware Evildoers, wherever you are." In the light of the later film, this line may well suggest the notion of an avenger-God, who sees even one's secret evil actions with his all-seeing heavenly goggles. Even so, the Avenger is played by Wallace Shawn, the small, chubby, balding actor who played Jeremiah, Mary Wilke's unlikely lover in MANHATTAN. The actual appearance of the actor makes his dire warning to evildoers comical. His power over the young minds in his audience depends on their imagining his appearance, just as God's fearsome threat to punish evildoers maintains its power only because the human imagination maintains its notion of an all-powerful Creator and Judge. If God exists at all, perhaps, Allen suggests, he is just a fragile actor who has great skill in projecting an illusion of power.

Conversely, the person of faith, according to Allen, may simply need to create an all-powerful God to be able to understand

and endure the existence of evil in the world. This realization, still posed tentatively by Allen, may hold the key to Mickey's question to his father in HANNAH AND HER SISTERS: If a loving God exists, why is there evil and why were there Nazis? (331) A believer can recognize and tolerate the presence of monstrous evil like Nazis only by creating a Masked (therefore hidden) Avenger God, who sees all things, judges and punishes the evildoers, if not in this life then in the hereafter. If that faith vanishes, and there really is no one to see and judge and punish, then human action has no moral value and life has no meaning. If faith is eliminated altogether, then Tina Valente could betray Danny Rose and enjoy her success with Lou without having to ask for forgiveness, and Uncle Abe should enjoy his pork chops on Yom Kippur without the slightest touch of queasiness. This is a step Allen is not quite prepared to make.

Woody Allen's search has taken him a long way through this series of "The Experiments." On one level, he is much more at peace in his world, and much more adept at enjoying its many pleasures. Yet the theological and ethical questions remain, more sharply focused and more pressing than ever. Allen has solved his old problem of anhedonia, but he has not yet exhausted the material for his films or his inquiry. He has not yet unmasked the avenger, and perhaps he never will, yet he continues to experiment and probe, ever in search of certainty yet ever more content with life.

NOTES

1. Nancy Pogel, *Woody Allen* (Boston: Twayne, 1987), p. 175, discusses several points of comparison to "Citizen Kane."
2. Sam B. Girgus, *The Films of Woody Allen* (New York: Cambridge Univ., 1993) p. 88., quoting Eric Lax, *Woody Allen: a Biography* (New York: Knopf, 1991), p. 371.
3. Woody Allen, ZELIG in *Three Films of Woody Allen* (New York: Vintage, 1987), p. 40. Subsequent page numbers in the text refer to this edition of the script.
4. Stephen J. Spignesi, *The Woody Allen Companion* (Kansas City, Mo.: Andrews and McMeel, 1992), p. 184, notes the relationship to MANHATTAN.
5. Maurice Yacowar, *Loser Take All: The Comic Art of Woody Allen* (New York: Continuum, 1991), p. 254, notes: "For her as for Zelig, salvation lies in a committed love."
6. Woody Allen, BROADWAY DANNY ROSE, in *Three Films of Woody Allen*. Subsequent page references in the text refer to this edition of the script.
7. Although Danny may be thinking of an imaginary screenplay for a movie yet to be filmed, MURDER INCORPORATED was in fact a mediocre crime drama directed by Burt Balaban and released in 1960. Actually, Tina's line is somewhat reminiscent of Tony Camonte's (Paul Muni) formula for success in Howard Hawks's "Scarface" (1932): "Do it first. Do it yourself. And keep doing it."
8. Yacowar, p.244, is particularly insightful in his reading of the final dialogue of the comedians. He compares Danny's relationship with Lou to Ike's with Yale in the anthropology classroom in MANHATTAN. Both Lou and Yale vanish from the narrative as irredeemable.
9. Woody Allen, THE PURPLE ROSE OF CAIRO in *Three Films of Woody Allen*, p. 342. Subsequent page references in the text refer to this edition of the script.
10. Yacowar, p. 246, also notes that the fictional characters in the story feel similarly trapped in their penthouse. They want to flee to Cairo or Morocco for a change of pace.
11. Douglas Brode, *The Films of Woody Allen* (New York: Citadel, 1991), p. 248, cites other critics who describe this West Side society as a decaying aristocracy whose world is rapidly disappearing.
12. Woody Allen, *Hannah and Her Sisters* (New York: Vintage, 1987). Subsequent page references in the text refer to this edition of the script.

13. Brode, p. 248, makes the point that in his earlier films, Allen has his characters search for an ideal love. Hannah represents the ideal and both Elliot and Mickey, her first husband, find her suffocating.
14. Yacowar, p. 253, ties this sequence of last-minute script alterations into a wider pattern of mutual betrayal in the various romantic involvements in the film. Standards and Practices betrays Mickey's artistic integrity, and Mickey almost immediately does the same to his writer.
15. The program was, of course, Orson Welles's radio adaptation of H. G. Wells's *The War of the Worlds,* broadcast on Sunday evening, October 30, 1938, as a Halloween prank.

CHAPTER V: THE INTERLUDES

Between the magnificent twin achievements of RADIO DAYS (1987) and CRIMES AND MISDEMEANORS (1989), Allen's artistic output takes a curious turn. He continues his startling pace of one film per year, and each of these films represents a new level of daring experiment. It is as though he were trying to test his own limits as an artist as well as the limits of his medium. Not all experiments are immediately perceived as successful, however, and as a result the films of this period may not have gotten the critical attention they deserve. On the basis of style these films may appear to be least characteristic of the Allen films, but the appearances are deceiving. In them, Allen returns to his usual questions, but he explores them from daringly different perspectives. If the entire body of his work is considered as a whole, according to the principles of auteur criticism, these three "minor" works, SEPTEMBER (1987), ANOTHER WOMAN (1988) and OEDIPUS WRECKS (1989) provide an important bridge from RADIO DAYS to CRIMES AND MISDEMEANORS, both widely considered among his finest works.

Allen does not appear as a character in either SEPTEMBER or in ANOTHER WOMAN. These two films have been understandably criticized for their absolute absence of humor, their staginess and their obvious debt to Ingmar Bergman. They join INTERIORS (1978) as Allen's trilogy of "serious" movies, and not surprisingly they are his least watched and least beloved. Unlike INTERIORS, however, the later films reflect Allen's hard won truce with reality. His characters examine the unrelieved grimness of their surroundings and gather up the resources to keep living. Unlike the heroes of the earlier films, they succeed to a certain limited extent. At the end of their ordeals, the future holds more promise than simply being able to recall simple transient moments of happiness in the past, whether these are real or imagined through art.

While the characters of the films of this Bergman period search for meaning in their very harsh surroundings, the explicit question of God's existence seems to slide into the background somewhat. This appearance may be deceptive. The progression of Allen's ideas on the subject reasonably leads to the suspicion that he continues to use his naturalistic characters to paint a picture of what God would look like, if he did indeed exist. Surprisingly for one whose religious thinking is rooted in the Jewish patriarchal imagery of God, Allen joins a more contemporary theological trend by stressing the feminine attributes of God. His congruence with a recent theological thought is probably accidental, and it certainly provides a less-than-complimentary picture of either God or women.

OEDIPUS WRECKS breaks the somber mood of Bergmanism. It is the third short film in a trilogy collectively entitled NEW YORK STORIES (1989), and to the delight of everyone, it brings the Woody character back to the screen. It is funny, and critics, probably relieved that Allen had not abandoned comedy altogether, loved it.[1] The other two contributions to the film were Francis Ford Coppola's embarrassing LIFE WITHOUT ZOE and Martin Scorsese's masterly LIFE LESSONS. Coppola's effort is a sentimental clinker about a child's life on Central Park South, and Scorsese's a brilliant, penetrating look at an angry, manipulative artist in Greenwich Village. Woody Allen ends the trilogy on the up-beat. He sets his film on his home territory, among his affluent Jewish friends on the Upper West Side. It was a homecoming for both Allen and his audiences.

Critics and audiences may have been so enthusiastic about the return of the old Woody Allen, that many of the serious elements of the film may have been missed during its initial release. In a mere 40 minutes, he addresses his old questions about Jewish alienation in a gentile universe, anhedonia and the search for love, meaning and the ground for moral behavior. At the same time, he returns to his questions about God as an all-seeing Masked Avenger, which he will explore explicitly and brilliantly in his next film CRIMES AND MISDEMEANORS. Like SLEEPER, OEDIPUS WRECKS hides its serious intent under a veneer of comedy. Like the best of Allen's work, it provides wonderful entertainment for those who need a salutary laugh, while at the same time it runs knitting needles into the mind.

SEPTEMBER is the most difficult of all the Allen films to watch. It encompasses a triple love story, like A MIDSUMMER NIGHT'S SEX COMEDY, but without the humor and without the happily romantic outcome. Like the earlier film, its characters are isolated in a country home to sort out their lives. Howard (Denholm Elliott) loves Lane (Mia Farrow). Lane, however, is captivated by Peter (Sam Waterston), but he in turn is strongly attracted to Stephanie (Dianne Wiest), who is married and ultimately chooses to return to her family in Philadelphia. The action is totally confined to the summer house in Vermont. It lacks the expansive outdoor world of A MIDSUMMER NIGHT'S SEX COMEDY or even the alternate world of New York City included in INTERIORS, which also unfolds in a summer house.

Lane serves as the Allen surrogate. In most dramatic terms she has recognized the world as hostile terrain. Her trauma only gradually comes to light. Diane (Elaine Stritch), Lane's mother, left her husband Richard, Lane's father, to live with Nick, a Sicilian gangster, who beat her repeatedly. Nick is shot and the story sold to the press is that Lane killed him.[2] The truth, brutally revealed late in the film, is that Diane in fact murdered him, and Lane, only 14 at the time, did what the lawyers told her, confessed the crime and was exonerated because of her youth. Like the earlier Job figures, Boris and Danny Rose, she is an Allen hero who is burdened by guilt and persecuted by life even though she has done nothing wrong. Her life has come to nothing, and months before the opening action she attempted suicide, a common Allen option for dealing with an unfair world. She has come to the old family estate in Vermont to regain her strength and her composure. The plan will work, but not before she undergoes the torments of the damned.

A Christian may be tempted to see Lane's ordeal as an image of Purgatory, the period of temporary cleansing in the afterlife before one enters eternal bliss. It may even suggest a form of death and resurrection, which Allen approaches gingerly in his frequent use of Easter references and especially in the fight scene in front of the crucifix in THE PURPLE ROSE OF CAIRO. More properly, however, Lane's struggle and triumph may reflect the classic *agon,* or ordeal, that precedes the vindication of the Greek tragic hero. Lane's struggle offers a particularly appropriate example of an Allen dramatic device that legitimately opens itself to a religious interpretation in the context of his developing treatment of these ideas in other films. The theological critic, however astute and well-intentioned, must be cautious in assigning explicitly religious meanings to the text too readily. The sequences of events and the development of the characters, however, can provide an entry into Allen's thought patterns as he continues his investigation of ultimate realities.

The possibility of love is certainly one of his concerns. Love is available to Lane, but like many Allen heroes, she cannot recognize it or respond to it properly. Howard, a recently widowed neighbor, spends time with her during the first winter months after her arrival. They walk and listen to music and enjoy each other's company. He drank heavily after his wife's death, but after Lane's arrival, he seldom touches anything. Her presence has had a saving effect on his life. Considerably older, he teaches French at a local school, but ironically he cannot communicate his feelings to her. Late in the film he explains that he said nothing because he did not want to upset or confuse her. Like Andrew in his pursuit of Ariel in A MIDSUMMER NIGHT'S SEX COMEDY, he has a sad record of missed opportunity. By contrast, Stephanie, first seen practicing her French with Howard, tells the story about spending the summer with a French pianist in Paris. They shared their feelings and love, even though they too could not communicate in language.

Lane might have responded to Howard, but she was distracted by Peter, a handsome young writer recently divorced, who rented the cottage on the grounds for the summer. Howard holds Peter, his successful rival for Lane's affection, and his work in utter contempt, even suggesting that he should return to writing beer commercials, since that pursuit is worthy of his talent. Peter has begun work on his novel "The History Professor." His book is a fictionalized tribute to his father, a professor who is fired and blacklisted during the McCarthy period. Peter admires him because he is a survivor. Denied a livelihood in his chosen profession, he kept the family together by playing poker and betting the horses. Like Lane, Peter's father has taken a mighty blow from life, but his character compels him to fight back.

Peter admires his father's brand of courage, but he has little strength to imitate him. Blaming his recent divorce for his writer's block, he cannot get the story onto paper. He tears up each chapter he writes, as though the past, the history of the professor of history, can be rewritten again and again until he finds it satisfactory for his own present needs. While Peter professes appreciation of his father, the survivor, he whines and laments about his own life. He is not content with what has already been written in the book of life, his own as well as his father's. He makes progress neither on the book, nor his life. Like Lane, he cannot let go of the past.

In his search for love, Peter looks first to Lane. They spent time together and even made love one night by the lake, but when he discovers her fragility, he turns to Stephanie, Lane's best friend. He did not believe, he says, that their relationship meant anything to Lane, and thus he can drop it without looking back. After a series of emotional conversations, he eventually persuades Stephanie to join him in the cottage. Again, he uses his divorce to excuse his irresponsible insensitivity to both women. The next morning, Lane discovers Peter and Stephanie kissing passionately, and the discovery of Stephanie's role in Peter's rejection of her contributes to her decision to try again to take her own life. Stephanie, for her part, regrets her foolishness, tells Peter she must return to her family, which is located in Philadelphia, Allen's capital of the gentile establishment. Ever level-headed, despite momentary lapses of good judgment, Stephanie is the one who discovers the missing sleeping pills and prevents Lane from ending her own life as her response to the humiliating betrayal she has suffered.

After her brief dalliance with Peter, Stephanie resolves to return to a stale and possibly loveless marriage to her husband Ken, with whom she has had several curt conversations on the telephone. She says that he is a radiologist, but she will never let him take an X-ray of her, because if he ever sees what is inside he would never understand and would be hurt. In the very first scene of the film, as Stephanie practices her French with Howard, she admits that she would probably forget it if she ever got back to Paris. As a mature woman, she is trying to learn the language she did not have during her summer romance, but she realistically understands that both Paris and youthful romance will be unlikely possibilities in her future.

Thus at the end of the film, each of the principal romantic characters has sought love in this inhospitable, sterile world in the country house, and each has failed. Howard is simply left alone, sitting on a couch and staring at the floor. Peter has neither his novel nor his loved one. He rolls billiard balls aimlessly around on the table as a reminder of the random, meaningless impact these events of the past few days have had on his life. Stephanie will return to her radiologist husband, and a marriage that is far distant from her Paris romance but one that offers her stability and a meaning in her life. She affirms life once more by thwarting Lane's most recent suicide attempt. Finally, with Stephanie's encouragement Lane will leave both Howard and Peter, sell her house and try to begin a new life alone in an apartment in New York. Stephanie tells her that maybe she will fall in love and maybe she won't. For Lane, the thousands of petty details that a property sale and moving demand will give her a reason to keep going.

Perhaps, Allen suggests in this ambiguous ending, human life is filled with meaningless distractions, like Stephanie's having to buy new shoes for her children as they return to school, but these small activities offer a reason, however tentative, to continue living. Allen has traveled a far distance from his early days of anhedonia and meaninglessness. He admires Lane's ability to feel pain, because suffering makes her human, and in the final scenes, when she faces death and draws back from it with the encouragement of Stephanie, a friend who has betrayed her with Peter, Lane has made her option for life. She does not need art like Mickey Sachs with his Marx Brothers' film or an escapist imagination like Cecilia or happy memories like Alvy Singer to give her a reason to live. The ordinary events of a human life, like moving and starting a new business, provide enough to keep Lane going simply because they are human acts and she is alive to perform them.

The catalyst for Lane's rite of purification is her mother Diane, a husky-voiced dynamo of a woman, whose vigor and strength stands in harsh contrast to her mousy, bespectacled daughter, whom she says dresses with as much style as a newly arrived refugee from Poland. Lane was apparently content trying to put her own life together, when Diane arrives for a prolonged visit along with her current husband Lloyd (Jack Warden), a nuclear physicist. Lane is furious. In an overly obvious symbolic reference, Lane complains that her mother picks flowers from the garden but neglects to put them in water. As a result, they soon wither and die. Allen forces the association between Lane and the flowers, whose lives are disrupted unto death. Diane interferes with their lives and then leaves them to die alone.

Diane is a strong character in her own right, the most terrifying mother figure in Allen's work. She is domineering, and self-centered like Eve in INTERIORS; energetic and intrusive, like Tess in RADIO DAYS; more violently destructive than a drunken Norma in HANNAH AND HER SISTERS. Diane, however, becomes doubly fascinating as an image of God, which Allen seems to suggest. As mother, she is the creator of life for Lane, but because of her self-centered life, she put her creation in impossible circumstances by leaving Lane's father, murdering her step-father and shifting the blame to Lane herself. As whim and her own happiness dictated, she left Lane to her own devices, even though the fragile daughter went through an apparent emotional collapse and suicide attempt. When Lane seems ready to take charge of her life again, Diane suddenly reappears, putting everything into chaos. She answers to no one, never explains her motivation or justifies her actions. She simply does what she does because she is Diane. As played by Elaine Stritch, Diane is the most powerful figure in the film. The other characters may hate her, but they have to admire her.

Although Allen is not using Diane as an obvious God symbol, he does use her to show the devastating effects of capricious action, exercised by one with little concern over the well-being of her children. She is an image of the God of Job, used so often in Allen's films. Because of her, others suffer without reason, and she remains happily unconcerned about their feelings. She feels no need to explain her action, other than admitting a certain lack of skill in practical matters, even though her ineptitude devastates those around her. She will be judged only on her own terms.

Although not Lane's rival for Peter in the usual sense of the romantic triangle, Diane is a distraction. Before Diane's arrival, Lane kept her hope alive that Peter would eventually respond to her. Peter is fascinated by this older woman; he entertains her and listens to her stories to such an extent that he no longer has much time for Lane. Peter and Lane plan to go to a Kurosawa movie in town, but Diane tells them to change their plans because without telling anyone she has invited the Richmonds over for a drink. Peter is distracted from his book about his flesh-and-blood father and plays with the idea of doing a biography of Diane, whose adventures are an endless source of anecdotes. He finds her a survivor, too. He is especially interested in retelling the story of the shooting, because that is what people want to read about. Diane's insistent intrusion into his life has turned him away from his worldly concerns to a world of illusion and half-truths. Lane's horror at reliving her past through his writing concerns neither Peter nor Diane. For some, believers and those who hover on the edges of belief, God's presence distracts from this world and pointlessly stirs up memories of guilt that may or may not be real.

By far the most painful scene Allen has ever filmed occurs moments after Lane has discovered Stephanie and Peter in each other's arms. She has made plans to sell the house to pay the debts she incurred during her illness. A family of potential buyers natters through the house, asking about mosquitoes and black flies. They cannot go upstairs because Diane is still in bed. The real estate agent takes them outside, and as Lane sits in the living room, stunned by what she has seen, Diane clumps down the stairs, jabbering about the Las Vegas stories she can tell Peter. Without changing the tone of tempo of her chatter, she announces that she and Lloyd have decided to stay in the house indefinitely, making it their permanent home.

Distraught to begin with, Lane becomes hysterical. All her plans for the future are shattered because of Diane's thoughtless, capricious decision to take possession of the house Lane believes belongs to her. When Lane reminds Diane that she had given her the house years ago, Diane merely smirks and wonders if she was drunk at the time. She cannot see, or refuses to see, the reason for Lane's reaction, or if she does see, it concerns her not in the slightest. Lane blurts out the truth about the murder, which was not her fault but Diane's, and Diane accuses her daughter of wasting her life for spite. At this moment, the buyers return, but Diane throws them out abusively. Moments later, seemingly without motivation, Diane changes her mind again and tells Lane to keep the house, if it means so much to her. By this time, of course, the potential buyers are gone. If Diane had taken a moment to think or feel compassion for her frail daughter, that dreadful argument need never have taken place.

The next morning, Lloyd piles luggage in the doorway, and he and Diane prepare to move out of Lane's life as thoughtlessly as they once moved in. As they gather around the mountain of suitcases, Diane makes the off-hand comment that life is too short to dwell on tragedies. She cannot accept the fact that she is the source of the tragedy in other people's lives. As a peace offering, she passes out trinkets, a brooch to Lane and a bracelet to Stephanie, tiny gifts compared to her immense resources piled in suitcases beside them. She asks for her make-up case, because, as she jokingly reminds them, it contains her diaphragm, which she should donate to the antique fair. Once capable of giving or withholding life, Diane now makes a joke of the power she once wielded. Diane, like God, is a relic of forgotten strength. She is best banished from the arena of human concerns so that the earthly enterprise can go on its own way without her. When she leaves the scene, everyone feels relief, not regret. In keeping with the underlying metaphor, God has become a troublesome nuisance, best banished from the human arena and forgotten so that life can go on.

Lloyd and Diane seem an unlikely couple, as indeed they are if SEPTEMBER were simply a romantic melodrama. Lloyd, in fact, embodies one possible human strategy for dealing with Diane. During their evening together while the summer guests wait for the Richmonds, who never appear, a violent thunderstorm causes a power outage. They are plunged into darkness, where they must look inward to examine their own lives and their relationships with one another during this dark night of their collective soul.

As the weather clears, Lloyd plays pool by candlelight with Peter, who asks if Lloyd ever worked on the hydrogen bomb. Lloyd argues that his work is far more terrible than destroying the world. When Peter asks what that could possibly be Lloyd explains that his work establishes the random character of the universe. It makes no difference if the world is blown up or not, since it came out of nothing and will eventually disappear into nothingness. Space and time are but momentary accidents.

Peter remains a man of the arts, even though he is not very successful at his trade. He points to the clearing sky, and asks how Lloyd reacts to all the beautiful stars he sees. Lloyd responds that he finds them just as lovely as Peter does. He admits that their presence suggests some truth (possibly a God) that remains just out of reach. He is grateful for his professional expertise that enables him to withdraw from these fanciful reflections and see the universe as it really is: random, without morality, and unspeakably violent. When Peter, humorless as ever, says they should discontinue this conversation because he has to sleep alone that night, Lloyd tells him that he clings to Diane so that he will not have to dream of physics.

Lloyd is Allen's consummate intellectual. As a physicist he understands the material nature of the universe, but as a human being he clings to something irrational, like Diane or God, to give him a moment of warmth and solace in his very cold world. He maintains his relationship to a difficult, aging woman, as people cling to outmoded concepts of God, simply because they must. Diane is honest with him when as they are dressing she reminds him of her ulcers and gall bladder problem. She refers to herself as a piece of machinery that is gradually wearing out. She allows Lloyd to pick her dress. She will have whatever appearance he wants, since humans often create a God to match their current tastes and expectations. Later, as she looks into the mirror of her dressing table, she says she will have to change her make-up, complaining that her appearance betrays her age, even though she still feels like a young woman. It is unfair, she thinks. Doubly unfair is the discovery that personal resources that once supported her are gone and when she studies her face in a mirror she realizes that what is missing is her future. Someday, she believes, even the relic-God will pass away. As they prepare for bed, Diane gives Lloyd a back rub, the moment of comfort he needs in his random, haphazard universe of unimaginable violence.

While Lloyd and Peter discuss the meaninglessness of the universe, Diane sits at her old ouija board, recalling her dead husband. Slightly drunk, she pushes the marker to suit her whim, and she contacts whoever she wants. No one is there to observe her or judge her. She asks Richard to contact Lane with a message of forgiveness, since she cannot do it herself. Forgiveness is a human responsibility. Diane refers to herself as one tough lady, who can forget past wrongs. Sadly, fragile humans like Lane are not that fortunate.

In the final scene, Stephanie and Lane discuss the details of selling the house, and Stephanie encourages her: "It's going to be okay." With or without a God, human activity will be enough to sustain them. The camera leaves the two women together at the kitchen table, and in a long travelling shot wanders through the well ordered house. Prominent are pictures of Diane in her younger days and the liquor bottles that are associated with her irrational behavior. The house encompasses all the human activity of these six vulnerable mortals. It is the only constant, like the universe itself. These human characters have tarried within its walls and soon will move on, only to be replaced with new residents, new pictures on the walls, new conflicts and new resolutions. The human drama continues as long as the universe perdures.

ANOTHER WOMAN (1988) presents another female character as the Allen surrogate. The questions Allen looks at are quite different, however. In SEPTEMBER Lane is nearly destroyed by the unfeeling actions of a capricious God, her mother, explodes in a torrent of emotion and finally reaches a plateau of peace with her own vulnerable humanity. Marion Post (Gena Rowlands) embodies another side of Allen's character. Like Allen at the time of the film's production, she has just passed her 50th birthday, and she wonders about the person she has become. What she discovers is a cold, methodical person who values academic productivity over humanity, and to achieve this dubious status as an intellectual she has systematically repressed anything that compromises her life of the mind. Looking once more at a theme he touched upon in Howard, the aging teacher in SEPTEMBER, Allen allows her to discover in her life a pattern of missed opportunities for happiness.

The title of the film is brilliantly ambiguous. Years earlier, Marion was "the other woman" because of her adultery with her present husband, and as the story continues, her safe little world will collapse when she discovers that there is again "another woman" in his life. Marion comes to terms with her life through her chance relationship with her younger, pregnant alter-ego, another woman who reveals what Marion's life might have been. Finally, and most tellingly of all, the title refers to the other flesh-and-blood woman she discovers under her layers of self-deception and convention.

While Lane in SEPTEMBER is a victim of others, Marion has built her own life deliberately. In her opening monologue, as she prepares to leave for her office, she says that by all accounts as she reaches her fiftieth birthday she has achieved a reasonable level of fulfillment both professionally and personally. She directs undergraduate studies at a fine women's college, but has taken a year's leave of absence to write another book on German philosophy. With her hair set in a tight bun, her gray, textured clothing and her shoes stylish but sensible for one who delivers her lectures standing several hours each week, Marion is Eve in INTERIORS, but without the fragility. She warns her audience that she has no intention of probing her inner life. She feels that her life is working well enough, and if this is the case, why bother to probe its depths. She is, she avers, not afraid of this kind of investigation, but she simply does not see the point of it. Throughout the film Allen asks whether despite its obvious success, her life (or his) is really working all that well after all.

Before the titles begin to appear on the screen, Marion leaves her apartment and closes the door, glass with iron security bars over it, as though she were leaving a jail cell. She has sublet another cell, a small apartment in Greenwich Village, to assure perfect privacy for her work. She believes that in beginning a new book she must close herself off from all possible distractions. This line of reasoning is actually the story of her life. In this she echoes Peter in SEPTEMBER, who likewise believed he could shut himself off from the real life of real men and women to work. Both discover that the life of the heart will not be denied.

Life seeps in through a heating duct for Marion. She leaves her comfortable apartment uptown because construction noises in the neighborhood distract her, but soon other uninvited noises will enable her to reconstruct her own life.[3] In the adjacent apartment, a psychiatrist listens to the story of his patients, and the voices slip through the ductwork into Marion's study. As she begins to work on her study of German Idealism, she hears voices, first of a young man confused about his sexual identity, and later in the day of a young woman complaining that life is full of deceptions. The woman explains that she wakes up sweating and asks her husband to hold her. As part of her therapy, she explains that her dream was a revelation, as though a curtain had parted and she could see herself, but she was afraid of what she saw. Her vision of self-discovery recalls Renata's looking through the window in INTERIORS or Tina's staring into the mirror in BROADWAY DANNY ROSE. Like many an Allen character, this as yet unseen woman thinks of suicide as a way to deal with her life. Marion is both repelled and fascinated by her experience of eavesdropping. The patients in the psychiatrist's office next to her apartment reveal a kind of uncertainty about themselves that she has never known. More to shut out the distraction than because of ethical scruple, she puts sofa cushions over the vent to block out the sound, but eventually she goes back to listen again.

Through a series of flashbacks, conversations and dreams, Marion reviews her life, not as the catalogue of superficial, professional details she had listed in the opening monologue, but as a series of events that might have altered her life, if only she had let them. Marion has had three men in her life. Sam (Philip Bosco), her first husband, was her teacher, and as she begins her professional academic career, he is her guide and inspiration. They encourage each other in their work. In a tender dream, she recalls giving Sam an ivory theatrical mask, which he holds to his face as they kiss. What masks stood between them, she might have wondered. By identifying it as a mask from the French version of "La Giaconda," she reveals that she is more interested in information than the sentiment behind the gift. In a dream, she watches a play in which she is a central character, and Sam tells her that a life of sharing information and ideas was suffocating for him.

As the dream-play continues Marion realizes her part in Sam's suffocation. Fifteen years after their divorce, Sam dies alone in a hotel room, due to a mixture of drugs and alcohol. She will not admit that it was suicide. The cause of death on the coroner's report was "suffocation." During their marriage, Marion had conceived and aborted, but did not tell Sam until after it was over. Her ostensible reason is that having a child at this time would interfere with her career just as it is beginning. Later, another character says that Marion was afraid of the feelings she might have had for her baby.

Getting along in years, Sam is crushed at the lost opportunity for having a child, and he is furious with her secretiveness, which he sees as a lack of trust. His reaction is human, but hers is philosophical. She reminds him of his teaching about the pointlessness of the universe, and she argues that it is inconsistent to want to bring a child into existence. Sam is like Lloyd in SEPTEMBER. He can compartmentalize his life, confident in the validity of his intellectual convictions, yet willing to live a human life of instinct and passion. He loves and wants children because he is a man. Marion accepts no such distinction. The life of the intellect is her only life. Throughout his film-making career, Allen has gradually accepted the fact that the intellectual answers he had been craving are unattainable. As Mickey Sachs discovered in HANNAH AND HER SISTERS, a Marx Brothers movie can be far more important in life than proof about a purpose in the universe. Marion is not yet able to understand this.

After her separation from Sam, Marion marries Ken (Ian Holm), a mirror image of herself, even down to his perfectly styled hair and preference for gray, tasteful but unexpressive clothing. He is, as Marion explains, a cardiologist who looked into her heart, liked what he saw and married her. (Stephanie in SEPTEMBER was sure that her husband, a radiologist, would be afraid of what he might find inside her.) In flashback, Marion recalls their engagement party, when Kathy (Betty Buckley), Ken's first wife, storms in and denounces Ken for committing adultery with Marion at a Holiday Inn, while she was in the hospital having her ovaries removed. Neither Ken nor Marion seemed deterred by the circumstance at the time. Ken responds coldly that he acknowledges her condemnation, as though that put an end to the matter. In his ice-encrusted world it does.

Married to Sam, Marion, ever the eager young scholar, could not accept a world of values outside her intellectual life. Because of her career, it was not logical to have a child, therefore other considerations, like Sam's feelings, meant nothing to her. During her adultery with Ken, however, she opts for an irrational act of passion, despite her disdain for anything outside her intellectual life. During a meal in a restaurant with friends, a strange woman interrupts their conversation. She introduces herself as one of Marion's former students whose life was changed by a brilliant lecture on "Ethics and Moral Responsibility." Marion's insight into moral living did not deter her affair with Ken, and Kathy's feelings of outrage at the adultery were as irrelevant as Sam's. In both cases, her sphere of morality is purely cerebral, and this world of concepts is clearly more important to her than the feelings of others. Her actions, either the secret abortion of Sam's child or the casual adultery with Ken when his wife is undergoing surgery, have little relationship to her ideas. Paradoxically, in both cases she acts on self-centered impulse. Marion is a moral solipsist.

Her past returns to haunt her when she discovers that Ken is now having an affair with her best friend Lydia (Blythe Danner). At a party Lydia's husband Mark (Bruce Jay Friedman) had publicly embarrassed her by telling a story about their being interrupted as they made love on the living room floor. Ken reacts stiffly and with some uneasiness to the story, but later in the conversation returns to it, embarrassing Lydia once more. Clearly, Lydia suggests a level of spontaneity and adventure for him that Marion cannot provide. Lydia's feelings, of course, mean nothing to him. Some time later Marion by chance sees Lydia and Ken together in a restaurant and accuses Ken of adultery, recalling their previous affair when he was still married to Kathy. He claims the two cases are completely different, but then adds the words he coldly spoke to his first wife, accepting her condemnation.

Allen's understanding of moral living in a universe that may or may not be meaningless has developed a healthy social dimension. His own ideas on "Ethics and Moral Responsibility," to use the title of Marion's brilliant lecture, now radiate outward in a clearly horizontal direction. He does not need a Masked Avenger in the sky, as in RADIO DAYS, to reward or punish human deeds. It is possible, without the help of German Idealism, to look at the consequences of one's actions to others and make a judgment about their moral value. Ken blithely accepts condemnation, but it means nothing to him. He is beyond redemption and simply vanishes from the narrative. Marion begins to see that people can cause pain to one another by their insensitivity and selfishness. Scholar that she is, she will learn from her past, as Diane in SEPTEMBER could not.

The final man in Marion's life is Larry Lewis (Gene Hackman) a writer who aspires to be a novelist. Unlike Peter in SEPTEMBER he shows promise of success as an artist, and he is honest in his pursuit of Marion. In flashback, at the party celebrating her engagement to Ken, moments before Kathy's dramatic entrance, Larry follows Marion to the kitchen, kisses her and asks him to abandon plans to marry Ken to live with him. Her hair is done in a loose pony tail, far less severe than the Marion of her 50's. She reacts warmly, but only for a moment. She has made her commitment, and rejects this passionate, and thus irrational, complication in her life.

After Kathy's unwelcome intrusion into the party and her expression of outrage, Marion and Larry return to the kitchen, and Larry repeats his petition, calling Ken a prig. When she claims that she and Ken enjoy each other and read books together, Larry tells her that it is all merely intellectual. She accuses him of trying to undermine Ken, something Ken would never do to him, but Larry asks if Ken would have the courage to undermine a rival if he loved a woman passionately, with the assumption that Ken is incapable of loving anyone or anything passionately. She dismisses the remark, saying that he is drunk, but, Larry retorts with the threatening but true observation that she is becoming frightened by the conversation. He has touched a level of feeling in her that defies her rational categories. Larry would do anything, even betray a friend, for the woman he loves. She cannot admit this kind of passion into her life.

The scene may appear troubling since Allen seems to be saying that passion excuses betrayal. His negative treatment of Lou Canova in BROADWAY DANNY ROSE and Stephanie and Peter in SEPTEMBER, however, puts a serious challenge to this conclusion. Allen is not gentle with adulterers. More to the point here, however, is Allen's insistence that love holds a priority over friendship. Love between a man and a woman includes passion, and it is open to the possibility of new life. At this point Allen is trying to weigh the value of passion in a human life. At 50, Marion is discovering how much she has missed because she never loved deeply. She is alone, while Larry, a man of passion, eventually marries, moves to Santa Fe, has a daughter and completes his novel, something Peter could never do.

Near the end of the film, Marion picks up Larry's novel and looks for the character Helenka, whom Larry says he modeled after her. As she reads, she imagines the action and realizes how close the fictional story touches her own life. Purely by chance, the Helenka of the novel (Rowlands), the younger Marion with her hair once again done in a loose pony tail, meets the Larry surrogate (Hackman). They have a drink, walk in Central Park where she talks about her coming marriage to his best friend, as though she were trying to convince herself that she had made the right choice. They are caught in a downpour, and as they huddle for shelter under an overpass, he kisses her and she responds with delight, but then, struggling to regain control of her feelings, she raises the wall between them once more. Larry concludes his story with the comment that from that moment he knew Helenka was capable of great passion, if only she would allow herself.

Marion's own philosophical writing has been going well. She closes Larry's novel and wonders if memories are a legacy one possesses or a record of things lost. She feels a mixture of wistfulness and hope, she says. The film ends with her subtle mysterious smile, as though finally she understands what has been missing from her life, and she realizes that as long as she has life she has the capability of finding love.

Other characters help her along this path of discovery. Her father (John Houseman) is a retired professor of history, like Peter's father in SEPTEMBER, who has achieved some distinction in his field and sits on the board of the Smithsonian Institution. When Marion and her stepdaughter Laura (Martha Plimpton) visit him in his Connecticut home, he wants to give them all his dead wife's possessions. He does not want to be reminded of her, saying that even a historian should give up the past. Marion wants him to move to the City, but he does not want his routine interrupted. Laura asks if he thinks he can fall in love again, and he responds that he hopes by his age he has been able to establish an immunity to such things. When Marion tells him that his son Paul is divorcing his wife, the old man snorts that Paul's activities are of no interest to him whatever. He feels Paul has been a failure in life because he never learned to apply himself. Only later, as she reflects on this scene through a dream that is set in the psychiatrist's office with her father as an imaginary patient, will Marion realize that her father is the image of what she will become. It is a chilling realization that she is destined to become as dead and loveless as her father.

As they look through the family photographs, Marion remembers the past. She once painted, but did not continue. She recalls her dear friend Claire, now an actress, who enjoyed walking in the garden by herself. Painfully, she remembers her brother Paul, who was an unsuccessful student and was forced to begin work in a paper-box factory so that Marion, a brilliant scholar in her father's estimation, could begin her studies at Bryn Mawr. In this recollection, she remembers that her father had taken the year off himself to continue his own private studies on the Continental Congress. When Paul learns that his father has determined his future in commerce, he stands alone in the summer house banging his head against a cupboard door, which significantly remains closed to him.

Most evocative of all the memorabilia Marion unearths is a copy of Rilke's poems. With her mother she delighted in the poetry, but while her mother's tear stains remain on the page, Marion's interests turned from poetry to philosophy. Once again she rejected the arts in favor of the colder, more rational field of philosophy, especially German Idealism. As she handles the volume, she remembers at age 15 doing a paper on "The Panther," who looked out from his cage and saw death.[4] Caged and past her 50th birthday, she is becoming ever more conscious of her own approaching death. Reading the volume alone in her home later that night she dwells on the lines from "The Archaic Torso of Apollo": "For here there is no place/ that does not see you. You must change your life."[5] Changing her life is the project Marion has begun, although she does not yet realize it. Rilke's and Allen's all-present eyes of God are watching her progress.

Marion has grown apart from her brother over the years. One morning she has made an appointment to meet Paul's wife Lynn (Frances Conroy), but Lynn is caught in traffic and arrives late. Marion refuses to enter a conversation with her because she must keep to her writing schedule, which the traffic has disrupted and Lynn must somehow be responsible for. Lynn says that she and Paul are separating, and she needs a loan, but Marion cannot discuss the matter at present; she must get to her books and typewriter. Nearing desperation as Marion turns away, Lynn tells her that Paul admires her but hates her, an assertion that Marion rejects. Ending the conversation, Marion says that she refuses to allow herself to become involved in this type of conversation.

After another eavesdropping session at the vent in her office sets loose more memories, Marion walks around the city and visits her brother Paul (Harris Yulin) at his modest office. They talk about their drifting apart over the years. Yes, she learns, Lynn was right. Paul has hated her. He recalls verbatim a critique Marion had given of something he had written, The youthful critic found the work of her brother overblown. His dreams, she felt, were interesting only to him and had no meaningful relationship to objective reality. His overly emotional reflections were little more than an embarrassment. Looking back over the years, Marion cannot believe she spoke so cruelly to her brother, but it is one more instance of her eventually realizing that what she considers objectivity is in fact hurtful and has isolated her from others. Many of Allen's alienated, lonely characters find themselves unfairly plunged into a hostile universe that they must learn to endure. Marion's universe is one that she has fashioned for herself. By this point Allen would take exception to Sartre: Hell is not the other people; it is the unloving self.

Her step-daughter Laura wisely analyzes Marion's strained relationship to her brother as a paradigm for her relationships to everyone else. When Marion accidentally discovers Laura and her boyfriend making love in the country home, she discreetly turns away. Laura tells her embarrassed partner that Marion is great, but she is judgmental. Laura is aware that Marion puts herself in a superior position and evaluates other people, and as an example, she cites Marion's comments about her brother. If she feels free enough to make harsh judgments about him, she will certainly treat her the same way. When Marion informs Laura about her forthcoming divorce from Ken, Laura remarks that she is not really surprised because she viewed their relationship as wrong because it was too comfortable.

Near the end of the film, Marion learns that Lynn and Paul have changed their plans to separate. Paul explains with some puzzlement that he and Lynn fight all the time but will remain together. He notes the irony that Ken and Marion have a perfect marriage and never fight, but they are getting the divorce. Marion and Paul agree that they should renew their childhood closeness to each other. As Allen continues his truce with the real world, he proposes that an imperfect but authentic marriage is more lasting and offers more happiness than a perfect but artificial one in which passion has no place.

Throughout his film making career, Allen has thus gradually refined his search for love through three stages. At first he sought the perfect, but unattainable love for his own self-actualization. Often the criterion for this kind of love was sexual gratification. From SLEEPER (1973) on, he seems to grow in the awareness that love is mutual. It involves giving as well as having. In addition, he discovers that an imperfect love can offer the happiness he long sought in his pursuit of an ideal. Finally, beginning with HANNAH AND HER SISTERS he begins to question whether a perfect partner may not only fail to bring happiness but may even be a source of suffocation. Hannah is certainly a more loving person than Marion, but she is, in her own way, just as "perfect," and in both cases the "perfection" and seeming absence of personal needs and even personal fragility drives people away from them.

Two women also help Marion discover the truth about herself. After many years without contact, Marion meets Claire (Sandy Dennis), her childhood friend, who is now an actress. Having a drink with her and her husband Jack (Jacques Levy), Marion monopolizes Jack's attention until Claire explodes in a jealous rage.

Jack is shocked. He and Marion have a great deal in common, like their interest in the German playwright, Berthold Brecht. He finds Marion's conversation enjoyable, he admits, but he sees no reason for Claire's outburst. Claire accuses her of flirting subtly with Jack, as she did several years ago with David, a man Claire once loved but who is otherwise unidentified in the script. Marion dismisses the allegation, but Claire insists, noting that Marion must assert her superiority, even if the men in question mean nothing to her. Marion, she claims, has caused her to doubt her own life, and their drifting apart during the years is deliberate on her part. Marion is speechless, but she has a great deal to think about.

In a dream, Claire takes Marion's part in a play, and with the objectivity of staged dialogue with Ken, Marion can see that the love has gone out of their marriage. When she asks him about this, Ken says he tries not to notice. Her guilt rises to the surface when he asks her not to call out for Larry in her sleep. Larry appears and tells her about his novel, his wife and daughter, and tells her about Helenka, the character in his novel that he based on Marion. In the final scene in the dream, she confronts the realization that Sam, her first husband, may have taken his own life because of her. The pattern is consistent: She discovers more truth about herself in novels, plays and poetry than from people. Art bears more meaning for her than life, and more than the German Idealism she has immersed herself in for so many years.

The other woman who leads Marion to her personal epiphany is Hope (Mia Farrow), the young woman Marion overhears in the psychiatrist's office. Hope is hugely pregnant, and her size is exaggerated by the layers of sweaters and shawls she wears. A younger woman, she is the image of what Marion might have been. Marion is intrigued by the fears and angers Hope reveals to her analyst. After several tentative attempts to meet her, Marion finally stumbles upon her crying in an antique shop, where Marion had hoped to find an anniversary gift for Ken. Hope has been frightened and moved to tears by a reproduction of "Hope," a manifestly pregnant nude by the Austrian stylist Gustav Klimt (1862–1918). Marion tries to comfort her by talking about their mutual interest in painting, which they both gave up years earlier. They have lunch together, and Marion drinks most of the bottle of wine and does most of the talking. She confides to Hope that she did not mind turning 30 or 40, but 50 has been traumatic because one sees the present and realizes that it is impossible to go back to the past. Finally, Marion admits that it would have been nice to have a child. With that remark, Marion recalls in flashback her argument with Sam about the abortion.

By way of parentheses, it is revealing to reflect on Marion's (and Allen's) fascination with German culture. Marion is a specialist in German philosophy. She was once moved by Rilke's poetry, and she is knowledgeable about Brecht's "Mother Courage," even to the point of criticizing the translation of the New York version. With Hope, she discusses the paintings of the Austrian Klimt and the school of painting he belonged to in Vienna, a forerunner of German Expressionism.[6] In one as broadly educated as Marion, one might expect to find references to other cultures as well. It may be that Allen's obsession with Nazis and the Holocaust leads him to rely on stereotypes of German culture to show the destructive effects of extreme orderliness and reason on human life. Although scarcely suggesting that Marion is in any sense a Nazi, Allen may want to raise the suspicion that Marion's "Germanness" allows her to live in her own moral vacuum.

In any event, listening at the vent in her office some hours later, Marion hears Hope's reflections on their luncheon conversation. Hope is terrified at the prospect of turning out like Marion, who, she believes, had her abortion not because of her career but because she feared the feelings she might have for her child. As her therapy session unfolds, Hope continues the story of their meeting by including Marion's chance discovery of Ken and Lydia together in another section of the dining room. Marion weeps as she hears the story of her profound humiliation at the realization of her husband's infidelity.

A few days before her luncheon with Hope, as Marion dozes in her office and begins a tangled network of dreams and memories, she imagines herself in the psychiatrist's office, just as Hope finishes a session. Hope is upset about the world's cruelty, but her analyst tells her to forget the world and get her own life in order. The doctor tells Marion that he must hurry with his treatment, because he must stop Hope from killing herself. The process has already begun. He adds that Hope began the process of suicide when she was a young woman. This process, however, remains undetected because Hope cannot do anything dramatic. It is more her style to be slow and methodical. In this analysis, Marion sees the image of her own life as one who has been spiritually killing herself, methodically and undramatically.

Marion's confident affirmation of interior peace and her smile in the final scene are reminiscent of Prof. Isak Borg's peaceful vision at the end of Ingmar Bergman's WILD STRAWBERRIES (1957), after which Allen clearly modeled ANOTHER WOMAN.[7] Both professors reach a milestone in their careers, review their lives and discover that the loneliness they find in their later years is really the result of their own coldness. The revelations are painful, but awareness of the presence of love in the world, and the conviction that this love is still available to them in their remaining years, naturally brings not regret but hope. Allen seems not only to have reached a truce with the universe, but to have acknowledged his past exaggeration of its hostility. One who finds the world an unloving place may in fact simply be an unloving person.

OEDIPUS WRECKS (1989) looks back to many of the earlier Allen themes and resurrects the comic Woody character. This much is obvious. Less obvious is the film's relationship to SEPTEMBER. Once the Bergman period had passed and Allen was able to turn away from his tormented gentiles, he used this cinematic short story to offer a delightful Jewish reinterpretation of SEPTEMBER, with its theme of the Mother as God, the celestial Masked Avenger of RADIO DAYS. The traditional Jewish mother jokes serve his purposes beautifully in this daring conceit.

Sheldon Mills (Woody Allen) has changed his name from Millstein, a fact that his mother eagerly points out to him or anyone else within earshot. Even his psychiatrist (Martin Chatinover) slips one day and calls him Mr. Millstein. Sheldon cannot escape his Jewishness, even though he has become a partner in a prestigious gentile law firm and plans to marry Lisa (Mia Farrow), a *shiksa* who is divorced, has a home in Vermont, like Lane in SEPTEMBER, and three children. His mother says that with a blond wife and three children he should be an astronaut. According to all the usual external norms, Sheldon has assimilated perfectly into mainstream society, and this would be true if only he could get past the problem of his mother.

Sadie Millstein (Mae Questel, once the voice of Betty Boop in the cartoon series), his mother, will not let him go. In the opening sequence, Sheldon tells his psychiatrist about a dream in which his mother is dead. In full livery, he is driving the hearse, when Sadie starts back-seat driving from inside the casket. When Sheldon the chauffeur expresses some impatience with her complaints about his driving, she tells him that if he's going to be nasty, she won't go. Sheldon offers the dream as an example of his feelings about her, but the psychiatrist tells him that he must stop reacting like a child and have a sense of humor about her foibles. Sheldon wishes she would simply disappear.

If Sadie can be understood as representing a God-image, and the possibility becomes quite plausible in the context of Allen's on-going preoccupations and especially of his somber reflections on the topic in SEPTEMBER, then Allen has begun to move away from his notions of a Creator as a philosophic construct needed to supply meaning and moral structure for human activity. Allen is now thinking of the God of his childhood, the God of Abraham, Isaac and Jacob. This God/Mother/Creator/Masked Avenger will not let Sheldon assimilate.[8] Even though Sheldon might want to believe that God is dead, as did Nietzsche, the fashionable theologians of the 1960's and 1970's and most citizens of modern secularized society, God's voice continues to haunt him. Precisely, this Mother/God wants to direct his life from beyond her death, even condemning his driving, his marriage to a *shiksa* and just about any other direction of his life. She scorns his pretensions as making him like a Wasp astronaut, as though he could soar into heaven through human technology alone. By continuing to try to control his life, Sadie keeps him in an infantile state, a criticism of God directed toward religious traditions by nonbelievers and uneasy adherents alike.

Sadie's custodial care over morality extends beyond her Jewish family. When she and Sheldon's stone deaf Aunt Ceil (Jesse Keosian) arrive unannounced at his office, they call him from an important meeting. When Mr. Bates (Ira Wheeler), the senior partner, comes out to bring Sheldon back inside, in a voice loud enough for Aunt Ceil, Sadie refers to Mr. Bates as the one who keeps a mistress. Sadie's outspoken traditional Jewish morality embarrasses Sheldon in front of his associates.

Sheldon tries to have his mother accommodate to Lisa. In their first supper together, Sadie excludes him from the conversation and tries to regulate his eating much as God does with his Kosher dietetic laws. She reminds him of his inherited baldness. She drags out the photo-album, and recalls Sheldon's childhood history, even to his bed-wetting. The album becomes a modern version of the historical books of the Bible, where even the most terrible tribal records of self-incrimination are preserved for everyone, even gentiles, to study.

Lisa tries bravely to persuade Sadie to change her mind about the engagement, not realizing that the God of the Judaeo-Christian tradition is immutable. They meet for lunch on Sunday, the Christian holy day, at the Tavern on the Green in Central Park. Sadie kvetches relentlessly about eating outside on the terrace, and when they take the children to a magic show, she announces in a stage whisper that she doesn't care for magicians either. In scenes reminiscent of the failed entertainers in BROADWAY DANNY ROSE, the magician calls Sadie up to participate in the show and asks her age, as Danny the aspiring comic had once done during his Catskill resort performance for senior citizens. Sadie tells everyone that Sheldon has changed his name. With the help of an assistant, Sadie climbs into the box, which the magician seals and pierces with several swords as Sheldon smiles approvingly. When the magician opens the box, he discovers that the trick has misfired, and Sadie has mysteriously vanished. The magician cannot recall her, any more than the inept hypnotist in BROADWAY DANNY ROSE could revive his own elderly volunteer from the audience. Sheldon is furious, for a while.

At first Sheldon worries about his mother, but gradually he finds renewed energy. A burden has been lifted from his shoulders. His love-making with Lisa is sensational. He enjoys the freedom, and tells his private detective, Mr. Flynn (Paul Herman), to forget about the search. He first offers a plausible explanation of her disappearance and then lies by claiming that she has returned. Sheldon likes the freedom of his life without his mother. In the process of assimilation into secularist culture, Sheldon is happily rid of his God, and does not want anyone, detective or theologian, to bring her back.

Sadie, however, will not stay away for long. As Sheldon buys his lunch from a Jewish delicatessen owner, he hears a hubbub on the street and when he goes outside he sees his mother's head and shoulders floating over the West Side like a Macy's float. Complete with glasses, she is the Masked Avenger in goggles looking down on human life, telling her son not to get married and gathering support from perfect strangers on the street. God has returned to his life to try to dictate his actions, and following the usual tactic of the Divinity, reproach and guilt take precedence over suggestion and encouragement. Simple, unthinking people, of course, are willing to agree with the Mother/God and add social pressure to curtail his freedom. Sheldon's response is to contemplate suicide. In the customary Allen response to a personal crisis, Sheldon says that he needs air, and then claims that he needs cyanide.

Sheldon repeats the suicide threat later that night. As he watches television with Lisa, newscasters recount the story of the strange apparition in the sky. They reveal that little is known of Sheldon Mills except that he changed his name and is a bed wetter. Stand-up television reporters on the street ask bystanders if Sheldon should marry Lisa. Sheldon tells Lisa that he is humiliated and wants to kill himself. When Lisa suggests moving to another state, Sheldon says they would have to live in the subway to avoid her gaze. Sadie has become for him the all-present eye of God. Days later, Lisa will discover Sheldon wetting his finger and sticking it into the socket of a light fixture modeled after a multiple bulb candelabrum, possibly suggesting a menorah. His comic suicide attempt fails.

Lisa, the *shiksa,* cannot understand Sadie's pattern of aggressive interference. Lisa complains that Sadie has been calling her *koorva,* and she winces when Sheldon tells her it means "whore". She whines that Sheldon does not understand her anguish because he grew up with this monster mother. As an outsider Lisa is not used to this kind of treatment. Sadie goes to Queens to tell everyone about Sheldon's hiatal hernia, and at night she blabbers about his security blanket. Sheldon has no secret that is not made public. Ed Koch, who is Jewish and the former mayor of New York City, appears on television as the classic A.C.L.U. liberal lawyer who defends Sadie's right to hover over the City and say the things she has. Besides, the mayor remarks, she has helped spot criminals. Again, she functions as the Masked Avenger, whose motto threatened malefactors with discovery wherever they are. When Sheldon, who like Danny Rose has done nothing wrong other than wanting to marry Lisa, tries to sneak out of his apartment to avoid the press, the eye in the sky catches him and points him out. With camcorders at the ready, the television reporters take after him. He cannot avoid the publicity and public ridicule, as punishment from God for some alleged crime he did not commit.

Sheldon is desperate. When he tells his analyst about his plans to commit suicide, the doctor suggests the remedy of last recourse, a spiritualist. The psychiatrist argues that there are some mysteries that science cannot explain, as Leopold found out in A MIDSUMMER NIGHT'S SEX COMEDY. Through his death Leopold, however, discovered a fanciful realm of fairies and fantasy, while Sheldon's world of the inexplicable involves the mystery of God. Sheldon is shocked by the analyst's suggestion and claims that he does not believe in that stuff, but the doctor responds that maybe it is time to begin.

Treva (Julie Kavner), the spiritualist, is a younger version of Sadie.[9] In her loud nasal voice, she greets Sheldon by commenting that he looks thin. In the tradition of Jewish mothers, she offers him food, a gift that in the Allen corpus implies sex. Trying to keep his distance from this mad psychic, Sheldon asserts that he does not believe in all her nonsense. He is a man of logic, science and rationality. Her reply is curt. He can rely on all the science and rationality he wants, but his mother is still floating over the Chrysler Building. Duly abashed when confronted with mystery he cannot fathom with his intellect, Sheldon submits to her series of rituals. He dances in Tibetan costume, listens to Treva read the Tarot cards, burns incense and sprinkles crushed pig bones throughout Sadie's apartment, where they leave a voodoo doll resembling the missing mother. All this seems nonsensical to Sheldon, and Allen plays it for its comic potential, but during the purge of Sadie's apartment, Treva sits down at the piano and plays beautifully. She has never taken a lesson, she explains, but in a previous incarnation she was a pianist. It is enough to shatter Sheldon's conviction that he is involved with a lunatic. Maybe there is something of value in Treva's demented liturgies.

Three weeks pass, and the meaningless rituals have failed to make contact with Sadie. Sheldon's patience is exhausted and he explodes. He calls her a fraud and accuses her of not knowing what she is doing. He says she should have taken her act to California, where she could have a swimming pool and her own church. In self-justification, Treva sobs that she has kept her hope. The world contains more than the visible. It is filled with hidden meanings and mysteries. Unfortunately, her attempts as a medium to fathom these realities never work. Even though Treva, the priestess of the unseen, expresses discouragement at limitations of her power, they are both forced to continue because they are confronted by the mystery of Sheldon's mother, who is still floating in the sky above New York City. For that there is no scientific explanation. Treva admits that she was only an unsuccessful actress, but an astrologer friend told her to go into the business of psychic phenomena, claiming that people flock to psychics because their lives are so empty. She says she lacks the gift to be successful as a psychic. It is a gift one must be born with, and Treva feels she was not.

Allen's commentary on faith and organized religion in this exchange is complex. The clerical caste has little success in leading many of the faithful to a solution of the mysteries in their lives. These professionals keep trying and hoping, but they have little to show for their efforts. At times they may even feel themselves failed actors. For their part, the followers keep coming back. They want desperately to believe in something because otherwise their lives are empty. Faith, Allen suggests through Treva, is something people are born with. Without it, the questions of life are unanswerable. Without faith, rituals, hymns, dances and prayers are no more effective than reason in helping a person make sense out of the universe. The God of Judaism hovers up there in the sky for Sheldon, but he cannot find any way either to make him intelligible or to get him off his back.

When all else fails, Treva resorts to guilt, the common tactic of clergy of all faiths and Jewish mothers. She sobs that she has let him down. She refuses to take his money. Sheldon tries to console her by assuring her that she did her best. The relationship shifts dramatically when he invites her to dinner. Afraid that Sadie will spot them, Treva offers to cook the meal herself. Boiled chicken, of course. During the meal, Treva insists on his eating more, and failing that, she wraps the left-overs in foil for him to take home. Their conversation is eerily reminiscent of Sadie's concern about Sheldon's health. Their parting is awkward and halting, as though either might want to prolong the evening but neither knows how.

When Sheldon returns home, he finds a note from Lisa. She is ending their engagement and taking her children back to Vermont. She writes a simple explanation that she woke up one morning and discovered that she was no longer in love. Human love, especially the gentile variety, cannot endure trials. The love of a Jewish God/Mother, as burdensome as it is, goes on forever, and ever. With the *shiksa* gone from his life, Sheldon opens his package of leftovers and stares lovingly at a drumstick dripping with chicken fat. He has come home, spiritually and romantically.

In the morning, Sadie's voice from the clouds awakens him, and both Sheldon and Treva emerge from the apartment to greet her. Treva, acting more like a Jewish mother than a fiancée, tells Sadie that she likes her son, but observes that he could use a little fat. Confident now that her son is in good hands, that is, hands much like her own, Sadie descends from the clouds and perches in the living room, where Treva asks to see pictures of Sheldon. The film ends with Sheldon's bemused and resigned expression. His mother has become his wife. He realizes that he has been unable to assimilate, and that he finds true peace in the continuation of his Jewish heritage.

Allen's truce with the universe now includes a theological dimension. He is comfortable not only as a human being, but as a Jew. The eyes of God are intimidating, and they do tend to reduce one to a juvenile state on occasion, but it is better to live under the gaze of someone who cares than to live alone. In RADIO DAYS Allen made peace with his Jewish heritage as his cultural legacy, but in OEDIPUS WRECKS he extends his cease-fire to the God of his fathers. . . and mothers.

NOTES

1. Douglas Brode, *The Films of Woody Allen,* (New York: Citadel, 1991), p. 270, offers examples of critical reaction.
2. Brode, p. 258, points out that the inspiration of the story was the scandal involving Lana Turner, whose lover Johnny Stampanato was stabbed to death by her daughter Cheryl Crane.
3. Maurice Yacowar, *Loser Take All: The Comic Art of Woody Allen* (New York: Continuum, 1991), p. 265, makes the connection between construction and reconstruction.
4. Rainer Maria Rilke, *The Selected Poetry of Rainer Maria Rilke,* ed. and trans. by Stephen Mitchell, (New York: Random House, 1982) p. 25.
5. Rilke, p. 61.
6. Alessandra Comini, *Gustav Klimt* (New York: Braziller, 1975), p. 6, explains the influence of Klimt's erotic style and his connection to a fellow Viennese, Sigmund Freud. Paul Vogt, *Expressionism: German Painting 1905–1920* (New York: Abrams, 1979), pp. 29–30, traces the influence of the Viennese school to the German Expressionists primarily through Oskar Kokoschka (1886–1980).
7. Richard A. Blake, "Women's Wear" in *America* (Dec. 17, 1988), p. 517, notes several points of comparison between the two films. The scene of self-discovery and peace appears in Ingmar Bergman, WILD STRAWBERRIES in *Four Screenplays of Ingmar Bergman* (New York: Simon and Schuster, 1965), p. 239. After reviewing his life, the old man says: "Yet I wasn't sorry about that; I felt, on the contrary, rather lighthearted."
8. Yacowar, p. 273, sees Sadie's appearance in the sky as "an Old Testament proof of Jehovah's power and pertinence in an alien land."
9. Annette Wernblad, *Brooklyn Is Not Expanding: Woody Allen's Comic Universe* (Rutherford, N.J.: Fairleigh Dickinson Univ., 1992), p. 134, maintains that Treva's and Sadie's differences are more important than their similarities. Treva offers hope, whereas Sadie is the reincarnation of "The Castrating Zionist," the title of the story Isaac Davis wrote about his own mother in MANHATTAN. The point is arguable, depending on what one foresees in Sheldon's marriage to Treva in the years to come.

CHAPTER VI: THE MORAL FABLES

Woody Allen's most recent phase, 1989–1993, traces a parabola of moral inquiry. Beginning with CRIMES AND MISDEMEANORS (1989) he faces the mystery of evil in the world with new clarity and in the context of his own Jewish religious tradition. In ALICE (1990) he investigates good and evil from his understanding of the Catholic tradition, which he no doubt puzzled over at some depth during his long, and at this time still loving relationship with Mia Farrow, the product of a strong Catholic upbringing. Revealed religion seems to offer Allen, if not a justification, at least a serviceable explanation of moral behavior. In SHADOWS AND FOG (1992), however, Allen returns to his agnostic position, but in a more personal, limited way. Everyone else may know the mysterious "plan" in a universe marred by irrational evil, and that is fine for them, but his hero can never quite join them. He is still the outsider. Finally, in HUSBANDS AND WIVES (1992) Allen returns to his beloved Manhattan, and while exploring the casual infidelities of his sophisticated characters, the best he can conclude is that their behavior is irrational.

After so many years of inquiry, while Allen drew ever closer to a religious resolution to his questions about meanings and moral structures, he seems, in the end, to have drawn back from the edge of a faith commitment to his own native agnosticism. It will be the task of the psycho-biographer to relate this rise and fall of religious interest to the events in his own personal life. The task of the critic, even one interested in his religious ideas, rests upon the films alone.

During this period, between ALICE and SHADOWS AND FOG Allen accepted an acting role in Paul Mazursky's SCENES FROM A MALL (1991), written by Mazursky and Roger L. Simon and co-starring Bette Midler. It reprises the later Woody character in Nick, who is both a neurotic nebbish but who at the same time has been quite successful as a lawyer who negotiates celebrity endorsements of consumer products. Midler is Deborah, a best-selling pop psychologist, but even on that lofty rung of the professional ladder, the character is vintage Midler, bold, brassy and very funny. The plot revolves around a marriage that falls apart through the discovery of mutual infidelities, and then comes back together when the couple decides to forgive each other's failures.

Despite all the classic Allen ingredients, the recipe flopped, even for die-hard Allen and Midler fans. The reasons one might propose to explain the failure of this ersatz Allen film are pertinent to the concerns at hand. The film is set in a Beverly Hills shopping mall, even though it was shot in a mall in New Jersey.[1] The Los Angeles setting drains the characters of their color and separates them from their cultural roots. They are Jewish characters who have assimilated so perfectly that they fit into the antiseptic world of chrome and glass just like everyone else. They might even order sandwiches with mayonnaise on white bread. The tang of rye and Kosher dill is gone. Although most of the other shoppers are buying Christmas presents to commemorate the Christian feast, Deborah and Nick match their behavior patterns by shopping for anniversary gifts for each other. Without the conflict that comes from cultural alienation and at least some residual religious sensibility, the plot is just another romantic comedy. Their angst comes from cancelling a holiday party for their friends rather than from their desperate search to find love in an unloving universe. If they separate, neither will be devastated. The surface is Allen, but there is nothing inside.

SCENES FROM A MALL, a Mazursky film, represents only a parenthesis in Allen's work and ideas. The role of religion in this latest phase of Allen's film-making grows naturally out of his previous works. His exploration of the God/Mother in SEPTEMBER and OEDIPUS WRECKS led him to a peaceful acceptance of the notion of a divine presence in his life. God, as Allen understood the concept, meddles in his affairs and brings repercussions that vary from embarrassing to destructive. For all of this, Allen opted for a kind of peaceful co-existence. Allen's God, the God of Job, may do terrible things to him, even reduce him to an infantile state, but the Allen characters discover that they have the resources to move ahead and perhaps even enjoy life, at least a little.

In SEPTEMBER Allen concluded that life must go on, and possibilities for the future, however ill-defined, justify endurance.

Lane endures the onslaught of her mother, witnesses the alienation of Peter due to Diane's interference and only barely survives the apparent collapse of her plans for a new life when Diane decides to take back the house. With Diane driven off the scene, at least for a time, Lane can set aside her plans for suicide and design a new life for herself. She accepts the trinket Diane throws her way, and moves on, apparently without bitterness, although if they meet again, it is certain that the old wounds will be reopened. Allen seems to have grown comfortable with the possibility of an inscrutable God, who may condone or even orchestrate terrible events in his life, as long as this being can be sent into exile, far from the present consciousness. Like Lane with her mother, Allen finds God crowding him; he needs his breathing space.

In OEDIPUS WRECKS, Sheldon survives without having to eliminate his God from his life. With his mother safely off the scene and his Jewish roots hidden behind a gentile name, Sheldon thinks he is free, but banishing his mother is no more effective than changing his name in transforming Sheldon into a gentile secularist. The borders between cultural and religious Judaism become blurred through Sadie, as the Jewish mother who becomes the eyes of God. In a matter of days, Sheldon's Jewishness reasserts itself, and he finds himself actually renewing his tradition by marrying a woman who turns out to be a younger version of his mother. If Sheldon, the Allen surrogate, can make sense out of this mysterious world, it will have to be as a Jew, and he seems quite content with that arrangement.

ANOTHER WOMAN appearing as it does between SEPTEMBER and OEDIPUS WRECKS provides Allen with a respite from God. Marion, like Allen, has entered her fifties wondering about the meaning of her life. German philosophy is her only religion, and it provides her with few guidelines for her personal behavior. As Marion looks back over her life, she realizes that she is capable of extraordinary cruelty, but she never entertains the idea that a revealed religious tradition could help her understand the moral value and disvalue of her actions. She fails in the natural virtues: generosity, kindness, compassion and honesty. Her sins against civility have eviscerated her life and rendered her empty of love. While looking through this sad history, however, she does undergo a form of conversion. Just like the person of faith, she hopes for something better in the future. Not having the luxury of an afterlife and a God to reward her struggles in eternity, she resolves to make the best of the days left to her on earth. She fashions her own reward. Through Marion, Allen proposes that regardless of their belief system, people must take responsibility for their own lives, and regardless of age, they can be optimistic about the future.

Moral living and religion preoccupy Allen during the period of these three films, but he chooses to treat them as distinct issues by emphasizing one or the other in separate works. The questions of God and morality will carry over into the next period, but in this final period the questions will be linked, examined and in the last instance, separated again.

CRIMES AND MISDEMEANORS (1989) may be Allen's richest and most complex work to date. In it comedy and melodrama, violence and gentleness, ideas and entertainment blend into an exquisite whole. Like the best of Allen, it delights on first viewing yet continues to yield its riches through repeated screenings and reflection.

This film, more than any previous work, lends itself to a rewarding psychoanalytic reading. According to this interpretive device, in this film Allen does not rely on a single character, the "little man" who is the participant observer in the actions of others, but rather once again he fragments his own character into several others, each of whom represents a facet of his own personality. The characters, many of whom appear in pairs, become different, even antagonistic sides of Allen's character that he tries to explore, understand and reconcile. Since he has not been able to accomplish these goals after years of psychotherapy, he will not cheapen the effort by presenting easy solutions in a single film that lasts less than two hours.

Allen's most daring innovation in CRIMES AND MISDEMEANORS is to shift the Allen surrogate, the searcher for love and meaning, from Cliff Stern, the character similar to those Allen frequently plays, to Judah Rosenthal (Martin Landau). The biblical Judah, son of Jacob and father of one of the tribes of Israel, represents the religion of all the Jewish people, as the word Judaism suggests. By choosing this name for his hero, Allen looks beyond Judah, the individual, and lets him represent the Jewish people as a whole.[2] Through him, Allen tries to understand the relationship between Jewish morality, revealed by a personal God, with that of the majority secularist culture, which is derived from reason, convention or simply good manners. Judah Rosenthal, however, maintains that he is not religious at all. He is proud of being a man of science, like Lloyd in SEPTEMBER, and he appears perfectly assimilated. He knows the best restaurants and hotels in Europe, collects art and speaks knowledgeably about music. By profession, Judah is an ophthalmologist, a man who helps people see, just as Allen the film maker does. Like Allen, too, he is successful, prosperous and respected.

In his moral life, however, Judah finds that happiness and certitude elude him. As the film opens, he receives accolades from friends and colleagues for his role in building a new ophthalmology wing for the hospital, yet later he realizes that his improper use of those funds for personal gain could be considered criminal. At the testimonial dinner in his honor, the toastmaster praises him for his devotion to Miriam (Claire Bloom), his wife of 25 years, and his family. Judah is indeed a dedicated family man, but he can coolly enter into an affair with a flight attendant and then arrange to have his mistress murdered when she becomes inconvenient. During his own speech, Judah jokes about his father's belief that "the eyes of God" look down upon his life, a notion he cannot completely abandon despite his conviction that he is a man of science.

While Judah experiences moral and religious ambiguity within himself, he finds the tension increased through contact with two figures who pull him in opposite directions. One of his patients is Ben (Sam Waterston), a friend of many years. Benjamin is the name of the youngest of the sons of Jacob, and it has become a traditional Jewish name through the centuries. Ben is a rabbi who is rapidly losing his vision altogether. No longer relying on the comic orthodox rabbi with his Yiddish accent, Allen creates in Ben a cultured, urbane figure, who despite his outward assimilation remains a figure of deep religious commitment as well as a man of extraordinary human compassion.

Although the secularized Judah cannot share Ben's religious beliefs, he does find him a man to trust with a discussion of his personal life. He tells Ben about his infidelity to Miriam and the increasing demands of his mistress. Ben advises complete honesty with Miriam, in the hope that through forgiveness and mutual trust their marriage can be reborn into a new, stronger relationship. While Ben gently calls the adultery a small infidelity, Judah sees it as two years of scheming and dishonesty. Through the eyes of a loving God, the rabbi is willing to forgive; through the logic of the secular world, Judah is harsh toward sin and sinner alike.

While Judah listens politely to the rabbi's advice, he finds sterner solutions, offered by the other side of his personality, may be required to solve his problem. He turns to his own brother Jack (Jerry Orbach), a man with known connections to the underworld, and as such the pole opposite to Ben. Jack, the name is often used by Jewish men as an assimilated form of Jacob, advises direct action. He knows how to have Judah's demanding mistress killed for a price. Judah is shocked. He dismisses the notion of a contract murder as a moral abomination. He is aghast at Jack's suggestion, but Jack argues that his solution is the only one appropriate in the real world. He scorns Judah's protected existence.

One night, unable to sleep after Dolores (Anjelica Huston), Judah's mistress, had become increasingly hysterical in her demands to speak to Miriam, Judah sits in front of the fire and thinks about the rabbi's advice. In his reverie, Judah imagines Ben's presence as the rabbi explains that he could not continue living without the firm conviction that the universe includes a moral structure, meaning, forgiveness, and ultimately some form of higher being beyond the power of the human senses to perceive. Ben explains that without this belief, there is no basis to know how to live. Judah cannot move from his own belief that God is a luxury he cannot afford. In the end, he calls Jack and tells him to go ahead with the murder. He has begun the downward spiral of corruption that began with adultery and misuse of hospital funds and eventually leads to a murder of convenience.

Judah's disintegration, however, has only begun with his decision to kill. He initially retains some sense of moral value based in religious belief. When Jack calls during a dinner party to tell him that the killer has been successful, Judah responds with a desperate prayer for God's mercy for what they have done. At first he feels remorse for his deed. Clearly upset he leaves his dinner guests to visit Dolores's apartment. He looks into the eyes of the dead woman, where he sees nothing, and then removes items that may link her to him. During the visit to the scene of the crime, he recalls his father in the synagogue, wrapped in a tallith, or prayer shawl, reminding him that the eye of God sees everything. Judah will begin a long-term project to blind that eye.

Some days later, in his office, Judah checks up on Ben's deteriorating eyesight. When Ben asks if he has resolved his personal problem, Judah lies, by saying that it is over because his mistress finally became reasonable about his predicament. Ben congratulates him on his good fortune. In the next scene, Judah meets Jack again. As they walk through Riverside Park, Judah tells Jack about returning to the apartment and seeing only a void in Dolores's eyes. Annoyed at Judah's imprudent visit to the apartment, Jack assures him that it is over. He should forget about it and get on with his life.

For Judah, however, it is not quite over, not yet. He drives through the Brooklyn Battery Tunnel to his childhood neighborhood in Brooklyn. When the landlady (Frances Conroy) allows him to step inside his childhood home, he fantasizes about a long-past seder with his family. Allen has used this technique, which he borrowed from Ingmar Bergman's WILD STRAWBERRIES, in ANOTHER WOMAN. Judah stands at the doorway while his religious father, Sol (David S. Howard) argues with his chain-smoking Marxist Aunt May (Anna Berger). May is impatient with the Hebrew ceremonial that is part of the ritual. She wants to get on with the meal. She is a cynic, arguing angrily that might makes right and that there is no moral order. Hitler, she believes, got away with his sins. Judah interrupts his dream to inject his belief that if someone does evil, he will be punished. An uncle answers that he will be punished only if he is caught, and May adds that if he is not bothered by ethics, he is home scot-free.

When Judah's father offers the opinion "murder will out," Judah is startled at the reference to murder and denies having brought up the subject. The family continues the argument on the value of their rituals and Hebrew prayers honoring an unseen God. They seem to conclude that faith is something one is born with. When May dismisses the ritual magic act as not being logical, Judah's father asks why logic must always govern human thinking. He says that he will always choose God over truth. Judah, the man of science, is clearly torn between the opposing positions of his father and Aunt May, but to survive, he must make the option for the ideas of May, whom he finds abrasive, even if that choice means deliberately rejecting the faith of his beloved father.

Lying becomes a habit for Judah. A detective questions Judah about his connection with Dolores. When Judah offers transparent lies about his relationship to her as a patient, giving vague, improbable explanations, the detective never questions the responses or asks to see any records. Luck remains on Judah's side. Getting away with murder is easier than he would have imagined. Later, during a second walk with Jack in Riverside Park, Judah again mentions his guilt and again wonders aloud about turning himself in. Jack's response is clearly a threat: He, too, is involved and will not let that happen. Judah recognizes that he has been trapped in a web of evil, and he cannot escape. Later, he will return to Dolores's apartment once more, and as he parks across the street, the camera focuses on the headlight as Judah extinguishes it. The eye of God, this heavy-handed symbol suggests, has at last gone out. Judah does not enter the building.

In one last glimmer of remorse, Judah loses control as he dines with his wife and daughter at a fashionable country-club. Miriam comments on his moods and his recent heavy drinking, and Judah, apparently somewhat drunk, lurches from the table, shouting his affirmation of belief in God, a topic that has preoccupied his thought if not his conversation during the meal. He has reached the conclusion that with a God, the world is little more than a sewer.

Time will eventually bring success to Judah's efforts to exorcise God from his life. In a moving climax to the film, when the two story lines come together, he talks drunkenly with Cliff Stern (Woody Allen) about a fictional murder he thinks would make a good movie plot. His imaginary killer is tortured by sparks of the religious background he gave up years before. Inexplicably, one day he discovers that life goes on in the world despite his deeds. He has a family he loves and he happily takes them on a vacation trip to Europe. The crisis of conscience has passed, and as the weeks and months slip by he realizes that not only has he escaped punishment, but he prospers. He settles into a secure, comfortable world of affluence. When Cliff expresses doubt in the possibility of a life without guilt, Judah counters with his belief that everyone has some burden of sin, and once in a while it may bother them, but eventually all the evil memories fade away. Judah's story has been autobiographical, of course. He is the man who has outlived his guilt and now can peacefully look forward to leading the rest of his life of wealth and privilege untouched by the memory of his crimes.

Allen, however, is not altogether at peace with Judah's assessment of crime without punishment and without guilt. In the next room, Ben is dancing with his daughter at her wedding reception, and with his dark glasses it is clear that Ben has lost his sight completely.[3] The eye of God has grown blind, and the rabbi goes through the motions of his former life, yet in that dance he is a sublimely happy man. Perhaps, Allen suggests, faith and moral living bring their own rewards, despite terrible human suffering, like blindness. In the final moments of the film both Judah and Ben are happy men in their own respective ways, but Allen clearly makes Ben the more heroic figure.

Cliff, too, is not convinced by Judah's story. He insists that the fictional murderer must turn himself in to the authorities and accept punishment. Judah finds this absurd. He argues that people in the real world rationalize or deny their evil acts, or they can't go on living. Cliff maintains that in the absence of God or something, the killer is forced to assume responsibility for himself, and that would be doubly tragic. Judah rejects this argument as mere fiction, a kind of celestial Hollywood movie. The existence of a judging and forgiving God is like a stock happy ending in the movies. Judah himself realizes that his own acceptance of responsibility for his acts, without a God or other agent of human justice, is not a happy ending. He has no one or nothing with whom to make a reconciliation. His hope rests in the passage of time and its convenient erasure of memory.

The ending is not particularly happy for Cliff Stern either. Although Judah does not know Cliff's story, the film's second plot line, Cliff and his brother-in-law Lester (Alan Alda) represent a second set of polarities that the audience can ponder as Judah might. In every conceivable way, Cliff is a loser, while in the eyes of the world, Lester is a big-time winner. Cliff's personal life is a disaster. At the beginning of the film, he realizes that his marriage to Wendy (Joanna Gleason) is obviously in its final stages. He complains that they have not made love in over a year. His sister Barbara (Caroline Aaron) reflects his desperation. She is divorced and so eager for a new relationship that she takes an ad in the personals section of a magazine. She finds a man she likes, but after the third date he sexually humiliates her. Her story shocks Cliff, but when he tries to share his revulsion with Wendy, she coolly comments that sex is filled with mysteries. The mystery exerts an unbearable pressure on Cliff's life, and he has not the slightest clue about how to solve it. Even more, he scarcely realizes it at the time, but he will be similarly humiliated and degraded.

Cliff inhabits a world shaped by idealism. He makes documentary films on socially relevant topics, like leukemia, that no one will pay him for and few audiences will ever see. His current project involves a series of taped interviews with a Jewish philosopher, Louis Levy (Martin Bergmann), a man who survived the supreme evil of the Holocaust and yet maintains an optimistic view of life. Levy's first appearance on screen introduces the question of God that underlies the entire film. Levy explains that the ancient Israelites conceived of a God who cares about people but insists that they behave morally. Yet no sooner had they reached this insight than they presented him as ordering Abraham to kill his only son Isaac. He concludes that we have never been able to conceive of an all-loving God. These are the kinds of ideas that Cliff, like Allen, finds intriguing, and he wants to use the film medium to present them to a wider audience.

In contrast to Cliff, the struggling artist, is Lester, a fabulously successful producer of mindless television sitcoms and mouther of endless inanities. Lester, with his perfectly assimilated name, is the brother of Ben the rabbi and Wendy, Cliff's wife. As Lester's brother Ben stands for spiritual values in Allen's mind, Lester himself represents everything that is materialistic and venal. A television crew follows Lester around to film a program about his life and ideas for "The Creative Mind." Lester's self-serving, pompous comments approach self-parody, but of course he takes himself with utmost seriousness. He hires and fires on whim, and he promises wonderful professional opportunities to starlets who are willing to get to know him better, and apparently many are. He hires Cliff as a favor to his sister Wendy, and then fires him dramatically when Cliff's presentation of Lester crosses the boundary from objectivity to character assassination. As a film maker, Lester stands for everything that Allen despises about the industry and fears about his own commercial successes. Cliff maintains an integrity that Allen admires, but no one ever sees his films. The two fictional film makers embody the dilemma that continually faces Allen about his own work.

The contrast between the two men reaches beyond art and into their personal lives as well. Desperately lonely in his disintegrating marriage, Cliff meets Halley Reed (Mia Farrow), an ambitious assistant producer working on "The Creative Mind" program featuring Lester. Equally put off by Lester's arrogance, the two form an instant friendship. Halley visits Cliff's studio and finds the material on Louis Levy so fascinating that she offers to try to have Cliff's Levy documentary included in the fall schedule. During her next visit to his studio to view more of the Levy material, she hears the philosopher explain his opinion that falling in love is really the attempt to recreate childhood attachments by discovering in the beloved the important people in the past. This process helps people correct past evils.

Among the evils of her past, Halley reveals that she had been married to an architect, but that marriage failed, as has Cliff's. Lester interrupts their conversation by calling and arranging a business meeting with Halley in his hotel room later that night. Cliff voices certain reservations about the meeting and that time and in that place, but Halley dismisses his fears. In order to pass the time before the meeting, Cliff opens his only bottle of champagne, sends out for Indian food and they watch a 16 mm. print of SINGIN' IN THE RAIN, a mutual favorite. Some days later, Wendy reveals that Halley and Lester have become close, and in disbelief, Cliff calls Halley's home at midnight. Lester answers. Cliff now knows he faces competition for Halley's affection.

Cliff's life takes several cruel turns, professionally as well as personally. From his answering service, Cliff learns that Levy has taken his own life, and the film he has shot about this wonderful, resilient optimist is now worthless. Sitting alone in his studio, Cliff listens once more to Levy's ideas about the universe. The philosopher maintains that since the world is a cruel place, people need a lot of love to keep them going. Sometimes people must reach the conclusion that the struggle is no longer worth the effort. Levy had apparently reached this solution himself, and one wonders if an absence of love in his own life had led him to this end. Suicide threats and attempts are common in Allen's films, and many Allen characters conclude that self-inflicted death is the only reasonable option in dealing with a hostile universe but only Levy and Eve in INTERIORS are successful in taking their own lives, the others are not. His suicide note reveals nothing about his thoughts or feelings. It simply states the obvious fact that he has gone out the window. By his death, Levy has betrayed Cliff not only artistically but philosophically, since through Levy Cliff had found a way to cope with his own cruel world.

Upon hearing the news about Levy, Halley comes to the studio to console Cliff. She tries to help him make sense of Levy's decision and explains that no philosophic system, however elaborate, is complete. Halley thus voices Allen's realization that the intellect alone cannot impose order on a universe that contains inexplicable mysteries, like the self-inflicted death of a good man or the Holocaust. She has taken the side of Judah's father in his seder debate with Aunt May. Halley and Cliff kiss warmly, but she withdraws, saying she has not yet recovered from her divorce, and she reminds Cliff that he is married. She leaves Cliff's studio, and once more he is alone. Some time later Halley reveals to Cliff that she intends to go to London to produce a few television programs on her own. Cliff is devastated, much as Ike was when Tracy finally left for London at the end of MANHATTAN.

At the wedding of Ben's daughter, Cliff assumes the role of the outsider, claiming that everything he wears is rented, even down to his shoes and underwear. He feels that he doesn't belong there, and he feels more alienated when he discovers that Lester has paid for everything. Wendy asks him to try to be pleasant, since they will never have to appear together again. Their marriage has definitively ended, and in fact, Wendy confides to a friend that she has already found someone else. Lester and Halley arrive together and announce that they have become engaged in London. Lester quips that he sent her white roses every day, like Lou, the treacherous adulterer in BROADWAY DANNY ROSE, until he discovered that she is allergic to them. Cliff sits glumly through the wedding ceremony, wearing his yarmulke and listening to the traditional blessings of the rabbi, but once the party begins, he withdraws to an outer room to brood alone, until Judah joins him for their conversation on murder and guilt.

Morally, Cliff is an ambiguous character.[4] Despite his idealism as a film maker, he cannot serve the role of moral exemplar in contrast to either Lester or Judah. He tries to commit adultery, but while Judah had a successful affair for over two years, Cliff fails in his one attempt with Halley. He has lofty artistic standards, but since he needs the money, Cliff accepts the position as film maker for the biography of Lester, whom he despises. After having sold out his personal integrity to make such a film, Cliff tries to redeem his self-respect by using his skill as an editor to cut the film in such a way that he unfairly makes a fool of Lester by interpolating shots of Mussolini and Mr. Ed, the Talking Horse. Lester, of course, fires him right in the screening room. Cliff's jealousy and resentment preceded Lester's winning Halley. He could not endure Lester's success and the adulation he receives from people who regard him as an artist and humanitarian.

In contrast to Lester and especially to Judah, Cliff stands out as a man of moral sensibility, however flawed, who tries to do the right thing but who fails consistently, often through no fault of his own. His misdemeanors never become crimes. His unsuccessful attempt at infidelity never leads to murder, nor does he forget the ideals he has as a film maker, even though he takes a job on an odious film project because he needs the money to finish the Levy documentary. Judah has crossed the boundaries of moral integrity deliberately and spectacularly, and Lester has forgotten where they lie, if he ever knew or cared. Cliff is a poor human being who tries to be moral and sometimes fails. The mystery of the moral universe, in Allen's thought, is that such a man ends up alone in a hotel dining room with nothing. Lester has Halley, Judah has Miriam, and both manifestly prosper. In such a world, can there be a just God who looks over the deeds of his creatures to reward the just and punish the evil doers? If there is a Masked Avenger or a Sadie Millstein up there in the sky, he conceals his presence very carefully. Job and Cliff Stern are brothers in their lamentation.

Allen's view of women becomes exceedingly cynical in CRIMES AND MISDEMEANORS. The autobiographical element may be at work here; perhaps strains in his own relationship with Mia Farrow are already beginning to appear. That is scarcely the point under consideration at present. In the earlier films the Allen character searched for an idealized love to give meaning to his life, like Annie in ANNIE HALL or Tracy in MANHATTAN. Gradually, he found happiness with women who are less than perfect, like Tina in BROADWAY DANNY ROSE or Holly in HANNAH AND HER SISTERS. Some of his women became so strong and self-contained that they frighten him, like Diane in SEPTEMBER, Marion in ANOTHER WOMAN or even Sadie in OEDIPUS WRECKS. In his films, the female characters generally represent a sign of love and peace in a universe that would otherwise be unbearable.

In CRIMES AND MISDEMEANORS the women consistently threaten and betray their men. Dolores, unable to admit that their affair is over and unwilling to accept the role of Judah's ex-mistress, displays progressively more neurotic, destructive behavior, endangering both his family and his reputation in the community. Like many an Allen character, when the pressure of life becomes too much for her, she threatens to commit suicide. Moving ever closer to Judah's home, she goes beyond letters and phone calls. She drives to a gas station in his neighborhood, calls and threatens to enter his house unless he leaves his birthday celebration and meets her immediately. This hysterical conversation convinces him that he has no solution but Jack's.

Wendy does not threaten Cliff with violence, but she is a destructive force in his life. She holds both Cliff and his work in contempt. Her reluctance to continue the sexual side of their marriage only underlines their isolation from each other. When she confides in Lester with some pride that she has found someone else, Wendy reveals that she has been more successful in adultery than her husband. Cliff's sister Barbara is equally isolated, even resorting to a desperate ad in the personals section, which leads to her horrifying debasement.

At first, Halley offers the hope for renewed love in Cliff's life, but when she chooses Lester, she both humiliates Cliff personally and cheapens all the values he once thought they had shared. She betrays both the man and his ideals. Miriam, Judah's proper, professional wife, becomes a bit of a nag during Judah's crisis. The starlets tolerate or even encourage Lester's advances to further their own careers. Ben, who represents spiritual values and happiness in defiance of his hostile, merciless world, dances at his daughter's wedding, but his wife never appears on screen. If Ben has reached peace, he has apparently done it without the support of a wife or any other woman.

Jenny, Cliff's niece, is the significant exception to the rule. Poised at the cusp between girlhood and womanhood, Jenny remains as yet untainted by the world. Cliff takes her to vintage movies at the Bleecker Street Cinema and buys her a book with pictures of old New York. Movies and New York are the true, constant loves in the lives of Cliff and Woody Allen, and he enjoys sharing them with her. They eat pizza together, the Allen constant sign of companionship, while he discusses his feelings about Halley and Ben with her. The clue to their relationship appears in the very last scene in the film, as Louis Levy explains in voice-over that human happiness is not part of the universe. The human capacity for love, however, can imbue this brute universe with meaning and give people a reason to continue living and to keep trying. Sometimes, according to Levy, people can discover joy in their families, their work and especially in their hope that future generations may discover more about the world than we have at present. For Cliff Jenny represents that hope that she will understand the world in ways that he cannot. She inspires him to "keep trying." He shares his cultural history with her, films and New York, and confides the movements of his heart to her, in the hope that she will learn from them and find the happiness that eludes him.

Levy's words and Ben's dancing provide the key to Cliff's questions about the seemingly capricious and unfair relationships between good and evil, reward and punishment in this present world. The wedding functions as a sign of a new family, new life, the continuation of the species.[5] To underline the theme, the camera lingers on unidentified children amusing themselves as their elders drink and dance. Ben has found happiness in his belief in a superior being and acceptance of his own disability. He is the Job of the final chapters of the book. His morality justifies his existence. While others have rejected the God of their fathers, Ben remains steadfast in his Jewish tradition. Because of his daughter's marriage, Ben can look to the future in hope, as Louis Levy suggests. As Miriam and Judah leave the reception, they too look toward their own daughter's wedding. Even Lester is planning for the future by announcing his marriage to Halley. Thus Ben the saint, Judah the monster and Lester the charlatan find happiness as they look to the future with new families, new life and new possibilities. Cliff, the morally ambiguous and thus most human character, sits alone, away from the wedding party, with nothing. His face reflects pain as he wonders why happiness and hope are the lot of just and unjust alike.[6] Morality or immorality has little to do with their success. For his part, Cliff tries and fails continually, as though happiness will ever remain beyond his grasp. Allen cannot solve this cruel mystery; he merely invites contemplation.

ALICE (1991) continues Woody Allen's search for meaning in the universe, but the prism switches from his familiar Jewishness to the less familiar world of Catholicism. Since this is alien territory for him, he does not appear as a character in the film, but substitutes Mia Farrow as his surrogate. Since his Jewish religious tradition seems unable to solve his questions about evil and meaning with clarity and certitude, as he concluded in CRIMES AND MISDEMEANORS, he now asks if another tradition can provide any more satisfactory answers. Mickey Sachs in HANNAH AND HER SISTERS also tried Catholicism, but he found, as he tells a Hare Krishna leader, that despite his effort and study, Catholicism never quite worked for him.[7] He seemed particularly unhappy with the notion of an afterlife that held the possibility of punishment for sins. No matter how hard he tried, Mickey could never escape his Jewish background.

In ALICE, Allen confines his inquiry to wealthy post-Christian gentile inhabitants of Manhattan. If these sophisticated New Yorkers mention religion at all, it is in the past tense. Their references to religion, if made at all, would include lines like: "I was raised a Catholic," and anyone who speaks the language knows that the unspoken second clause is understood: "but I've outgrown all that by this time." Allen's search for meaning in this film is vested in Alice, and thus it involves the traditional Catholic neuroses, based both in real sins unforgiven and guilt over imaginary crimes, as opposed to Allen's more familiar Jewish brand of guilt with its roots in the strong mother figure. The Woody character, of course, has no place in this kind of residually Christian world.

Alice Tate (Mia Farrow) is a gentile princess. A graduate of Sacred Heart Academy on Fifth Avenue, she married Doug Tate (William Hurt), scion of a wealthy family who resolves that the family fortune will not diminish under his stewardship. He is a man of his word. Although he never mentions religion at all, his name and the old-wealth of the family point to Episcopalian roots somewhere. In all likelihood, then, Alice "married outside the Church," a sign of her juridical separation from membership in the Catholic Church. In the film, she never mentions attending any religious service or any concern for the religious education of her children. Alice Tate, however, can be no more successful in becoming an ex-Catholic than Mickey Sachs is in becoming an ex-Jew. Cultural and religious roots run too deep in both characters.

The Tates' Manhattan apartment bristles with wealth and servants. The children attend a private nursery school that will increase the chances of their acceptance into an Ivy League college, and the Tates' interior decorator (Julie Kavner) arrives with a

$9,000 eel trap that could be made into a lamp or something. With all her wealth, Alice is bored with her life. She describes herself as one of those women who spends her days shopping in the finest boutiques, gossiping and getting pedicures. She advises her maid on the purchase of healthy, chemical-free chickens and fiber rich fruit for her diet and preferred skin creams and moisturizers for her bath. As a symptom of her discontent, she develops an intractable backache. When her personal trainer (Billy Taylor) arrives in the apartment for her supervised work-out, she asks if she should hire a Swede to walk on her spine, but the trainer recommends acupuncture from Dr. Yang.

Allen places Alice face-to-face with a basic option, constructed along the lines of the polar opposites he proposed in CRIMES AND MISDEMEANORS. Her first option is her husband Doug, who promises security and wealth, but who has little sympathy for Alice's boredom and restlessness. His idea of a wife is a mother for his children and a manager of his social calendar. While she dreams of being a writer, he suggests helping the wife of a friend run a sweater boutique, since she is good with people and knows sweaters. When she wants to take a course in writing, he tries to tell her gently that he does not think she is bright enough to become a professional script writer.

The opposite to Doug, her bastion of security, is Joe Ruffalo (Joe Mantegna), whose Italian name shows that he, like Alice, had at least some Catholic influence in his life. Joe plays jazz saxophone. They meet at the nursery school as they deliver their children, and they notice each other when by chance she drops a copy of the poetry of Edna St. Vincent Millay, which he retrieves and hands to her with the comment that it is romantic. That momentary contact changes Alice's life. She cannot put him out of her mind, and she confesses her infatuation to her friend Nina (Robin Bartlett) as though it were a major affair. The gossips cluck that Alice is a Catholic and not the type to have an affair. Alice's friends in the beauty parlor are amused at her imaginary liaison and suspect, correctly, that Alice's marriage to Doug may be going through a troubled period. Alice, however, does not yet recognize the problem. In the midst of their conversation, one of the girlfriends incidentally mentions Dr. Yang, the acupuncturist and herbalist, and Alice is startled when she hears the name a second time.

Taking the coincidence as a sign, Alice with her chauffeur and destroyer-sized limousine arrive in Chinatown. Dr. Yang (Keye Luke) has little patience with her self-diagnosis of her back problem. Using the formal, third-person title, he barks with a touch of anger that the source of Mrs. Tate's problem is not her back, but her heart and her head. Under hypnosis, Alice reveals her fantasy about penguins, who, Alice says, mate for life. Dr. Yang laughs at the thought that she must think penguins are Catholics, a joke that recalls Ike's comment to Tracy in MANHATTAN, when he tells her that people should be like pigeons or Catholics and marry for life.[8] During the fantasy a strange man kisses her, so the joke touches on the question of marital fidelity that Alice must resolve precisely as a Catholic. Allen's Jewish characters, by contrast, often face wrenching, painful divorces, but these are human events. Religious beliefs and traditional morality never apparently enter their minds.

In the second part of her hypnosis-induced fantasy, Alice talks with Doug and expresses discontent with her present status as wife. One of her roles, she feels, involves looking attractive so that Doug's friends will admire his taste: She reminds Doug that she once had ambitions to be a costume designer in the theater, but he dismisses her talents by saying she was only a small-town girl with a Catholic-school education, as though both of these factors had ill-prepared her for the real world. She recalls their early romance, and his proposal of marriage to her in an amusement park. Doug says he has wealth already, but he wants her to be a wife and mother to his children. Alice, however, wants a different role in life. Dr. Yang asks if she resents her present status, and Alice replies that she is not angry; she is just lost and a bit confused about her future.

Dr. Yang, however, is neither a Catholic nor a penguin. For him a life-long commitment to one mate in an unhappy marriage is not an overwhelmingly positive value. He feels that Mrs. Tate must confront her passions, including her attraction to Joe. While she returns to the ways of vanity, taking out her compact and brushing on make-up, as though blusher would make her magically attractive, he prepares an infinitely more powerful magic potion for her to drink before she meets the children, and possibly Joe, at school. Dressed in her signature colors of red and black, with a stylish school-girl hat, she sits down next to Joe on a bench in the school's corridor. In a scene of glorious comic dialogue, Alice engages him in a skillfully seductive dialogue that suggests years of working the bars at convention hotels rather than studying poetry at Sacred Heart Academy. She looks into his eyes and strokes his cheek gently as she asks about his music, and to her own amazement as much as his, she speaks knowledgeably about reeds and Coltrane's harmonics. Before they are interrupted by a teacher, Joe agrees to meet her in the Penguin House of the Central Park Zoo the next day.

When the potion wears off, Alice is stunned at what she has done. She tells her friend Nina that she is not trying to find an episode of meaningless sex, but Nina asks what she *is* looking for. Although she expresses horror at the idea of meeting a strange man, Alice wonders about what to wear and worries about having gotten fat recently. Plans for the still innocent tryst run into a psychological roadblock when Doug mentions that night that they have been invited to a benefit for Mother Teresa at Sacred Heart. Mention of the saintly nun and Sacred Heart stir the embers of Catholic memory. The next afternoon, bareheaded in the rain, Alice gets as far as the seal pond but never enters the Penguin House. Joe waits inside, eventually realizing that he has been stood up.

Alice confesses her failed tryst to Dr. Yang, mentioning Mother Teresa and her upbringing as the reasons she could not meet Joe. Dr. Yang cannot change the values she developed throughout her life history, but when she mentions that she knows nothing about Joe, he gives her another magic potion that will make her invisible. Thus she will be able to follow Joe around and see what kind of man he is. She sees more than she expected. Following Joe into the office of Vicki (Judy Davis), his ex-wife, Alice watches in amazement as the two engage in spontaneous and passionate sex on the office sofa. Unfortunately, the elixir wears off and Alice hides behind the couch trying to mix another dose to restore her invisibility and permit a discreet departure from the scene.

While Joe more clearly than ever represents adventure and passion in her life, Doug remains true to his stodgy form. At home that evening he looks through brochures, trying to decide which luxury car to buy next. Alice wonders once more about being a writer, but Doug is far too practical to encourage her interest in the arts. Joe calls her at home to ask if she is all right, and she declines the invitation to another meeting. The choice thus becomes clearer and more inevitable.

Dr. Yang continues his treatment by offering yet another magic herb, this one to be burned at midnight. He asks if she believes in ghosts, and when she hesitates, he offers the opinion that all Catholics believe in ghosts, a remark that he repeats. By this comment, he apparently refers to Catholic belief in a life after death, but his mocking tone is belied by the serious strategy he plans for Alice with his magic herbs. He must believe in ghosts as well.

At midnight, Alice burns her magic herbs and calmly joins Doug in their huge bed. Moments later, she rises and enters the living room, where she meets Eddie (Alec Baldwin), an artist and her first love. Eddie died when his sports car ran into a truck nearly 20 years earlier. For some inexplicable reason, for a long time Alice felt guilty about Eddie's death. Reunited now, she tells him about Joe, who is much like him: temperamental and irresponsible but cute. She tells him that their relationship has not progressed very far, and Eddie remarks: "Thou shalt not commit adultery." He adds that this line is not his, it is merely something he has read. As they speak, he picks up a hippo of Steuben glass on the end table, as though this frivolous extravagance contrasts with the Spartan life and lofty artistic aspirations they once shared.

In an invisible form, Eddie stays with Alice as she meets Joe the next day in school. When Joe wants to meet her again in the zoo to show her a polar bear with blue eyes just like hers, Eddie is impressed. He asks how long it has been since Doug used a line like that. She declines the invitation, but when Joe suggests taking their children to the Big Apple Circus, Eddie tells her that she won't go to hell for taking her kids to a circus. Eddie remembers her Catholic fear of going to hell for a serious sin, like adultery, and uses the traditional language to remind her that going to the circus with her children is no serious sin.

That night, Eddie helps Alice relive her romantic past with him. They soar over Manhattan like Superman and Lois Lane on their way to the Moonlight Casino, which burned down 10 years earlier. They dance dreamily in the empty, darkened hall. She recalls that falling in love with him was scary, and Eddie encourages her to find out how she feels about Joe. He reminds her of the nude painting of her he sold, and like Lee and Frederick in HANNAH AND HER SISTERS, the art work represents their intimacy. When she asks how many other women he made love to, he is evasive, but he adds that she was the only one who seriously considered becoming a nun. They recall the night she burned the dinner, her first roast duck, and the time Eddie argued politics with her mother, who accused him of being a Communist. Eddie wants them to have a child together, even if they do not marry. At the end of her fantasies, Eddie simply fades away.

The next day Joe, Alice and their children attend the circus, and she prompts him to speak of his former wife. He found her passionate, but they were each too opinionated for the marriage to last, he explains. They visit the Museum of Natural History, where Ike and Mary first realized that they were in love in MANHATTAN, and finally they visit a roof-top overlooking Times Square, much like the scene of Sally's amorous escapades in RADIO DAYS. All the while they are eating, a sure sign in Allen's films that they have begun to communicate on a personal level. Some days later, Alice continues to ask about Joe's former wife. He explains that she is an advertising executive, and he met her when he was doing a commercial for detergent. A half-hour later, he boasts, they were making love in the ladies' room. Alice is impressed by his irrepressible passion, and reluctantly agrees to meet him for a friend's recording session later that night. She refers to their meeting as a date.

At home that evening, Alice again brings up her need for a career, and Doug mentions his friend's wife's sweater boutique. Doug has his regular backgammon game, but as she waits for him to leave, he receives word that the game has been cancelled. She lies about having to see her sister, leaves the apartment and changes clothes in the lobby. When she finally meets Joe in front of the school, Alice is distraught. She is upset about lying to Doug, and Joe tells her she is upset not about the lies, but because she has discovered she is capable of lying to her husband. Alice is beginning to realize that her deeply held religious and moral values are crumbling very, very rapidly. Furious, she rejects Joe's offer to drive her home. She hails a cab.

Alice does not go home, however. She arrives at Dr. Yang's office and discovers that the place has become an opium den for Dr. Yang and his friends. She takes one hit to be polite, then relaxes and asks for more. Drifting into sleep, she dreams of her sister Dorothy (Blythe Danner), a successful attorney who has just moved to New York from Philadelphia, Allen's bastion of the gentile establishment. The two sisters meet outside the now dilapidated family home in the country. As they speak, Dorothy admits her revulsion for Alice's trivial life and frivolous wealth. Alice assures her that she has not yet begun cheating on Doug, and Dorothy cynically comments that Alice probably still believes all that the nuns told them in school. Alice claims that she stopped being a Catholic at 16, around the time she met Eddie. Dorothy says her days as a Catholic ended when her mother discovered her diaphragm. Through this exchange between the sisters, Allen presents the cliché perception that Catholicism can be reduced to an anti-romantic sexual morality, a common belief among Catholics and non-Catholics alike. As the film progresses, Allen will challenge and repudiate this idea.

Alice admits that she misses the music and the rituals. In the background walk two nuns in traditional garb, although not of the type once worn by the members of the Religious of the Sacred Heart of Jesus. Alice enters a confessional that has miraculously appeared on the lawn, and muses not about her potential infidelity but about her fear of raising her children without proper values. Alice recalls her adolescence and the times when she prayed with the sisters in the chapel with her arms outstretched like Jesus on the cross because she wanted to be a saint. She recalls that she was never happier than when she was able to assist sick and elderly people.

Only at the close of her dream does she recall her infatuation with Joe. Alice's Catholic tradition then consists of something more than a list of unrealistic sexual restraints. Catholic spirituality, which involves both prayer and good works, remains deeply embedded in her life, and she regrets not being able to pass these along to her children. Dorothy has touched a nerve in criticizing her current affluent and vapid life style with Doug.

The next day, when they meet outside the school, Joe kisses Alice, and she immediately looks around to see if anyone, even perhaps the eye of God, has seen them. In the evening when Alice attends the benefit for Mother Teresa with Doug, she is deeply moved and weeps copiously, but in the next scene, possibly the next afternoon, she sits on the bed in Joe's apartment while rain pours on the skylight. This time not even Mother Teresa could derail her plans for adultery. After their love making, both lovers ask about their performance, and each tries to persuade the other that it was something special. Alice next appears in a class in creative writing at Columbia, a clear indication that she has gained the courage to move out of Doug's orbit intellectually as well as sexually.

Alice's inhibitions drop away like autumn leaves. She meets Joe openly at Barbetta's restaurant, and after they finish a bottle of wine, she playfully shares her disappearing herbs with him, and the invisible pair enjoy a pleasant journey along Madison Avenue. He wants to make love to her on top of a mail box, but even invisible, she has some sense of restraint. They enter an expensive boutique, where Alice eavesdrops on her friends and learns that Doug has had his own series of infidelities. The gossips don't blame him, since they think Alice is the mousy mother-superior type. Scarcely interested in such gossip, Joe prefers to follow model Elle McPherson into the dressing room.

Life quickly unravels for Alice. Emboldened by her disappearing herbs, uninvited and unannounced she drops in on Doug's office Christmas party, just as Doug brings an attractive young executive into his office. Without much preliminary conversation, they begin to make love just as Joe and Vicki had. From their conversation, Alice realizes that their affair has been going on for some time. She understands then that Doug may have passion in his life, but she has no part in it. She serves only as his trophy. As her potion wears off, she becomes visible and surprises the lovers in *flagrante*. By this time it is clear, even to her that the marriage is over. Later that evening, both Doug and Alice deny their infidelities, and their lies confirm the end of their love.

Before his dose of disappearing potion wears off, Joe turns from Madison Avenue and eavesdrops on a session between his ex-wife Vicki and her therapist. He learns that Vicki still loves him. When Alice meets him in the rehearsal studio, he tells her what he did, and as a result, he and Vicki have decided to try to restore their marriage. He and Alice will not see each other again.

With Doug and Joe both gone, Alice returns to her last friend, Dr. Yang, who is packing for a trip to Tibet to learn about new potions. He tells her that love makes human beings most unpredictable. He explains that where there is no logical thought, there can be much romance and much suffering. He offers her one last herb, which is a strong love potion. When she decides which man to choose, she will give him this draught and he will fall irretrievably in love with her. The potion becomes a joke, both in the film and in her life, when a maid drops it into the eggnog at a Christmas party and ardent suitors nearly start a riot to gain her affection.

As Alice walks alone along Fifth Avenue on her way home from the Christmas party, she thinks deeply about her life. She meets two wealthy women wrapped in furs who talk about liposuction and Palm Beach. This is her future, and she wants no part of it. At home, Doug admits his guilt and offers a trip to Barbados to restore their lives to what they were before. She does not want that either, and she announces that she is going to Calcutta to work with Mother Teresa. Although she does not intend to take the vows of convent life, she at last fulfills her adolescent dream of becoming a nun and serving those in need.

The gossips at the beauty parlor snidely narrate the final phases of Alice's story, which includes her journey back from Calcutta to a poor neighborhood in New York where she works in a settlement house and spends every available minute with her children. In their eyes, Alice is deranged, but they excuse her folly with the observation that she always had a Catholic streak in her. In the final shot, Alice pushes her children on a playground swing, as happy in her new life with her family as Ben was dancing with his daughter at her wedding at the end of CRIMES AND MISDEMEANORS.

The similarity is not accidental. Both Alice and Ben take great strength from their respective religious traditions. Both find great happiness precisely from living out the premises of their faith. Through his belief Ben finds the courage to accept his blindness, and through hers Alice discovers happiness in her own ability to sacrifice herself for others. Neither wealth and security with Doug, nor passion and adventure with Joe were able to make her happy, but living a moral, even a heroic saintly life as shaped by her religious tradition is itself enough to give her a sense of fulfillment and meaning.

Despite his wisdom in matters of the heart, Dr. Yang could only bring Alice part of the way along her journey. He could not grasp the depth of the Catholic influence in her life. Dr. Yang is another of Allen's limited men of science, but one who oddly combines this role with that of the magician.[9] He opened her to a world of human emotions and passion, and this was the necessary first step, but at the end he can do no better than offer her one more magic potion to help her find another man to love. The frantic search for love becomes a transparent fiasco at the Christmas party. Like Cecilia in THE PURPLE ROSE OF CAIRO, Alice finally opts for reality over magic. She underlines her independence by pouring the rest of the herb down the drain as she tells Doug about her resolve to fly to Calcutta.

Alice's family, as they appear to her in fact and fantasy, furthers the work that Dr. Yang began. Alice's mother (Gwen Verdon) appears while Alice tries to organize her past life into material for a script she is writing. Her Muse (Bernadette Peters) puts on Allen-like glasses and helps Alice see the truth about her family before she tries to process her life into art. Alice had convinced herself that her mother, a minor screen actress, sacrificed a promising career for marriage. The truth, her mother explains, is that as she began to show signs of aging, the studios lost interest and she was happy to have a husband to take care of her. Without him, she would have committed suicide, the standard Allen option for handling a difficult time. When he did die, she did drink herself to death with Margaritas. Through her mother, Alice gains insight into the danger of her present need for Doug to protect her, and she becomes aware of the risk of future self-destruction if she surrenders her own independence as her mother had.

Dorothy presents a fascinating critique of Alice's life. As Alice's older sister, she experienced similar childhood influences from faith and family, yet Dorothy went on to become a successful lawyer, while Alice abandoned her career ambitions immediately after high school. One chooses independence, the other surrendered her freedom to have someone take care of her. Quite early in life both reject what they learned about sexual morality from the sisters at Sacred Heart, and by her own testimony, each considers herself no longer Catholic. Dorothy, however, keeps her own "Catholic streak" by objecting to Alice's life of conspicuous consumption. Dorothy holds the riches of this world as slightly suspect. As a lawyer, she affirms in her life a kind of Catholic incarnationalism. She sees the world as an arena where human activity and divine grace interact, although she would certainly no longer put it that way. That is something else the nuns once told her, and even though her thinking may have become completely secularized, she still wants to make a difference in the world. Alice has drifted into a most un-Catholic passivity. Her security rests upon closets filled with clothes and nurseries filled with expensive stuffed animals. Dorothy can explain this to her bluntly. They speak the same religiously-grounded language, while Dr. Yang does not.

Like Dorothy, her girlhood friend Nancy Brill (Cybill Shepherd) exposes Alice to a role model for professional success, but one that Allen reveals as empty. As a lawyer, Dorothy can occasionally do something worthwhile for people, but Nancy deals in schlock television scripts. For a time, Alice thinks she wants to be like her. On two occasions, Alice visits her former friend, hoping to gain her help in breaking into script writing, but as they talk Nancy looks at her watch, thumbs through typescripts on her coffee table and eventually escorts Alice to the door. Nancy buys scripts for a cable television company and cannot imagine that Alice could produce the adult fare she needs. She wants blood-and-guts stuff, and the heroines must be sexy and unscrupulous, scarcely the kind of material Alice would be likely to create, given her own sheltered background. Once again Allen uses commercial television to represent an artistic sell-out, and Alice, ever the Sacred Heart girl, values life and art too much to enter that world, even though for a time she has a feeling that she would like to.

In his chronicle of Alice's journey, Allen shows a remarkably sympathetic understanding of Catholic culture. Many of the characters he creates for ALICE seem to take for granted that Alice is a victim of repressive Catholic sexual morality. They seem to suggest that if she could simply forget what the nuns told her about adultery, and enter a nice healthy, liberated affair with Joe, or anyone else, she would find happiness. Eventually, she does, and it doesn't work for her. She wasn't overwhelmed with Catholic guilt, and in fact she was willing to continue to see Joe, but the passion she shared with him was simply not enough to bring her lasting happiness. Some time spent with Mother Teresa, however, changes her life and makes her extremely happy. Alice's exuberant joy should be enough to confound and silence the gossips at the beauty parlor.

Douglas Brode, a long-time student and critic of Allen's films, summarizes Allen's conclusions in ALICE as clearly having religious content: "Woody is not suggesting that every one of us should run out and convert to Catholicism. What he is saying, however, is that in order to be happy, we must reclaim the most decent and traditional values, learn to walk away from not only capital gains [Doug] but also hedonist pleasure [Joe], idealistic romance [Eddie] and even artistic ambition [Nancy]. Essentially, [Allen is] calling for a return to the most basic of Christ's teachings. . . ."[10]

SHADOWS AND FOG (1992) reveals that Allen's exploration of religious traditions in his previous two films had produced little of lasting value to help him with his perennial problems of meaning and morality. Judaism helped Ben through his acceptance of blindness, and Catholicism provided a meaning in life for Alice, but neither religious tradition, Allen concludes, can offer much to him. In these earlier two films, Allen conceded that others may indeed discover a kind of happiness through their beliefs, and that was fine for them, but in SHADOWS AND FOG, the organized religions take on a sinister quality, menacing the life of the Allen surrogate, Max Kleinman, whose name translates from German as "little man." Religions may provide answers for believers but they can be quite hostile to ordinary, every-day agnostics like Allen.

In SHADOWS AND FOG Allen scrupulously re-creates the look of the German Expressionist movies of the 1920's and 1930's. The action takes place at night, and the narrow cobblestone streets are invariably damp, while stone walls and fog absorb light from pathetically inadequate street lamps. Grotesque shadows distort commonplace reality beyond recognition. The plots of such films are convoluted and filled with loose ends. Terrified characters find themselves menaced in stairways, tunnels and blind alleys, and as they search for solutions to their problems, they are more victims of coincidence than agents of their own destiny. These stylistic traits, of course, are more than visual tricks designed to provide horror-show thrills. They reflect the inner turmoil of the soul in a state of metaphysical dread, and as such they "create states of anxiety and terror."[11] This visual style of the German Expressionists will eventually develop into the form of American Expressionism known as the film noir, which became the cinematic language of choice for American detective stories in the 1940's and 1950's.[12]

Allen's use of Expressionist lighting and sets is no mere exercise in film history. In the context of Allen's development as an artist and thinker, the dark and ominous look of this unnamed central European city provides the perfect image of the universe as Allen perceives it. This represents a return to his earlier, darker view of the world, where he could justify life on this grim planet only by cherishing crumbs of human happiness, like memories of a love he had lost in ANNIE HALL or a Marx Brothers movie in HANNAH AND HER SISTERS. As Allen began to work through his various questions, the later films contained a more nuanced view of life that is reflected in the visual style. In CRIMES AND MISDEMEANORS, for example, the scenes of darkness in Judah's living room or office or the exteriors around Dolores's apartment on the night she is murdered are balanced by scenes of light, such as the several formal dinner parties or the conversations in the open spaces in parks and gardens. In ALICE, the heroine wears bright red costumes and meets Joe in well lighted rooms, while Dr. Yang's office is dark and many of her dreams take place at night. By their visual styles, both of these films offer a richly textured pattern of happiness and desperation.

In SHADOWS AND FOG, by contrast, the gloom is unrelieved even by the comic lines and situations. After offering reasons to hope for happiness in one's religious tradition in the earlier two films, Allen now slams the door on optimism and on religious belief. With SHADOWS AND FOG Allen reverses his theological direction altogether. Unable to accept the faith of either Ben or Alice, Allen retreats into a horrifying world that provides an uncompromisingly hostile environment for him. Morality no longer seems to bring its own rewards, and happiness is an improbable goal. This world offers few instances of love and many opportunities for betrayal.

Trying to survive in this universe is Max Kleinman (Woody Allen), whose wire-rimmed glasses give him an uncanny resemblance to Leonard Zelig. Kleinman describes himself as an ink-stained clerk and lives alone as a bachelor. He is ethnically Jewish, but at present a professed agnostic. Since ANNIE HALL Allen's heroes have been relatively prosperous writers, teachers or producers. Kleinman represents a throwback to a very early type of Allen character, like Virgil Starkwell the failed gangster in TAKE THE MONEY AND RUN, or Fielding Mellish the inept product tester in BANANAS. Kleinman has not even managed to be particularly successful in earning his livelihood. He refers to his employer, Mr. Paulsen (Philip Bosco), as your majesty, and as he competes with Simon Carr (Wallace Shawn) for a promotion in the firm, he becomes the complete sycophant. The universe is not a hospitable place for Max Kleinman.

After several still shots of the city establish both locale and atmosphere, the camera follows a mysterious man in a homburg as he lights a cigarette, and it reveals a large, sinister figure as he emerges from the shadows and tramps stiffly down a stone staircase. A band of vigilantes shatters the ominous silence by pounding on Kleinman's door and rousing him from bed. They are impatient with his slow response and ask if he is deaf. He tells them that he was in a deep sleep. Dressed only in his underwear during their most unfriendly visit, Kleinman learns that he must join the posse in searching for a homicidal maniac who prowls through the streets striking without reason. Kleinman says that he would rather leave the matter to the police and go back to bed. They respond that the police have had their chance, now it is time to take matters into their own hands. From their brusque orders Kleinman feels that he may be a suspect himself, but he is not sure of what crime he may be accused. Kleinman wants to know what he must do, but they tell him he will learn the plan in time. By the time he dresses and stumbles out into the street, they are gone, and he is alone.

Through this comic interrogation, Allen has sketched the outline of the philosophic inquiry of the film. Kleinman's universe is threatening enough to begin with, but the added presence of inexplicable evil, in the form of a homicidal maniac, makes the world even more hostile, and finding a solution becomes a matter of extraordinary urgency. They have to stop him before he strikes again. Kleinman may be deaf to what is happening in the world, as the vigilantes suggest, but he is actually asleep and prefers to continue sleeping, not bothering with the problems of the outside world. A man in his underwear seems especially "exposed" and vulnerable, and the image of Kleinman cringing and whining before his inquisitors reveals the frail status of the human person facing the terrible, incomprehensible forces loose in the universe.

The vigilantes speak of their plan, but they will not share it with him until some unspecified time in the future. Allen's world is unfair; there must be a plan, divine or human, to put order into the chaos of this universe, but he cannot find out what it is. Other people—like Ben or Alice, for example—seem to be able to depend upon their respective religious traditions to provide a plan to help them understand the world and cope with its evil, but Kleinman has no such help. Does God have a plan for his creation? Do human beings have a plan to deal with the universe, whether or not there is a God? The vigilantes appear certain that they have a plan, but they abandon Kleinman, and he must begin his search alone, a task that is doubly difficult since he does not know what he is looking for.

In a few brilliant comic moments, Allen has restated the agnostic's conundrum that has continued to haunt him from his earliest films. One reading Allen's films from a religious perspective, however, must be careful to avoid reducing SHADOWS AND FOG to a form of simplistic allegory. Searching for literal one-to-one relationships between fictional events and characters and the ideas they represent in Allen's mind could compromise the rich subtlety of the text. The homicidal maniac, for example, is not a malevolent God, but more accurately the irrational evil that remains unchecked in the world. This mystery nags believers and nonbelievers alike. God, if he exists, has designed a universe where such things are possible, and that is Allen's problem. In several other contexts, it may be recalled, Allen uses Hitler to represent the question of inexplicable evil in a world supposedly designed by a loving God. The vigilantes, who themselves vaguely suggest Nazi secret police, do not necessarily represent the various competing dogmatic denominations, but they do suggest all kinds of people—scientists, philosophers and artists, as well as theologians—who think they have clear answers to serious problems but do not, cannot or will not share them. Kleinman, or Allen, must wonder if they have these answers at all, or are merely bluffing.

One type of person who pretends to have the answers in Allen films is the man of science, like Leopold in A MIDSUMMER NIGHT'S SEX COMEDY or Lloyd in SEPTEMBER. As Kleinman begins his journey through the city in search of a plan, he first visits The Doctor (Donald Pleasence), whose laboratory is crowded with cadavers in various stages of dissection and jars filled with human organs. The Doctor conducts his experiments with great urgency because of the murders. He tells Kleinman that these horrific events have given him an opportunity to conduct experiments to probe the nature of evil. He boasts that when he finishes his work he will have the answers to questions he can presently only speculate about. When Kleinman asks if there may be something that he cannot see with his microscopes, the Doctor scoffs at the notion of spiritual realities, just as Lloyd and Leopold do. He lifts the sheet on one of his cadavers and tells Kleinman to ask him about the reality of life after death. Kleinman gags at the sight, and possibly the smell, takes a stiff drink and leaves, no more enlightened about the plan than he had been. As he returns to the street, he passes by a huge eye painted on the wall. Someone, or something, is watching him, but at this point it is not clear whether it is the eye of God or the vigilantes or the killer. Later in the film, Allen confirms the suspicion that God has little to do with Kleinman's life.

The Doctor continues his work, but later in the evening as he holds a human heart in his forceps, he realizes that the killer has entered the laboratory. He asks the maniac why he kills, and then reminds himself that it is foolish to ask a question of an irrational mind. He tells the killer that if he could examine the inside of his brain, he would find chaos. He wonders aloud where insanity stops and evil begins. By making this distinction between insanity and evil, Allen proposes the perfectly valid observation that the first can often be explained by medical science; the second remains a mystery. The Doctor thinks he can find a physiological, scientific cause for insanity, but even if he can, he realizes, too late perhaps, that evil transcends insanity. Bolting from the laboratory, The Doctor tries to escape, but soon finds himself in a blind alley, where the maniac murders him. Evil, Allen argues, cannot be explained in rational scientific terms, and The Doctor soon learns that his folly has led him into a scientific blind alley.

Not all Kleinman's encounters with science end in death. As he walks through the night with Irmy (Mia Farrow), the fog parts for a few minutes and they look at the stars. Irmy improbably takes the role of the scientist and points out that what they see in the sky is merely light from stars that ceased to exist millions of years ago. Kleinman is distressed by the thought and says he wants to know that what he sees is really there, but as they speak, the fog returns and Kleinman is no closer to certainty than ever. Irmy says the real mystery is that the two of them are there, as strangers, looking at the stars, but Kleinman responds that everything is in motion and the thought makes him nauseous. Restating the usual Allen remedy for Sartre's "Nausea," Irmy replies that her father used to tell her that everyone is happy but rarely recognizes the fact.

Where reason fails to provide answers to life's mysteries, Allen generally turns to love to give him a reason to keep living. His normally comic romantic conflicts take a decidedly sour turn in SHADOWS AND FOG. Irmy, the circus sword swallower, lives with The Clown (John Malkovich), who despite her pleading refuses to marry her, have children and settle down in a town like ordinary people. He claims he is an artist and needs room to grow, and yet he wonders why audiences do not appreciate him the way they once did. He leaves their wagon, and falls directly into the arms of the star aerialist Marie (Madonna). When Irmy discovers them, she attacks him physically and resolves to leave him forever.

Irmy appears to be the wounded innocent, but later that night as she wanders alone by the river bank she meets a streetwalker (Lily Tomlin), who offers her a place to stay as a guest in her brothel. These philosophic ladies-in-waiting are half-sisters to Tom Baxter's hospitable friends in THE PURPLE ROSE OF CAIRO. Their conversation at dinner opens new horizons for Irmy. The Lily Tomlin character explains that she turned to prostitution to pay her husband's medical bills, but when he recovered, he threw her out. Once again Allen points out that virtue is often punished. Another hostess (Jodie Foster), argues that the only love that lasts is unrequited love, and they agree that a good marriage is based on luck. These thoughts about the transient nature of love and the element of chance in marriage are familiar Allen themes. Their cynical views on love and marriage disturb Irmy, who shortly before wanted to leave the circus and begin a family.

An eager young customer named Jack (John Cusack) mistakes Irmy for one of the working ladies and bids for her favors. Irmy at first declines with some embarrassment, and the professionals scorn Jack for thinking he can buy anyone he wants. When the price reaches $700, however, Irmy's innocence evaporates. Like all the other women in the room, Irmy too has her price. Later, as Irmy and Jack compare notes on their performances, Irmy reasserts her innocence, saying that her activities that night do not reflect her real self. Jack responds that perhaps her true self had emerged for the first time. The remark is ambiguous. It may refer to her uninhibited passion, but it may reflect Jack's view that under the surface of innocence, Irmy is a whore at heart. Later in the film, when the Jodie Foster character offers her favors to Kleinman, he says he has never paid for sex before, and she replies that he only thinks he hasn't, offering the cynical suggestion that all sexual activity is prostitution and all women are whores.

Allen's misogyny, emerging clearly in CRIMES AND MISDEMEANORS and continuing with the gossiping girlfriends in ALICE, has taken a bitter, cynical turn in SHADOWS AND FOG. In the funny bordello scene in THE PURPLE ROSE OF CAIRO, the ladies of the evening are moved by Tom Baxter's innocence and his naive reflections on marriage and childbirth. They are so impressed by Tom's refreshing views that they even offer him a freebie. Tom wins them over to his point of view. In SHADOWS AND FOG, however, the cynicism of the whores prevails, and both Irmy and Kleinman, at first seemingly innocent, become corrupted and enter into the business of sex for money.

The police break in and arrest Irmy for practicing without a license. The Clown, now duly repentant, searches the city for her, and in his travels he meets Jack, who describes his own marvelous experience with Irmy. Since it was merely lust, not love, Jack explains, he no longer feels any attraction to her. When The Clown finally locates Irmy, after her stay in the police station, he wants both her and the money she earned. They argue and fight, but then they discover the body of a woman murdered in the street and her baby girl crying nearby. At first he insists on handing the infant over to the authorities, who will put her into an orphanage, but Irmy eventually persuades him to bring her home, where The Clown instantly becomes a doting father. After mutual infidelities, Irmy and The Clown have become reconciled, and the child represents the future and new life for them. In the past Allen frequently used a sin and reconciliation theme to show that couples must learn to tolerate each other's faults in an imperfect world. This child, however, enters their lives not as the result of their love, but because of chance, precipitated by a cruel, unmotivated murder.

Irmy and The Clown certainly act out Allen's familiar reconciliation ritual, but it is undercut by the notion that their good fortune and love stem from an act of unspeakable evil. Human actions, good or ill, have unpredictable consequences, unrelated to the morality of the agents. Allen thus returns to Job's and Cliff Stern's conundrum at the end of CRIMES AND MISDEMEANORS: Why is evil rewarded and virtue punished? The question of consequences becomes poignant for Kleinman as well. Kleinman has done everything possible for Irmy, and he has been rejected in favor of The Clown, a self-centered, grasping philanderer. Irmy and The Clown have each other and the child, and Kleinman, after a good-bye handshake from Irmy, is left alone, just like Cliff Stern. Kleinman's world holds little reason or justice.

During their journey together, Irmy leads Kleinman through an exploration of a type of Catholicism that is far less attractive than Alice's. Irmy's Catholic background is revealed through the small icon of Our Lady of Perpetual Help that she keeps on her dressing table in the circus wagon. As she and Kleinman wander through the city, she stops under a huge crucifix on the front of a church. The image moves her to repentance. To ease her conscience about her new-found source of wealth, she asks Kleinman to give the money to the church. She is ashamed to enter the building herself. Inside, Kleinman finds a priest and a police officer, two cold, impersonal authority figures, working together on a list of names. It is not clear what the list is for, but it seems ominous. They tell Kleinman they are busy. When Kleinman interrupts, they add his name to the list. When Kleinman gives them the money, the officer wants to know where it came from, but the priest looks at the money and discourages further questions. They take the money and erase his name. When money is involved, the church can conveniently and hypocritically turn the blind eye toward moral evil.

Outside Irmy and Kleinman meet a desperately needy woman with a baby, the same woman who is murdered later that night. Irmy tells Kleinman to return to the church and take back half of her contribution, which was intended for the poor anyway. He is reluctant because he believes that they use the money for costumes and velvet cushions, too, but finally he does as she asks. As Kleinman takes the money, the officer puts his name on the list once more and circles it.

In this sequence, Allen presents an image of Catholicism as cold, authoritarian and venal. Clergy and police act as one to keep lists of malefactors, a bit of business that uncomfortably recalls the charges of collaboration with the Nazis frequently directed against the Catholic Church. Charitable contributions, Allen suggests, may be effective to ease one's conscience, but when Irmy takes back half of the money for the hungry woman, Allen implies that earthly concerns are best left to direct human generosity, without the intervention of some ecclesiastical middleman. For some reason, Allen has become rapidly disenchanted with the work of people like Mother Teresa and "the Catholic streak" in her followers like Alice Tate.

The vigilantes and police function as agents of vengeance for an unknown power. Kleinman watches the police place the Mintz family under arrest, a sight that recalls Nazi round-ups of Jews on the flimsiest of pretexts. Complaining to the police, he repeats the Job theme that appears consistently since BROADWAY DANNY ROSE: Why are innocent people allowed to suffer, when they haven't done anything wrong. The chief assures Kleinman that he has nothing to worry about, since they won't go any further than the Orthodox elements. After dealing with Jews in varied states of successful assimilation and adaptation for his past several films, Allen now returns to his earlier concern with the Jew as threatened outsider. When Irmy asks if he believes in God and prays, Kleinman says that his people pray in another language and he was never sure they weren't calling down their problems on themselves. The irrational persecution of the Jews and God's failure to intervene reappear as Allen's greatest obstacle in finding a meaning in the universe.

The vigilante bands, however, cannot agree on a unified strategy and soon turn against one another. After the murder of one of the leaders by a rival group, one band captures Kleinman and tells him he must make a choice among the competing posses, but Kleinman maintains that he does not know enough to make a choice. As non-committed, he becomes everyone's enemy and is nearly hanged by the frenzied mob. Again the religious parallel is clear. Since he cannot choose among antagonistic sects, he is vilified by all.

Kleinman is rejected by Irmy, shut out by his fiancée Eve (Kate Nelligan) when he tries to get her to take in Irmy, and nearly shot by his former fiancée (Julie Kavner), who accuses him of having sex with her sister in a broom closet on the very day he failed to show up for his wedding to her. Since he has had such terrible relationships with the women in his life, none of them will take him in when the lynch mob closes in and he needs help. By chance, he wanders into the brothel, where no questions are asked and he is as welcome as anyone else.

When Kleinman arrives, Jack and the ladies are engaged in their deep philosophical discussion. They agree that bondage brings freedom from natural impulses, and thus provides an exhilarating experience. As a slave, one no longer has to assume responsibility for one's actions. Freedom is burdensome, a notion that Allen has not formally expressed since his play "God," published in 1975.[13] The notion does however coincide with Cliff Stern's sense of tragedy at the end of CRIMES AND MISDEMEANORS, when he tells Judah how terrible it would be if a man had to assume total responsibility for his acts.

Jack plays the cynic, telling the Jodie Foster character, that she is a true whore because her only God is money. She tops him in cynicism by countering that it is better to worship a false god than to believe in no god. Allen seems to be proposing the pursuit of wealth as a substitute for a higher morality or even romance, a position he resolutely rejected through his hostile treatment of Doug Tate and the idle, rich women in ALICE. At least, Allen implies, the tough prostitute is honest with herself and doesn't need illusions, like Alice.

One of the whores says life means having as much wine and as many men as possible, while another maintains that if this is all life means, she would kill herself. In this statement she reiterates the common Allen option for characters in distress. Still one other wants to die in her sleep and leave the scene quietly. Jack admits that he has thought of suicide himself, but only as a response to the problems posed by his intellect. His blood gives him lust, and so when given a choice he sides with his blood, and that gives him a reason to continue living. Kleinman has told them he cannot make any option, even the one between intellect and blood, and so the Jody Foster character makes the decision for blood and lust for him, offering him an experience of life in the back room. Kleinman, however, is so burdened by his intellectual problems that he is impotent and cannot complete the sexual act with her. Kleinman's impotence suggests both human powerlessness in dealing with the universe and the human's frequently unsuccessful quest for a loving relationship. In this scene, Allen has also returned to an early theme by inflicting Kleinman with a case of anhedonia, an affliction that seemed cured years earlier.

In the final moments of the film, Kleinman is chased in turn by vigilantes, the police and the maniac. His flight leads to the circus, where Kleinman warns Irmy just before the mad killer strikes. The killer follows Kleinman into a circus tent, where Armstead the Magician (Kenneth Mars), gloriously drunk, prepares his apparatus for travel. Armstead's illusions help Kleinman escape and then trap the killer, but he inexplicably escapes, free to continue his irrational mischief in an irrational world. Not even a magician can keep evil trapped in a steel cage and chains. Similarly, God, if such a being exists, seems to be equally inept in containing the evil running loose in his creation. No one can explain how the tricks worked, or how the killer escaped. Evil remains a mystery, and the killer is free to strike again. After some hesitation Kleinman accepts a job as Armstead's assistant. Armstead's final comment is that people don't only like illusions, they need them. With that, he raises his hand, and the screen goes black.

Like Cecilia in THE PURPLE ROSE OF CAIRO and Alice, Kleinman must decide between reality and illusion. Cecilia chooses reality, but for her, life is bearable only because she can escape into the movies; Alice finds life itself rewarding. Kleinman chooses to reject his real world and remain in the world of circus illusion. Allen suggests that when people face inexplicable evil, like a homicidal maniac, they will escape into an illusion, like God, not because they want to but because they need to. Allen shows Kleinman trying to perform a trick with coins, but he fails. Like Kleinman, Allen knows that such illusions are phony, mere feats of manual dexterity and stage props, yet this is the choice that Kleinman makes. But without illusion, Allen insists, life is simply insupportable.

HUSBANDS AND WIVES (1992) revisits the documentary style that Allen had not used since TAKE THE MONEY AND RUN (1969), if one distinguishes the documentary from the newsreel technique that he used in ZELIG (1983). In the earlier film Allen presented a parody of television biographies, which as he saw it, tended to inflate the importance of their subject, in this case Virgil Starkwell, nonentity. HUSBANDS AND WIVES uses the cinema verité style, complete with interviews conducted by an off-screen voice, while each of the principal characters sits alone wired with a visible microphone cord. The technique provides not biography, like the earlier film, but an extended session of psychoanalysis. The camera and interviewer become the analyst, loosing a whirlwind of memories and long repressed feelings. As the process continues, the characters reach new levels of honesty with themselves.

Each of these complex New York sophisticates in the narrative are interesting people in their own right, and thus their stories hold a value of their own. Allen may have an additional purpose in mind, however. He may be substituting the film maker for the analyst and presenting a record of his own psychological state through the comments of the different characters. Even without tying the persons and situations of the film to the events in this turbulent period of Allen's life, one can still perceive in the fiction reflections of different facets of Allen's own personality. Such awareness adds insight into the mind of the artist, but very little about his life. While the ruthless probing and questioning of the camera enables the documentarist to get inside the characters in this fictional narrative, it also provides a fascinating look at Woody Allen as he enters his late fifties.

HUSBANDS AND WIVES completes the downward movement of the parabola of Allen's religious reflections in this most recent period of his film making. As the story opens, Gabe Roth (Woody Allen), a modestly successful novelist and teacher of creative writing at Columbia, plays with the television dial. On the screen he sees an unidentified scientist (Nick Metropolis) talking about a symposium in honor of Albert Einstein, the paradigmatic "man of science." The television scientist recalls that on that occasion Einstein said God doesn't leave the universe to chance, but Gabe responds that he prefers to hide and let people try to find him. On another channel an announcer tries to sell a mail-order course in writing, and with that Gabe turns off the set in disgust.

Judy Roth (Mia Farrow) carries an armful of books, including a volume of Sartre, across the living room. Gabe comments on the ad, saying that no one can teach something like writing. Writing is a gift that people have or they don't. The best a teacher can do is expose students to great literature and hope that they are inspired.

This opening scene begins the narrative and introduces two principal characters quite effectively. One need go no further than that to appreciate this exchange. At the same time, however, in the wider context of Allen's preoccupations, it is significant that the film begins with a reference to God that Gabe dismisses with his cynical remark about hide-and-seek. A talent for writing, he insists, is an innate gift; it cannot be acquired. This is the same proposition Allen has consistently used to describe his own inability to make a "leap of faith" in a God that would give meaning to his world and its moral structures. This idea appears explicitly in the seder debate in CRIMES AND MISDEMEANORS. The best one can do is read the theologians and philosophers and hope to be inspired to believe. Allen has done the reading, but the inspiration to believe never comes to him or his heroes. Gabe turns the set off and walks away. For the duration of this film at least, Allen turns his back on his religious questions. God will play no role whatever.

Gabe and Judy prepare to spend the evening with their friends Jack (Sydney Pollack) and Sally (Judy Davis). As the hand-held camera darts and swoops through the confined spaces of the apartment, Sally announces quite matter-of-factly that she and Jack have decided to separate. While Jack and Sally are quite calm about their future, Judy becomes furious. As Sally observes later in the film, Judy was upset because they had done something that she wanted to do but could not. In her on-screen interview, Judy at first proposes that she was hurt because Sally had not confided in her, but as she continues to discuss the matter with her unseen interviewer, she admits that she wondered what it would be like to be single again.

As the story progresses, Allen reveals more about Jack, who may represent one side of Allen's own personality. Like Ken in ANOTHER WOMAN or Elliot in HANNAH AND HER SISTERS, Jack has become lonely in his marriage, a fact he foolishly reveals to a business associate. This friend sets him up with Shawn (Christi Conaway), an expensive call girl. At first Jack rejects the proposal, but as he finds Sally becoming ever more tedious, he makes the phone call and arranges a meeting at the Americana Hotel. During their first meeting he is impotent and suffers from chest pains, an echo of Uncle Abe's reaction to his guilt when he eats pork chops and shell fish on Yom Kippur in RADIO DAYS. Later, as Shawn reveals in an interview, Jack began regularly meeting her and then one of her girl friends as well, and thus the pattern of infidelity was set.

When Jack leaves Sally and moves in with his personal trainer, an aerobics and astrology expert named Sam (Lysette Anthony), he ends his relationship with the two call girls. Jack enjoys simple low-brow entertainment with Sam that Sally would never have tolerated. In a later interview, Sally tells about seeing Jack enter a lingerie shop on Lexington Avenue to buy a bra-and-panties set for his athletic young mistress when he had told her he was going to be in Chicago. Lies compound the evil of infidelity, and Sally realizes their marriage is ending. Allen has Judah in CRIMES AND MISDEMEANORS describe the threat to his own marriage as two years of plotting and deception. Loneliness and a desperate quest for love have driven Jack to outright foolishness, as they have many of Allen's heroes in the past.

Delight in this simple child-woman is destined not to last. At first Jack enjoys her mindless chatter about health foods, and he revels in his new diet and exercise regime, but as they leave a screening of Kurosawa's RAN, he expresses impatience at Sam's calling "King Lear" "King Leo," but Sam excuses her mistake by arguing that Shakespeare wrote in English, while Kurosawa used Japanese to retell the story. Their relationship ends violently when Sam joins Jack's sophisticated friends for drinks and argues with them relentlessly about the validity of astrological predictions. Jack, who has just been shaken by hearing that Sally is seeing another man, is furious. He drags Sam physically away from the party and drives to Sally's and his home in Riverdale. Allen portrays something pathetic in Jack's emotional immaturity and frantic quest for love. His eventual reunion with Sally, through yet one more restatement of his sin and reconciliation theme, affirms Allen's familiar proposition that imperfect relationships are preferable to the futile search for perfect love.

Sally is not without fault herself. While Gabe offers criticism freely, in the manner of all English teachers, he acknowledges quality as well. Sally's negativity is unrelieved, a dark, unpleasant image of Gabe's (and Allen's) relentless dedication to high standards. Just like Marion in ANOTHER WOMAN, Gabe offers devastating comments in the name of complete honesty, but he is at heart a gentle, polite man. In contrast, Sally is a volcano of rage. On the evening she learns that Jack has moved in with Sam within three weeks of their separation, she erupts. She calls Jack twice from the apartment of her dinner companion Paul (Timothy

Jerome) and screams obscenities over the phone. When Paul tries to calm her down by explaining that he has tickets for "Don Giovanni," Sally says that the opera is about Don Juan, who should have been castrated for his activities. Paul's stupefied expression indicates that this romance with this incendiary woman will go no further, even if he survives the evening.

Even when Sally meets Michael (Liam Neeson) and wants to gain his affection, she cannot control her tongue. She criticizes his taste in architecture and furniture. On the evening he plans to propose their entering into a more lasting relationship, she finds fault with the sauce served at his favorite restaurant, explains that the performance of Mahler was a bit slow and says she was a bit carsick because of his erratic driving. Sometime later, when Michael stays the night with her, they agree that they were distant during sex. Sally says that her mind is hyperactive, even when she is in his arms.

Their pillow talk ends when Jack breaks into the house. Quite drunk and still in a rage, he has just left the party with Sam. When he discovers Michael, he knows the gossip is true and his fury triggers a monstrous four-way screaming match. Nothing is resolved for the moment, but it is clear that Jack has had it with Sam and wants to come back to Sally. The Allen theme of sin and reconciliation has never been presented in a more harrowing scene. Allen never shows them embracing in a gesture of mutual forgiveness. Instead a voice-over narrator explains that two weeks later they are back together, as though they merely accepted the inevitable. In one final scene, they are in bed together and express satisfaction that they decided to forget about their concert tickets in order to be alone with each other. They had thought of giving the tickets to Gabe and Judy, but they know that things have changed between them.

Their insight is an understatement, since things have been changing between Gabe and Judy for some time. While Sally is violent and confrontational, Judy is manipulative. During an interview, Judy's former husband of five years (Benno Schmidt) describes how she cultivates her victimhood to get what she wants. What she wants most of all is another child, but Gabe, like Sam in ANOTHER WOMAN, does not think it fair to bring another life into this terrible world. Because she fears Gabe's criticism, she gives her poetry to Michael, a fellow editor at her office. She wants encouragement, she admits, not criticism. Later she admits that she wants Michael as well, even though she remains married to Gabe. Since Judy introduced Michael to Sally, he assumes that their friendship is platonic and Judy still wants to see him married to Sally. After Gabe and Judy separate and Jack and Sally reunite, Judy prepares a dinner for Michael, and he confides that he still loves Sally, and under these circumstances a relationship with Judy is not possible. Judy storms out amid a torrent of angry tears. Michael follows her and holds her in his arms to show his remorse for his thoughtless comment. He has fallen into the trap set by the expert victim. A voice-over narrator explains that a year and a half later they are married. Once again, Judy got what she wanted.

Gabe is less fortunate. He tries to satisfy Judy's needs, and even consents to their having a child if that will help, but Judy is offended at Gabe's suggestion that she needs help in keeping her marriage alive. During an all-night conversation, they share their frustrations and anger, but they remember the good times as well, like walks in the snow in Central Park and watching WILD STRAWBERRIES together on late-night television. In that film, Professor Isak Borg sorts through the memories of his search for love, as do Gabe and Sally in their conversation. For a moment they seemed poised for a classic Allen reconciliation, but it is not to be.

In earlier Allen movies, tender memories would be enough to keep them going, but not now. Alvy Singer takes delight in his memories of his adventures with Annie Hall. In RADIO DAYS, Allen begins to doubt the healing power of memories, when in his role as voice-over narrator he says that he will never forget those radio voices, even though each year they seem to grow a bit dimmer. Through Marion in ANOTHER WOMAN he asks whether memories are something one keeps or things that one has lost. After Gabe reminds her of the good times they had together, Judy comments that it's all over between them and they both recognize the fact. Those memories are nothing more than memories. The years have passed by. The off-screen narrator adds as a quiet coda to the scene the information that a few days later Gabe moved into a hotel. Allen has sent his hero back into the loveless, impersonal universe of his earlier films.

Like Cliff Stern at the end of CRIMES AND MISDEMEANORS, Gabe Roth is alone at the end of the film. For some time he had been attracted to a 20-year-old student, Rain (Juliette Lewis), but despite his obvious affection for her, the relationship never becomes romantic. Rain explains that she was named after Rainer Maria Rilke, Marion's favorite romantic poet in ANOTHER WOMAN, but the name also holds associations to the e. e. cummings line used in Elliot's pursuit of Lee in HANNAH AND HER SISTERS: "Nobody, not even the rain, has such small hands."

After class, Gabe praises her work extravagantly, and she blushes because his approval means so much to her. He takes a personal interest in her education. They walk in the Riverside Park and discuss Russian literature, much as Cliff taught his niece Jenny about classic films and New York. She brings him home to meet her parents (Blythe Danner and Brian McConnachie), who are thrilled to meet a near-famous author, although with his familiar in-joke, Allen has Rain's mother admit she preferred Gabe's earlier, funny stories. Gabe cannot play the genial guest, however. He remains shaken by the accusations of an abusive stranger (Ron Rifkin), who accosted them outside Rain's apartment. When they are alone, Rain explains that he is the therapist who treated her after simultaneous affairs with two older men had upset her emotional life. The therapist himself fell in love with her, and now he believes that Gabe has taken his place in Rain's affections. Gabe is stunned at the allegation and is perhaps more stunned at the realization that it may be true. The degree of sexual experience in one so young rivals Tracy's in MANHATTAN, and these two young women underline Allen's melancholy belief that romance is always available to the young and beautiful, while as he grows older, Allen finds his chances for love diminishing rapidly.

Gabe, now separated from Judy, buys an antique music box for Rain's 21st birthday. During the party in her parents' penthouse apartment, the lights go out during a thunderstorm, and Rain asks Gabe for an adult kiss. Gabe's hesitation indicates clearly that they have not been romantically involved before. He complies, however, but at a later date, he reconstructs the scene for his unseen interviewer. After their kiss, he recalls, she holds the music box, lets it play a few notes, then closes it saying that she knew their relationship would not pan out. Gabe leaves in the rain and thinks of going home to Judy, but he recalls that his marriage to her is over and he is alone. Alone, he thinks of Judy and realizes that he has failed her.

Allen's pattern of misogyny continues. Although Judy and Sally are very different personality types, they are both extraordinarily difficult women. The two younger women offer little more. Sam, with her exercise, health foods and astrology, is an amusing child who offers little promise of maturity. Rain, however, is mature beyond her years. If Gabe's judgment is correct, she has the talent and energy to become a fine writer. At the same time, her attraction to older men has sent her through one unhappy experience of therapy before her 21st birthday, and in all probability it will not be her last. Bright, but neurotic and manipulative, she has the potential to become another Judy. When Gabe reminisces about his first wife Harriet (Galaxy Craze), an intensely sexual woman who eventually had to enter a mental hospital, he tells his interviewer that as a writer he always picks kamikaze women who crash into him and bring him down in flames with them.

Rain does, however, provide Allen with the opportunity to present the most self-reflective passage in any of his films. Gabe's appreciation of her writing is all important to Rain, yet for some strange reason the opposite is equally true. The voice-over interviewer asks Gabe why he values Rain's opinion but not Judy's. He cannot answer the question, but he does not deny its premise. As they discuss literature during one of their walks in Riverside Park, Rain asks to read his work in progress, which he despises as unworthy of his talent and Judy resents because it is overly autobiographical and presents an unflattering picture of her. Rain wants to see it so that she can learn more about Gabe. At first he is reluctant, and like a parent who does not want to say no, tells her he will think about it. Eventually, he relents and gives it to her.

As Rain reads the novel, Gabe's voice-over describes his understanding of relationships between men and women in purely biological terms. While the camera shows hundreds of sperm cells trying to fertilize a huge ovum, he explains that men have millions of cells and want to spread them around, while women have a limited number of ova, and thus set unrealistically high standards for the privilege of fertilizing them. After offering his biological theory of love, Gabe continues his novel by telling the contrasting stories of two men: one is a rogue and has dozens of women in tow. He is miserable because with all his available sex, he admits that he is an extremely lonely man. The second has a perfect wife and family, but he is jealous of the first man and miserable because of his imprisonment in his marriage. Gabe says the only time this man and his wife reached orgasm simultaneously came when the judge gave them their divorce papers. In the case of the first man, the male principle is dominant, and in the second the female prevails, but both lead to personal disaster. Gabe's implication is that a perfect balance between the two is necessary if one is to achieve happiness in marriage, but this is all but impossible in the real world.

Rain is not pleased with what she reads. To her horror, she leaves the manuscript in a cab, but with extraordinarily good luck they are able to locate it. As they ride over to Brooklyn to retrieve it, Rain explains that her losing it was a Freudian blunder. She admits that she is competitive and suspects that she left it in the cab because she did not want to compare her own writing to Gabe's. As the conversation continues, however, her subconscious motivation may be quite different. She may simply have wanted to destroy it. When Gabe insists on hearing her reaction to the book, her candor cuts close to the core of both Gabe's manuscript and Allen's films. Rain finds his treatment of women and his attitude toward life offensive. She finds intolerable the endless series of casual, meaningless affairs that dominate Gabe's narrative. Gabe responds that he does not condone affairs, but exaggerates life for comic purposes. Rain challenges a basic premise of Gabe's (and Allen's) view of life when she asks whether we must oscillate between endless dissatisfaction and dull, suburban drudgery?" Gabe claims he is merely trying to show how difficult it is to be married.

Rain's criticism becomes even more pointed. She asserts that his main character views women as shallow and retrograde, and asks why Gabe allows him to waste so much time fantasizing over a woman he thinks is sexually perfect, but who is sick. She compares reading Gabe's book to viewing TRIUMPH OF THE WILL, a Nazi propaganda film; she appreciates the technique but hates the ideas. Being compared to a Nazi is too much for Gabe, and he snaps back that he doesn't appreciate an analysis of his morality from a 20-year-old student with pretensions. Quite correctly Rain realizes that her remarks must have hit close to home.

In their last exchange in the scene, however, Allen fights back and undercuts his critics. Gabe tells Rain that he would hate to be her boyfriend, because she must put him through hell. Rain hesitates, then smiles faintly and says that she is worth whatever pain she causes. By her final comment in the scene Allen has made her another one of his fascinating but neurotic heroines. Even without her psychoanalysis she knows she puts men through hell, but confident of what she has to offer, she enjoys her power over them. Near the end of the film, she will exact her adult kiss from Gabe, take her music box and walk out of his life, leaving him utterly alone, just like Annie, Tracy, Dorrie, Halley, Marion, Alice and Irmy. Allen has given himself the last word in his script, but the exchange with his 20-year-old student has left him shaken.

In their final joint interview, Jack and Sally reveal what they have learned from their failed divorce. They explain that love is not really about passion and romance. It is about companionship, a buffer against loneliness. Now that they are back together they realize that every marriage has problems, but if these cannot be resolved, they must be endured and simply swept under the rug. They seem content to try to do this.

Gabe, in his final interview, has not yet recovered from his disappointment. He admits his loneliness, but for the time being at any rate, he claims that he is content to be alone and concentrate on his work. Standing in for Allen, Gabe says that his next work will be more political and less personal. Growing uncomfortable under the relentless gaze of the camera, he finally asks: "Can I go now?"

NOTES

1. Douglas Brode, *The Films of Woody Allen,* (New York: Citadel, 1991), p. 285.
2. Sam B. Girgus, *The Films of Woody Allen* (New York: Cambridge Univ., 1993), pp. 110–112, is particularly insightful in discussing this film as Allen's serious examination of his religious, as opposed to cultural, Jewishness.
3. Stephen J. Spignesi, *The Woody Allen Companion* (Kansas City: Andrews and McMeel, 1991), p. 214, argues that Ben "symbolizes" God.
4. Brode, p. 275, is particularly critical of Cliff's smug sense of moral superiority.
5. Annette Wernblad, *Brooklyn Is Not Expanding: Woody Allen's Comic Universe* (Rutherford, N.J.: Fairleigh Dickinson Univ., 1992), p. 141, cites the golden colors of autumn, as photographed by Sven Nyquist, as another indication of the basic optimism of the film. Optimism may be too strong a word to apply to the film as a whole.
6. Maurice Yacowar, *Loser Take All: The Comic Art of Woody Allen* (New York: Continuum, 1991), p. 276, describes the mystery in terms of the two partners in the dialogue: "One person personifies evil rewarded, the other virtue punished."
7. Woody Allen, *Hannah and Her Sisters* (New York: Vintage, 1991), p. 144.
8. Woody Allen (with Marshall Brickman), MANHATTAN in *Four Films of Woody Allen* (New York: Random House, 1982), p. 197.
9. Yacowar, p. 283.
10. Brode, p. 284.
11. Lotte H. Eisner, *The Haunted Screen: Expressionism in the German Cinema and the Influence of Max Reinhardt* (Berkeley, Calif.: Univ. of California, 1973), p. 21, uses this phrase as she explains the translation of Expressionist ideas from literature and painting to film.
12. Bruce Crowther, *Film Noir: Reflections in a Dark Mirror* (New York: Continuum, 1989), p.39 ff, discusses the visual and philosophic relationship between American and German Expressionism.
13. Woody Allen, *God* (New York: Samuel French, 1975), pp. 33–34, contains a dialogue in which the Greek slave Diabetes explains his reluctance to accept his freedom. He says: "To know one's place is safe."

FILMOGRAPHY

WHAT'S NEW, PUSSYCAT? (1965)
Director: Clive Donner
Screenplay: Woody Allen
Cinematography: Jean Badal
Editor: Fergus McDonnell
Design: Jacques Saulnier

Cast Includes: Woody Allen, Peter Sellers, Peter O'Toole, Romy Schneider, Capucine, Paula Prentiss, Ursula Andress

WHAT'S UP, TIGER LILY? (1966)
Director: Woody Allen; Japanese Version: Senkichi Taniguchi
Screenplay: Woody Allen
Cinematography: Kazuo Yamada
Editor: Richard Krown
Design: Ben Shapiro

Cast Includes: Tatsuya Mihashi, Mie Hanna, Akiko Wakayabayashi, Tadao Makamaru, Susumu Kurobe

CASINO ROYALE (1967)
Director: John Huston, Kenneth Hughes, Val Guest, Robert Parrish, Joseph McGrath
Screenplay: Wolf Mankowitz, John Law, Michael Sawyers
Cinematography: Jack Hildyard
Editor: Bill Lenny
Design: Michael Ayringer

Cast Includes: Woody Allen, Peter Sellers, Ursula Andress, David Niven, Deborah Kerr, Daliah Lavi, William Holden, Kurt Kaznar, George Raft, Jean-Paul Belmondo

DON'T DRINK THE WATER (1969)
Director: Howard Morris
Screenplay: R.S. Allen, Harvey Bullock; play by Woody Allen
Cinematography: Harvy Genkins
Editor: Ralph Rosenblum
Design: Robert Gundlach

Cast Includes: Jackie Gleason, Estelle Parsons, Ted Bessell, Joan Delaney, Richard Libertini

TAKE THE MONEY AND RUN (1969)
Director: Woody Allen
Screenplay: Woody Allen, Mickey Rose
Cinematography: Lester Shoor
Editor: Paul Jordan, Ron Kalish
Design: Fred Harpman

Cast Includes: Woody Allen, Janet Margolin, Marcel Hillaire, Jacqueline Hyde, Louise Lasser

BANANAS (1971)
Director: Woody Allen
Screenplay: Woody Allen and Mickey Rose
Cinematography: Andrew Costikyan
Editor: Ron Kalish
Design: Ed Wittstein

Cast Includes: Woody Allen, Louise Lasser, Carlos Montalban, Navidad Abascal, Howard Cosell, Roger Grimsby, Don Dunphy

PLAY IT AGAIN, SAM (1972)
Director: Herbert Ross
Screenplay: Woody Allen
Cinematography: Owen Roizman
Editor: Marion Rothman
Design: Ed Wittstein

Cast Includes: Woody Allen, Diane Keaton, Tony Roberts, Jerry Lacy, Susan Anspach, Viva

EVERYTHING YOU ALWAYS WANTED TO KNOW ABOUT SEX* (*BUT WERE AFRAID TO ASK) (1972)

Director: Woody Allen
Screenplay: Woody Allen
Cinematography: David M. Walsh
Editor: Eric Albertson
Design: Dale Hennesy

Cast Includes: Woody Allen, Louise Lasser, Anthony Quayle, Tony Randall, Lynn Redgrave, Burt Reynolds, Robert Q. Lewis, Regis Philbin, Heather MacRae

SLEEPER (1973)

Director: Woody Allen
Screenplay: Woody Allen, Marshall Brickman
Cinematography: David M. Walsh
Editor: Ralph Rosenblum
Design: Dale Hennesy

Cast Includes: Woody Allen, Diane Keaton, John Beck, Mary Gregory, Don Keefer

LOVE AND DEATH (1975)

Director: Woody Allen
Screenplay: Woody Allen
Cinematography: Ghislain Cloquet
Editor: Ralph Rosenblum, Ron Kalish
Design: Willy Holt

Cast Includes: Woody Allen, Diane Keaton, Georges Adet, Frank Adu, Edmond Ardisson

THE FRONT (1976)

Director: Martin Ritt
Screenplay: Walter Bernstein
Cinematography: Michael Chapman
Editor: David Grusin
Design: Charles Bailey

Cast Includes: Woody Allen, Zero Mostel, Herschel Bernardi, Michael Murphy, Andrea Marcovicci, Remak Ramsey

ANNIE HALL (1977)
Director: Woody Allen
Screenplay: Woody Allen, Marshall Brickman
Cinematography: Gordon Willis
Editor: Ralph Rosenblum
Design: Mel Bourne

Cast Includes: Woody Allen, Diane Keaton, Tony Roberts, Carol Kane, Paul Simon, Shelley Duvall, Janet Margolin, Collen Dewhurst, Christopher Walken, Marshall McLuhan

INTERIORS (1978)
Director: Woody Allen
Screenplay: Woody Allen
Cinematography: Gordon Willis
Editor: Ralph Rosenblum
Design: Mel Bourne

Cast Includes: Diane Keaton, Mary Beth Hurt, E. G. Marshall, Geraldine Page, Maureen Stapleton, Sam Waterston

MANHATTAN (1979)
Director: Woody Allen
Screenplay: Woody Allen, Marshall Brickman
Cinematography: Gordon Willis
Editor: Susan E. Morse
Design: Mel Bourne

Cast Includes: Woody Allen, Diane Keaton, Mariel Hemingway, Michael Murphy, Meryl Streep, Anne Byrne, Tisa Farrow, Bella Abzug

STARDUST MEMORIES (1980)
Director: Woody Allen
Screenplay: Woody Allen
Cinematography: Gordon Willis
Editor: Susan E. Morse
Design: Mel Bourne

Cast Includes: Woody Allen, Charlotte Rampling, Jessica Harper, Marie-Christine Barrault, Tony Roberts

A MIDSUMMER NIGHT'S SEX COMEDY (1982)
Director: Woody Allen
Screenplay: Woody Allen
Cinematography: Gordon Willis
Editor: Susan E. Morse
Design: Mel Bourne

Cast Includes: Woody Allen, Mia Farrow, José Ferrer, Julie Hagerty, Tony Roberts, Mary Steenburgen

ZELIG (1983)
Director: Woody Allen
Screenplay: Woody Allen
Cinematography: Gordon Willis
Editor: Susan E. Morse
Design: Mel Bourne

Cast Includes: Woody Allen, Mia Farrow, Ellen Garrison, Stephanie Farrow, Susan Sontag, Saul Bellow, Irving Howe, Bruno Bettelheim

BROADWAY DANNY ROSE (1984)
Director: Woody Allen
Screenplay: Woody Allen
Cinematography: Gordon Willis
Editor: Susan E. Morse
Design: Mel Bourne

Cast Includes: Woody Allen, Mia Farrow, Nick Apollo Forte, Sandy Baron, Will Jordan, Corbett Monica, Milton Berle, Howard Cosell

THE PURPLE ROSE OF CAIRO (1985)
Director: Woody Allen
Screenplay: Woody Allen
Cinematography: Gordon Willis
Editor: Susan E. Morse
Design: Stuart Wurtzel

Cast Includes: Mia Farrow, Jeff Daniels, Danny Aiello, Dianne Wiest, Edward Herrman, Zoe Caldwell, Karen Akers, Milo O'Shea

HANNAH AND HER SISTERS (1986)
Director: Woody Allen
Screenplay: Woody Allen
Cinematography: Carlo Di Palma
Editor: Susan E. Morse
Design: Stuart Wurtzel, Carol Joffe

Cast Includes: Woody Allen, Mia Farrow, Barbara Hershey, Carrie Fisher, Michael Caine, Dianne Wiest, Lloyd Nolan, Maureen O'Sullivan, Max Von Sydow, Sam Waterston, Julie Kavner, Tony Roberts, Benno Schmidt, Joanna Gleason, Bobby Short

RADIO DAYS (1987)
Director: Woody Allen
Screenplay: Woody Allen
Cinematography: Carlo Di Palma
Editor: Susan E. Morse
Design: Santo Loquasto

Cast Includes: Mia Farrow, Julie Kavner, Dianne Wiest, Seth Green, Josh Mostel, Wallace Shawn, Danny Aiello, Diane Keaton, Tony Roberts

SEPTEMBER (1987)
Director: Woody Allen
Screenplay: Woody Allen
Cinematography: Sven Nyquist
Editor: Susan E. Morse
Design: Santo Loquasto

Cast Includes: Mia Farrow, Dianne Wiest, Denholm Elliott, Elaine Stritch, Sam Waterston, Jack Warden

OEDIPUS WRECKS in NEW YORK STORIES (1989)
Director: Woody Allen
Screenplay: Woody Allen
Cinematography: Sven Nyquist
Editor: Susan E. Morse
Design: Santo Loquasto

Cast Includes: Woody Allen, Mia Farrow, Mae Questel, Julie Kavner, Mayor Ed Koch

CRIMES AND MISDEMEANORS (1989)
Director: Woody Allen
Screenplay: Woody Allen
Cinematography: Sven Nyquist
Editor: Susan E. Morse
Design: Santo Loquasto

Cast Includes: Woody Allen, Mia Farrow, Martin Landau, Anjelica Huston, Alan Alda, Joanna Gleason, Sam Waterston, Martin Bergmann, Jerry Orbach

ALICE (1990)
Director: Woody Allen
Screenplay: Woody Allen
Cinematography: Carlo Di Palma
Editor: Susan E. Morse
Design: Santo Loquasto

Cast Includes: Mia Farrow, Joe Mantegna, Keye Luke, William Hurt, Alec Baldwin, Blythe Danner, Gwen Verdon, Bernadette Peters

SCENES FROM A MALL (1991)
Director: Paul Mazursky
Screenplay: Roger L. Simon, Paul Mazursky
Cinematography: Fred Murphy
Editor: Stuart Pappe
Design: Pato Guzman

Cast Includes: Woody Allen, Bette Midler, Bill Irwin, Paul Mazursky

SHADOWS AND FOG (1992)
Director: Woody Allen
Screenplay: Woody Allen
Cinematography: Carlo Di Palma
Editor: Susan E. Morse
Design: Santo Loquasto

Cast Includes: Woody Allen, Mia Farrow, John Malkovich, John Cusack, Donald Pleasence, Madonna, Lily Tomlin, Jodie Foster, Kathy Bates, Julie Kavner

HUSBANDS AND WIVES (1993)
Director: Woody Allen
Screenplay: Woody Allen
Cinematography: Carlo Di Palma
Editor: Susan E. Morse
Design: Santo Loquasto

Cast Includes: Woody Allen, Mia Farrow, Judy Davis, Sydney Pollack, Juliette Lewis, Lysette Anthony, Liam Neeson, Blythe Danner, Benno Schmidt

A SELECT BIBLIOGRAPHY

BOOKS BY WOODY ALLEN

Allen, Woody. *The Complete Prose of Woody Allen.* New York: Wings, 1991. Includes *Without Feathers, Getting Even,* and *Side Effects.*

Allen, Woody. *Four Films of Woody Allen.* New York: Random House, 1982. Includes "ANNIE HALL," "INTERIORS," "MANHATTAN" and "STARDUST MEMORIES."

Allen, Woody. *God.* New York: Samuel French, 1975.

Allen, Woody. *Hannah and Her Sisters.* New York: Vintage, 1987.

Allen, Woody. *Three Films of Woody Allen.* New York: Vintage, 1987. Includes "ZELIG," "BROADWAY DANNY ROSE" and "THE PURPLE ROSE OF CAIRO."

BOOKS OF WOODY ALLEN CRITICISM

Brode, Douglas. *The Films of Woody Allen.* New York: Citadel, 1991.

Girgus, Sam B. *The Films of Woody Allen.* Cambridge, England: Cambridge Univ., 1993.

Hirsch, Foster. *Love, Sex and the Meaning of Life; Woody Allen's Comedy.* New York: McGraw-Hill, 1981.

Jacobs, Diane. *. . . but we need the eggs: The Magic of Woody Allen.* New York: St. Martin's, 1982.

Lax, Eric. *Woody Allen: A Biography.* New York: Knopf, 1991.

McCann, Graham. *Woody Allen.* Cambridge, England: Polity, 1991.

Pogel, Nancy. *Woody Allen*. Boston: Twayne, 1987.

Spegnesi, Stephen J. *The Woody Allen Companion*. Kansas City: Andrews and McMeel, 1992.

Wernblad, Annette. *Brooklyn Is Not Expanding: Woody Allen's Comic Universe*. Rutherford, N.J.: Fairleigh Dickinson Univ., 1992.

Yacowar, Maurice. *Loser Take All: The Comic Art of Woody Allen*. New York: Continuum, 1991.

INDEX

Boldface folios refer reader to cited films' synopses

ABOUT THE AUTHOR

Richard A. Blake, S. J., is a Jesuit priest, currently teaching film and journalism at Le Moyne College in Syracuse, New York. After receiving his doctorate in film at Northwestern University, he became an associate editor, and subsequently managing and executive editor at *America* magazine, a weekly journal of opinion published by the Jesuits of the United States and Canada. During that time, he also served as regular film reviewer, a role he retained after leaving the magazine in 1985 to return to the academic world. In that year, he held The Jesuit Chair at Georgetown University and later moved to Le Moyne College. In addition to the regular film reviews, he has published many articles on the arts, and two books: *The Lutheran Milieu of Ingmar Bergman's Films* and *Screening America: Reflections on Five Classic Films*. His reviews in *America* have received four awards from the Catholic Press Association, and *Screening America* received a citation from Alpha Sigma Nu, the national Jesuit honor society.